MIND, MACHINE AND MORALITY

A treatise on the future of human-machine systems and the consideration of their manifest and more esoteric purposes.

Mind, Machine and Morality
Toward a Philosophy of Human-Technology Symbiosis

PETER A. HANCOCK
University of Central Florida, USA

ASHGATE

Published by
Ashgate Publishing Limited
Wey Court East
Union Road
Farnham
Surrey, GU9 7PT
England

Ashgate Publishing Company
Suite 420
101 Cherry Street
Burlington
VT 05401-4405
USA

www.ashgate.com

British Library Cataloguing in Publication Data
Hancock, Peter A., 1953-
  Mind, machine and morality : toward a philosophy of
  human-technology symbiosis
  1. Human-machine systems
  I. Title
  620.8

ISBN: 978-0-7546-7358-3

7025666

Library of Congress Cataloging-in-Publication Data
Hancock, Peter A., 1953-
  Mind, machine, and morality : toward a philosophy of human-technology symbiosis / by
  Peter A. Hancock.
    p. cm.
  Includes bibliographical references and index.
  ISBN 978-0-7546-7358-3
  1. Technology--Philosophy. 2. Human-machine systems--Philosophy. 3. Human engineering.
  I. Title.
  T14.H2855 2008
  601--dc22

                                                                    2008030264

Mixed Sources
Product group from well-managed
forests and other controlled sources
www.fsc.org Cert no. SGS-COC-2482
© 1996 Forest Stewardship Council
FSC

Printed and bound in Great Britain by
TJ International Ltd, Padstow, Cornwall

Contents

List of Figures

List of Tables

Preface

Among the immediate concerns of everyday life we often are so bound up in the needs and the minutiae of the moment that we forget to reflect upon the path we have each individually trodden. This book serves an explicit purpose for me personally, which is to collect and consider a number of the assertions that I have made, primarily about the link between humans, the technologies they create, and most recently the morality and the ultimate purpose behind what is often termed 'progress'. This issue has come to concern me ever more greatly, since I believe that the divorce between our purpose (that is, the reasons that we do something), from our processes (that is, the way that we accomplish whatever it is we want to do), is a very damaging situation. It promises to destroy us unless the rift can be first bridged and then healed. I view this divorce as one of the greatest challenges facing society in the coming century. This work then is part of my continuing effort to generate a modern philosophical renaissance based upon an understanding of the symbiosis of perception-action and its mediation through the technological extensions to all human capacities. Several of the present chapters have appeared previously in one form or another and I have tried to make explicit these respective antecedents. However, I have made many changes and updates while also adding new chapters. I hope that readers both new and old will find value in what I have presented.

The first chapter considers the nature and science of human-machine systems and what the link between human and machines seeks globally to achieve. The second is a more discursive exposition on this same theme, looking at the reasons for and nature of technology and sets the broadest of pictures against which ideas in subsequent chapters are contrasted. The next chapter considers one specific proposition which, briefly stated, is that human-machine technologies evolve toward a commonality of form and function over time and that the injection of requisite variability is consequently, the responsibility and mandate of innovative designers. This is followed by an assessment of how functions are currently allocated and may in the future be distributed respectively to human and machine. Dynamic function allocation certainly represents one of the first steps towards true human-machine symbiosis. Harmony characterizes the next chapter which seeks to provide visions and metaphors for how humans and machines might work in the near term and how technology can be embedded into the environment now and in the more distant future. Given these progressions in human-machine relationships, Chapter 6 questions the very nature of what we mean by work. It asks whether advancing technology could actually redefine one of the central pillars of human society. For example, as videogames become more realistic and advanced systems become ever-more like videogames, will there be a point at which electronic work becomes electronic play? In exploring the theme of work and technology, the next brief chapter provides an historical account of men without machines, a condition which resulted from a deliberate intention to punish the individuals who were so deprived. The specific example is taken from the story of the convicts of Sarah Island, Tasmania in the early nineteenth century. These circumstances provide a wonderful example of how profit rapidly overcomes moral rectitude when the two are set in direct opposition. This leads to my explicit consideration of machines and morality in Chapter 8. I look for solutions in the brighter aspects of social organization by asking whether we can use tenets such as 'life, liberty, and the pursuit of happiness' as moral design imperatives for the symbiotic systems we look to create. Finally, by using an explicit and unpleasant example, I try to explore the moral dimensions of the act of creation in technology and the subsequent moral divorce between such acts of design and fabrication and the later application and use of such technologies. In examining the darker side of the question of morality I hope to stimulate thinking on this critical matter. This text then is only a point of departure in a very long journey that seeks to examine a complete philosophy of technology. It is not even the end of the beginning, but it is a personal benchmark and one I want to establish for myself and very much hope that it is of use to others also.

I am most happy to acknowledge the support and contribution of so many people who have had significant influence on the present work. I am especially grateful to Dr. Mark Chignell and Dr. Steve Scallen, who have graciously allowed me to reproduce our collaborative work here. In respect of those whose insights and work I continue to rely on, I would especially like to thank Raja Parasuraman, John Wise, Tom Sheridan, Chris Wickens, Dave Woods, Kim Vicente, Erik Hollnagel, Richard Jagacinski and the many others from whom I learn on a daily basis. My particular acknowledgement must go to my colleague John Flach, whose integrity and insight is a constant source of inspiration. I am very happy to acknowledge the support of numerous agencies that have funded my research work over the decades. It has been both a pleasure and a privilege to work with them and I am most grateful for the numerous opportunities they have generated. Of course, the views expressed here are my own and do not represent the viewpoint of any of the agencies named. I must also express a particular debt of gratitude to Ron Westrum. In directing me to sources which frequently illustrate my ignorance, he never fails to interest and educate. I am most grateful for his guidance. I must express sincere thanks to Dr. Karol Ross, who read and commented on the whole manuscript; her observations are very much appreciated. Finally, this work has very much benefitted from the critical comments and helpful remarks of both Professor Neville Moray and Dr. Robert Hoffman; I am very much indebted to each of them for their time, patience, and insight.

Acknowledgements

The author and publishers wish to thank the following for permission to use copyright material:

Figure 1.6
Figure D.4 'The structural stability of the potential surface changes as a function of variations in the y-parameter' from '*Information, Natural Laws, and Self-Assembly of Rhythmic Movement*', Kugler, P.N. and Turvey, M.T., (1987), Lawrence Erlbaum, Hillsdale, New Jersey, reprinted by permission of the Taylor & Francis Group.

Figure 1.9
Figure 6.13b (p. 269) from '*The Origins of Order: Self-organization and Selection and Selection in Evolution*' by Kauffmann, Stuart A. (1993). By permission of Oxford University Press, Inc.

Chapter 2, pp. 20–21 and p. 29
Gibson, J.J. (1979), *The Ecological Approach to Visual Perception*, Hillsdale, New Jersey: Laurence Erlbaum, reprinted by permission of the Taylor & Francis Group.

Chapter 2, p. 31
'The Hammer' from '*The Complete Poems of Carl Sandburg. Revised and Expanded Edition*', © 1970, 1969 by Lilian Steichen Sandburg, Trustee, reprinted by permission of Houghton Mifflin Harcourt Publishing Company.

Figure 3.4
Cover art by David Sweeney from Klein, G.A., Orasanu, J., Calderwood, R., and Zsambok, C.E. (eds.) (1993) *Decision Making in Action: Models and Methods*. Norwood, NJ; Ablex, reprinted with permission from the artist and Greenwood Publishing Group.

Figure 3.5
René Magritte, 'Second Nature', 1965 © 2008 C. Herscovici, London/Artists
Rights Society (ARS), New York.

Figure 9.2
The barrel and the 'branks', Mary Evans Picture Library.

Figure 9.3
Figure 341 – The Water Torture – Facsimile of a Woodcut in J. Damhoudère's
'*Praxis Rerum Criminalium*' in 4to, Antwerp, 1556.

Every effort has been made to trace all the copyright holders, but if any have been
inadvertently overlooked the publishers will be pleased to make the necessary
arrangement at the first opportunity.

Reviews for Mind, Machine and Morality

'Professor Peter Hancock is the modern day Renaissance man, crossing discipline boundaries with ease. *Mind, Machine and Morality* treats us to a metaphysical account of the issues that touch our everyday lives. Peter tells a good story, often rooted in his personal experience, which draw the reader's attention to the crux of the big human-technology issues. This book will challenge your conceptions of the discipline of Human Factors; it will whet your appetite and leave you thirsting for more.'

Neville Stanton, Brunel University, UK

'A delightful and penetrating philosophy of purpose and process in human-machine-society interactions, as only Peter Hancock can render it—liberally spiced with history, humor and erudition.'

Tom Sheridan, Massachusetts Institute of Technology , USA

'*Mind, Machine and Morality* is a masterwork by one of the great scientists and thinkers of our time. Hancock's theory relies on notions of perception-action coupling and goal-orientation of human-machine systems. Thus, were I to reach into history, I would say that Hancock has taken Edward C. Tolman's *Purposive Behavior in Animals and Men* and James J. Gibson's *Ecological Psychology*, arguably two of the great works in psychology, and extended them into the computer age, and well beyond. Hancock does far more than present tales of caution about the impact of machines on people: he presents tales of celebration of the human ability to adapt and to exercise its moral faculty. Hancock's intellect, itself charged with a clear sense of right and wrong, races across history, using poetry, lithograph, allegory, metaphor, and tales of modern technological woes. Just the set of poems by great poets about the dangers and woes of mechanization and machines is itself worth the price of admission. Hancock's mind courses across history to bring tales of technology and morality, juxtaposed in crystalline relief. Only a mind as far-reaching and at the same time as scientifically grounded as Hancock's could draw links between antiquity and today, such as that between the drawings of William Blake, the words of R. L. Stevenson in *Treasure Island*, and the physics of Minkowski spaces. Hancock presents a grand vision of Human Factors as a socio-political science, standing at the center of a moral imperative for human-machine interaction, critical to the success and survival of the human species. Hancock makes the case that participating in the creation of user-hostile systems is immoral. Therefore it is a moral imperative to use Cognitive Task Analysis to insure that technologies are human-centered. I like that. If you work with technology, or if you work on technology, this masterwork will make you... no, it will help you think.'

Robert R. Hoffman, Institute for Human and Machine Cognition, USA

'An amazing breadth of ideas and concepts that will challenge readers to reassess the way they have framed human interaction with technology. Hancock makes a definitive break with Human Factors as "device advice" or "appliance science". Drawing upon sources as diverse as Aurelius and Asimov, Hancock compels designers to face fundamental philosophical and moral considerations concerning not just how technology will work with people, but why such technology is developed. Although no easy answers exist for such considerations, this book provides a broad foundation for shaping the increasingly intertwined relationship between people and technology.'

John D. Lee, University of Iowa, USA

Chapter 1
The Science and Philosophy of Human-Machine Systems

Science above all things is for the uses of life.

(Francis Bacon)

Preamble

This first chapter develops a theoretical structure for the science of human-machine systems. This structure is based on the premise that technology is the principal method through which humans expand their ranges of perception and action in order to understand and control the world around them. The theory presents a broad rationale for the contemporary impetus in human-machine systems development and the historical motivations for its growth. Unlike any other interdisciplinary fusion of knowledge, the science of human-machine systems is more than a convenient collaboration among proximal areas of knowledge. Through the identification of opportunities and constraints that derive from the interplay of human, machine, task, and environment, I point to this area of study as *the* vital bridge between evolving biological and non-biological forms of intelligence. Absence of such a bridge will see the certain demise of one and the fundamental impoverishment, if not the extinction, of the other.

Introduction

THE SECRET OF MACHINES

We can pull and haul and push and lift and drive,
We can print and plough and weave and heat and light,
We can run and race and swim and fly and drive,
We can see and hear and count and read and write.
But remember please, the Law by which we live,
We are not built to comprehend a lie.
We can neither love nor pity nor forgive –
If you make a slip in handling us, you die.

(Rudyard Kipling)

Humans and Technology

Rudyard Kipling's *The Secret of Machines* is as appropriate for the supervisor of modern-day complex systems as it was when it was written for the individual worker in the factory of the nineteenth century. Slips and errors in handling machines can and frequently do lead to death. Yet, we have built a global society whose dependence on technology grows daily. The way in which humans and machines integrate their actions lies at the very heart of this development. The emerging science of human-machine systems seeks to maximize the benefit derived from technology while exercising a continual vigilance over its darker side and its dangerous potentialities. It looks to turn human-machine antagonism into human-machine synergy.

Traditionally, the study of humans and machines has been represented simply as a discipline that makes technology more appropriate or palatable for human consumption. It also forces the human to adapt, as was foretold in the film *Metropolis*. However, this is a very reactive interpretation and is one that is usually cited or employed after some spectacular technological disaster has rendered this perennial issue momentarily 'newsworthy'. My purpose here is to take a proactive perspective and to represent this area of study as one that actually motivates *all* of science, engineering, and indeed the systematic empirical exploration of the human condition itself in the very first place.

As the quotation from Francis Bacon at the start of this chapter implies, in order to understand the motivation for science and its material manifestation in technology, we must first have a clear vision of what Bacon's 'uses of life' are. We need to understand how people use their capacities for perception, cognition, and action to decide on specific goals and then carry out meaningful and useful tasks in the pursuit of those goals. As well then as a fundamental examination of human purpose, this effort demands a rational analysis of tasks themselves, a psychological analysis of human behaviour and capability, and an engineering analysis of how humans interact with the tools and systems they have created so that they may accomplish these tasks.

Therefore, my first task is to address how humans use technology in the goal and task-oriented exploration and manipulation of their environment. It was Powers (1974, 1978) who asserted that goal-directed behaviour is organized through a hierarchy of control systems (but see also Lashley, 1951). Higher-order systems receive input from and subsequently control an assemblage of lower-order systems and it is these lower-order systems that interact directly with the external world. One of Powers' central points is that the flow of control is bi-directional, with control flowing upward from lower-order systems as much as it does in the downward direction from higher-order systems. Human activity has thus been characterized as an inner loop of skilled manual control and perceptual processing which is embedded within an outer loop of control that, among other capacities, features knowledge-based problem solving. Moray (1986), for instance, gives the example of a nested series of goals working from an extreme outer loop of very general goals (such as influencing society and raising children) to extreme inner loop processes (such as controlling the momentary position of a vehicle's steering wheel in order to negotiate a curve in the road). These different levels of temporal and spatial scales of perception-action can serve to frame our overall human exploration.

Unaided by any tools or instruments, human perception and action are necessarily limited. However, with the birth of technology, and its growth in each succeeding generation, the bounds of these respective capabilities have expanded and are in constant redefinition. To describe this historic line of progress, I start here with a description of the limits to unaided action and unaided perception. However, we must first recognize that the limit of human perception has always exceeded that of human action. We have always been able to see further than we can control. Imagine you are standing on the top of a high hill. You might well be able to see more than thirty miles into the distance on a clear day and yet, without technical assistance you can only exercise physical control over the few square yards of that spreading vista that surrounds you. The 'tension' that results from this disparity between what can be perceived and what can be controlled provides the major motivational force for human exploration. It is a major theme in the theoretical position I develop in this book. Indeed, the presence of this tension between perception and action may well underlie the fact that astronomy was arguably our first science, although perhaps geometry for agriculture may have evolved in parallel. The long days anticipating the harvest and the long nights contemplating the vagaries of the wandering stars and the fiery messengers they contained might well have started human beings on the road to formalized observation (Koestler, 1959). Thus the link between perception and action may explain *how* we humans explore the environment. However, it is the gap between the powers of perception and action which may explain *why* we humans explore the environment.

In regard to this exploration, technological innovations often generate a dual effect. That is, new technologies increase the range of our actions while simultaneously expanding the range of our perception. The further these respective bounds are extended from our everyday experience, the more complex the technical systems that are needed to support such exploration. At the point where even aided perception starts to become inadequate – and this occurs at the very edges of our understanding – there is an increasingly greater reliance placed on metaphorical representations of the spaces involved. The most obvious example is that at the limit of celestial mechanics and quantum mechanics it is indeed largely metaphor that we are dealing with. In elaborating this overall theme of expanding ranges of perception and action, I look to use the Minkowskian framework to describe the evolving vista of capabilities (see Moray and Hancock, 2009). For example, leaps of progress such as the genesis of tools (Oakley, 1949), and the more recent advent of 'intelligent' orthotics can be captured and expressed easily using this form of description.

There is, however, a dissonance when we contrast the progress of technological innovation and the advance not of perception and action, but of human nature itself. The latter appears to have changed very little across recorded history while technology changes almost daily. The result is an ever-increasing potential for a catastrophic disconnection or more colourfully our moral dilemma in exercising 'the power of gods with the minds of children'. There are strong constraints on human nature, but we are rapidly augmenting our basic perception-action abilities as we systematically explore and engineer our environment. Such environments serve to 'create' our future selves and we have seen more radical changes between the last two to three generations than we have in the fifty generations before them. The future of human beings is now bound to the co-evolution of biological and non-biological (computational) forms of life. This in turn implies the need to regard the goal-oriented interaction between humans and the perceivable environment as the basic unit of analysis (see Flach and Dominguez, 1995).

❖ ❖ ❖

Perception and Action in Space and Time

The personal and collective odyssey of humankind has been to find and establish our place and role in the universe. While this journey might be considered from one perspective as a spiritual endeavour, my focus here is on the goal-oriented use of technology as a process to provide mastery over the environment. While the environment is best measured by the physical metrics of space and time, the exploration of space and time is motivated by personal and collective goals that can be expressed as our desire for certain future states of our world. Our success or failure with respect to these goals is evaluated by the associated perceptual experiences that they engender. In this overall process, our behavioural strategies can be defined as the particular ways of achieving these desired goals. In contrast to strategies, tasks represent a finer-grained level of action, closer to the centre of the nested loops referred to earlier. Tasks are the steps by which strategies work toward goals (see also Shaw and Kinsella-Shaw, 1989). While a goal is a desired future state, strategies and tasks are supportive elements that provide the specific transitional steps to achieve that goal. In the case of a task, the transformation is explicitly an energetic one. That is, a task is only achieved with a formal change to the physical state of the world. Goal achievement relies on the success of strategies which are themselves composed of the successful and integrated completion of more than one task. From a thermodynamic perspective, tasks typically result in a reduction of local entropy (Swenson and Turvey, 1991) and the expenditure of energy toward a more ordered state of any sub-system. The idea of 'progress' is implied by the fact that transformations take time to occur. Therefore, the simple perpetuation of a system without any goal-directed alteration cannot be regarded as a task within this definition.

The demands a task places on an operator or the cost of performing the required transformation can only be measured with respect to what it is to be achieved. That is, a task is a relational concept. In human performance such costs are typically expressed as a function of the time taken to pass from an initial state to a following state and the accuracy with which that transition is achieved (that is, speed and accuracy). Transformation cost can also be expressed in terms of the cognitive effort or the muscular energy involved. Machines, as transformers of energy, act to increase the number of paths (or successful strategies) by which a goal can be achieved. Technology thus serves to broaden the horizon of achievable goal states (for example, an astronaut's presence in outer space).

While technology serves to open up windows of opportunity, environmental circumstances often serve to constrain and limit the goals which can be achieved (for example, contemporary astronaut presence on Mars). However, one hallmark of expertise is the ability to project what the future expected environmental constraints might be and to seek ways in which to 'navigate' around them. The environment also presents unexpected and unanticipated constraints that interrupt ongoing tasks and strategies and can, under certain circumstances, remove the desired goal from the range of possible outcomes. With respect to goals then, human-machine systems seek to expand ranges of possible achievement, while the environment can act to restrict them, although it can occasionally present surprising opportunities also. Unfortunately, it is the antagonistic aspect of the interaction between the human and the environment which has permeated much of the history of design. Thus, the idea of 'conquering' nature, although predominantly of Occidental origin, is one that has grown into a global preoccupation (see McPhee, 1989). Thus technological systems are often shaped to 'conquer' and 'control' the environment, rather than recognize and harmoniously incorporate relevant, intrinsic constraints. Ultimately, it is the ability to recognize and benefit from these mutual constraints and limitations to action that characterizes 'intelligence' on behalf of human-machine systems. Although there are few such systems operating at present, there is still hope and promise for the fulfilment in the future.

Goal-oriented behaviour is thus initiated in part by reacting to environmental constraints that limit the range and effectiveness of perception and action. The limitations of perception and action can be considered initially within a framework that views space and time as orthogonal axes. The environment may be scaled from the very small to the very large and from the very brief to the extremely prolonged. Within these continua there are ranges of space and time that relate most closely to our own physical size and our own perception of a lifetime's duration (Hancock, 2002). One representation of this in terms of orders of magnitude is illustrated in Figure 1.1 (see Hoffman, 1990).

Human-range (the innermost circle), illustrates the limit of unaided human action (for example, throwing a javelin). Perceptual-range (the horizontal lines envelope) illustrates the range of unaided human perception (for example, looking into the night sky). Orthotic-range (the vertical hashed-lines envelope) shows how the range of human action increases vastly with the addition of technology. Universal-range (the outermost envelope) illustrates the paradox that while technology expands the range of action it is vastly more effective in increasing the range of perception (for example, the Hubble telescope). These envelopes are expressed as

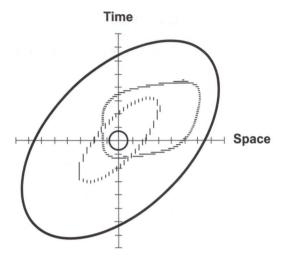

Figure 1.1   The ranges of unaided and aided human activity

functions of space and time. These regions are illustrative approximations and are not drawn to represent definitive boundaries which, given the dynamics nature of technology, would change on almost a daily basis anyway.

In identifying our own location in the universe, we humans almost always place ourselves at the centre. The history of the science of astronomy for example, can be seen as an account of our progressive physical displacement from this notion of a central position. In particular, the step from an earth-centred to a sun-centred solar system was one such step (Koestler, 1959, 1973). Yet, however much we recognize this displacement from a physically privileged location, we each continue to view the world around us from a psychologically privileged position – the self (Hancock, 2005; see also Gooddy, 1988). Thus 'human-range' is placed in the centre of Figure 1.1.

Human responses to the spatial dimensions of existence have been examined quite extensively, particularly in areas such as the study of psycho-physics. For instance, spatial discrimination at the lower end can be measured by Vernier acuity in vision, two-point threshold for touch, and by auditory spatial localization and discrimination in hearing (Stevens, 1975). In contrast, the study of human perception of temporal variation has a much more chequered history. It is true that human interest in the dimension of time has a long history, going back to the use of astronomical tables in early religion and agriculture (for example, Fraser, 1966). However, this interest has been more sporadic than systematic. In the modern world, interest in the temporal dimension is reflected by the ubiquity of timing devices to synchronize the actions of people and things (for example, De Cortis, 1988; Hoc, 1995). The relation of time scales to spatial magnitude is shown in Figure 1.2.

Scale (s)	Epoch	System	Level of Interaction
10^7	months		
10^6	weeks		Society
10^5	days		
10^4	hours	Task	
10^3	10 min	Task	Work Group
10^2	minutes	Task	
10^1	10 sec	Unit Task	
10^0	1 sec	Operations	Cognition
10^{-1}	100 ms	Acts	
10^{-2}	10ms	Neural Circuit	
10^{-3}	1ms	Neuron	Neurophysiology
10^{-4}	100 microsec	Organelle	

Figure 1.2   A time scale of human actions (after Newell)

Human-Range: Boundaries to Unaided Action

One of the first lessons we can learn from the ideas in Figure 1.2 is that direct human experience is an extremely small subset of the range of possible overall experience. Let us define the limits of unaided 'human-range' to mean without the assistance of other instrumentalities including natural entities or manufactured tools or machines. Given the physical constraints of our musculoskeletal system, unaided humans cannot manipulate objects smaller that about 0.1 mm in size (0.025 inch). Also, in respect to an upper boundary to this range, we might be able to throw a stone some hundred yards or so but without some form of assistance we could not exceed this distance to any significant extent. Of course, the specification of this spatial boundary includes assumptions about time. Throwing the stone implies a force exerted over only a very short duration. Thus, spatial constraints cannot be specified independent of time constraints and vice versa. This mutual dependency is as important for the human sciences as it is for the physical sciences (see Locke, 1690; and see also Hancock and Newell, 1985). Unaided, human beings can achieve quite a lot over their lifetime. However, in the greater order of the universe any such achievement is tragically limited, as illustrated by Shelley's classic poem *Ozymandias* (Shelley, 1818). With respect to the boundaries of time, the lower threshold can be viewed as the duration that divides the performance of two separate tasks, or what the pre-eminent psychologist William James referred to as the 'specious' present. The upper temporal boundary is most likely considered the length of an individual's lifetime, although we may want to say that many humans leave partial representations of themselves through communication, procreation, or recreation after their death.

Over a lifetime, unaided by tools or orthotics, a human may change the local environment significantly. However, history shows that few existing archaeological monuments were constructed without the use of the then existing highest state of technology. Indeed it might be argued that no totally unaided human manipulations of the environment survive for long, and even the wonderful cave paintings of Lascaux have to be protected against their slow dissolution. In the overall picture then, the spatial and temporal dimensions are interdependent and the collective range over which any unaided human may exert action (*human-range* in Figure 1.1) is highly restricted in comparison to the limits of unaided perception. This latter limitation is explored in the following section.

Perceptual-Range: Boundaries to Unaided Perception

If the boundaries to unaided action are relatively restricted, the same cannot be said of the boundaries of unaided perception or what I will call *perceptual-range*. The lower temporal boundary is usually represented by events that are separated by fifty to one hundred milliseconds in duration (Poppel, 1988; Stroud, 1955; but see Vroon, 1974). This period is said to represent the 'perceptual moment' (Gibson, 1975) or, as previously noted, the 'specious present' (Clay cited by James, 1890; and see Minkowski, 1923). Depending upon what it is we wish to observe, various limits to spatial perception might be offered. Unaided, the human observer can see objects down to about 0.1 mm and from their motions infer the presence of even smaller, but not directly perceivable particles. Although without aid, empirical microbiology is somewhat limited, it is not the lower bounds of space and time that represent such a great contrast to the limits on action. Rather it is the upper bounds to unaided spatial perception. As can be seen from the superimposed envelope of *perceptual-range* in Figure 1.1, it is the vast regions of space that we may perceive unaided, but over which we cannot act at all that represents the major disparity between the two envelopes. It is then, as I have noted, no coincidence that astronomical observation provided a major early impetus for what we now recognize as 'science' (Koestler, 1959).

It is the 'tension' created by the dissociation between perception and action (I can see further than I can act) that provides motivation for exploration, as epitomized in Browning's couplet '... but a man's reach should exceed his grasp, or what's a heaven for?' The contemporary vehicle for such exploration is our application of science in the form of technology. However, 'reaching' as the metaphor for exploration and the struggle for knowledge is not a new conception. Nowhere is this urge more clearly represented than in the wonderful illustration of William Blake, '*I want, I want,*' which is reproduced in Figure 1.3. In this picture

Blake expresses the essence of our human desire to reach beyond our frustrating restrictions on action. Here again we see that Blake's example is taken from the large scale of space, a reaching toward the nearest celestial body (the moon). Our manifest inability to exercise influence over far distant objects has been clear for many millennia. It is, of course, of more than passing interest that arguably the greatest engineering feat of the twentieth century – the Apollo programme – was designed to and achieved the specific aim expressed in Blake's etching. The numerous other themes within Blake's illustration, for example, the use of the ladder metaphor for ascent into the heavens, have been explored by others (as in Bronowski's *The Ascent of Man*, 1958). As with all of Blake's work, however, there yet remains more irony and pathos to be distilled.

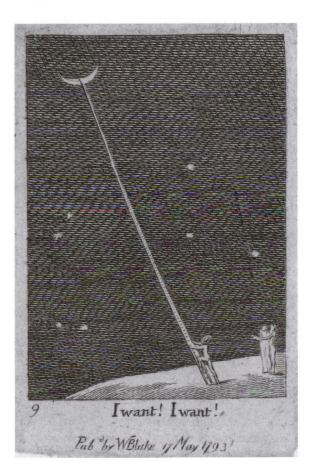

Figure 1.3   William Blake represents the eternal reaching of human nature in the illustration 'I want! I want!'. Reproduced by permission of the Fitzwilliam Museum, Cambridge, England

Orthotic-Range: Boundaries to Aided Action

In exploring and manipulating the environment with the aid of external implements, technology has always served two contrasting purposes. Tools increase the ranges of space and time over which an individual may act but this almost inevitably also increases the regions of space and time that can be observed. With respect to aided action, the envelope is expanded several orders of magnitude over the meagre limits of unaided action. Contemporary boundary markers to this *orthotic-range* are represented by elementary particle manipulations at the lower spatial range and the *Voyager* spacecraft and its physical presence beyond the edge of the solar system at the upper spatial range. It can be argued that humankind has exercised influence over a much larger spatial range if we consider any remaining information intrinsic to radiowaves that have left this planet within the last century and a half. The choice of which physical manifestation is used as the criterion may be subject to debate, but this difference merely extends the envelope of influence by some small multiple. The question as to specific numbers is not of particular concern here. Rather, the inevitable conclusion is that the advent of technology has increased the range of our capabilities by many orders of magnitude, a difference that continues to increase on a daily basis.

On the temporal scale, at the lower boundaries of time, we have now become familiar with pico-second measures (Rifkin, 1988). At the upper range of the time scale, modern data storage devices can preserve at least a small portion of an individual knowledge or expertise well beyond the individual's lifespan (Moravec, 1988). Indeed, history is the collective record of our individual actions and now goes back some five to six millennia. It may further be argued that procreation and the attendant information communication also perpetuate some portion of individuals' knowledge after death. According to allometric scaling, humans should live on average to approximately 27 years of age (see Schroots and Birren, 1990; and Yates, 1988). Already, our use of medicine and public hygiene as facets of technology stave off personal death for more than three- to four-fold our natural lifespan. Also, there is a trend with improvements in nutrition and personal fitness for individuals to perhaps live even longer. In spite of the limits on individual perception of spans of time, the scale for upper temporal boundaries of the things we create with technology are several orders of magnitude greater than any individual's lifetime. We have direct evidence that the constructions of our forebears have lasted some thousand years and we project that our own influence may probably last into the tens of thousands of years with intentional creations of steel and concrete and perhaps even hundreds of thousands of years with unintentional by-products (for example, nuclear waste). It is important however, to distinguish, at a number of levels, between mere persistence of effect versus creative and generative actions.

So far, we have contrasted ranges of unaided versus aided action and have looked at ranges of unaided perception. Now we must proceed to the examination of the largest expressed envelope that of aided perception. It is the most all-encompassing since it represents all that we can know of our universe.

Universal-Range: Boundaries to Aided Perception

Outside the orthotic scale then we find *universal-range*. This represents the boundaries of what we may perceive when aided by our technology. In essence, it represents the universe as it is known to us. Like other envelopes identified in this chapter, the universal-range continues to expand. An individual looking out into space is also looking back in time. This absolute interdependence of space and time has been recognized by physicists for over three centuries, while this combination (space–time) has also been explored with respect to human behaviour (Hancock and Newell, 1985; Moray and Hancock, 2009).

As I have noted, with the aid of contemporary technology the human range of perception is vastly increased. The resolution of the Hubble telescope has expanded the *universal-range* and has improved the knowledge of entities interposed between ourselves and that threshold. Like other forms of expensive and complex technical systems it proved vulnerable to failure (see Perrow, 1984; Reason, 1990), although it was successfully repaired. As with all such technologies, it is now coming close to its personal obsolescence as do all forms of technology and indeed all single human individuals.

At the aided lower end of the spatial scale, where observation fades into metaphor, we have begun to recognize the interaction of the conceivable and the perceivable, and the associated fusion of the potential with the actual. (There may in fact be absolute limits on the measurement of space and time at the Planck length and the Planck duration at 1.6×10^{-35} metres and 5.4×10^{-44} seconds respectively.) Comparable recognition at the upper extreme boundaries of space–time would represent a significant step forward. Nor is it happenstance that the very large often co-varies with the extremely prolonged and the very small frequently co-varies with the exceptionally brief. Such an observation exposes the fragility of using physical metrics to understand the basic living dimensions of experience for which humans is perhaps best described as a 'lifetime' (Hancock, 2002).

Synthesizing Scales

There is then a continual tension between these respective envelopes of aided perception and aided action. This tension is fed by the desire of humankind to exercise physical control over that which they can perceive. The inseparable nature of perception and action has been heavily emphasized in the ecological school of psychology as most eloquently expressed and championed by James Gibson (see Gibson, 1979). This approach affirms that what can be perceived is overwhelmingly the result of an individual's prior actions and what is then acted on largely results from the process of perception. What it means to perceive something is tantamount to what it means to have a history of interacting with that entity. Thus, for instance, a particular pattern of shapes might well impinge itself on the senses, but only in an act of perception is it apprehended as a sitting surface that composes a 'chair'. Traditionally, this linkage between perception and action has been illustrated as a circle in which perception and action are looped together (Neisser, 1976). However, if we now add our space-time framework to this conception, we can see these loops are actually elements in a spiral of development in which an individual learns from and expands upon their previous experience. Graphically, this can be shown as a perception-action spiral and this is illustrated in Figure 1.4. As noted, in this conception there is a continually expanding range over which the embedded perception-action loops function. In the modern world, technology plays an integral role in accelerating this spiral of exploration. It is indeed also one specific purpose of technology to resolve the inequities in the envelopes of perception and action. Therefore, we can recognize a companion view of technology as the vehicle which brings the *universal-range* in to *human-range* by representing entities at different scales, comprehensible at our specific human level.

In addition to the tension created by the dissonance between the disparate regions of perception and action, there is also a growing dissociation between activity and experience. For example, if a human operator (or more specifically a supervisory controller) interacts with a system via technically aided perceptions (displays) using technically aided actions (valves etc.), then the directness of everyday experience is replaced by a more abstract and indirect relationship (Sheridan, 2002). In essence, 'hands-on' experience disappears. Consequently, the further the envelopes expand away from the relatively fixed region of human-range, the further divorced is response from direct experience as, for example, in the control of Mars-based robotic exploratory vehicles. Such a difference is represented by the respective disparities in the envelopes of Figure 1.1.

Beyond the issue of 'tension', this leads to a second critical observation. As we progress in our efforts to perceive and influence the very large and the very small, we begin to rely exclusively on metaphorical representations of these entities with which, by constraint, we have had no direct experience. The necessary advisability

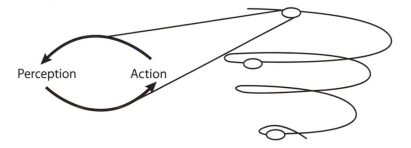

**Figure 1.4   Perception-action loops expand and interpolate into individual
and collective perception-action spirals**

of this strategy and some of the pitfalls and their possible remedies are the topics of other chapters in this book. The interim result is that technology must seek not only to expand *universal-range* but also to provide a representation of its content in a manner that is directly coherent within the *human-range*. This represents a major challenge to future development of technology in general, and to the science of human-machine systems in particular.

As we explore the ranges of our 'universe' that are ever further from our own personal experience, we have traditionally employed progressively more interconnected and interactive technologies to do so (Perrow, 1984). Indeed, it is the emergent properties of these interactions which frequently provide the challenge, the uncertainty, and the novelty that is sought alongside the expansiveness of exploration. However, problems mount as we move further from the *human-range* and as we use more complex orthotics to do so. It is, of course, a step of the imagination to understand that scale and, therefore, complexity are only relative to the entity under examination, whether it be human, machine or the human-machine dyad. It is such steps of imagination that are explored in the chapters which follow. However, before we can proceed in that direction, we have to take the present description and bring it to life. For activity is not static and neither should be our descriptions of it.

❖ ❖ ❖

Perception-Action in Space-Time

While the diagram in Figure 1.1 provides a first-pass representation of the envelopes of perception and action, it is a 'static' picture of what are essentially dynamic processes. However, in studying human activity we are primarily interested in an approach where the human operator dynamically 'navigates' through space and time in a goal-oriented fashion. One appropriate framework from which to approach the description of such dynamic navigation is the Minkowski space-time diagram (see Figure 1.5). For the present purpose the key idea of this representation can be encapsulated in the often reproduced quotation from Minkowski (1923) himself, in which he noted:

> space by itself and time by itself are doomed to fade away into mere shadows
> and only a union of the two would preserve an independent reality.

Minkowski went on to ask:

> who has been at a place except at a time, and who has experienced time except
> at a place?

Minkowski's space-time is a four-dimensional representation, usually illustrated for the purposes of simplicity as a two-dimensional diagram in which the three spatial dimensions are compressed into a single axis. The diagram, an example of which is shown in Figure 1.5, possesses four distinct areas which are parsed by a single point of intersection. The first of these quadrants represents the absolute past and contains the sum total of all knowable, previous events. This event landscape is composed of a series of what Minkowski termed 'world lines', one of which is illustrated here by the line labelled [A]. This represents the progress of a single individual or conscious entity. The sum of all world lines (essentially what becomes a world 'braid') represents the world (or the universe, depending upon the scale of one's analysis). Each active world line leads to an intersection between the absolute past and the absolute future. This intersection is labelled the 'specious' present. This represents the transition point between past and future and, as will be argued, implies the presence of a sentient observer (Hancock, 2005). Transition through the specious present sequentially reveals the absolute future as it passes on to become a deterministic component of the absolute past. On either side of the present, lies a symmetric region labelled the absolute elsewhere. Since the lines represent the speed of light and, as far as we know to the present nothing can exceed the speed of light, any observer within this framework cannot experience these regions of existence.

It is important to envisage what general characteristics compose the quadrants. Essentially, each is made up of distributions of energy. There are a number of visual representations of this and perhaps one of the most informative is a line-drawing from Kugler and Turvey (1987) as shown in Figure 1.6. Here, these authors present

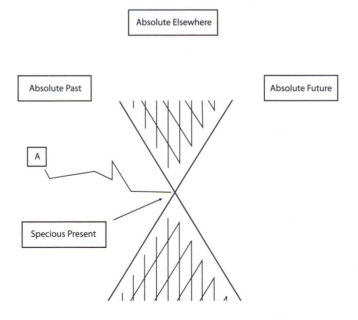

Figure 1.5   Minkowski's space-time diagram (1923)

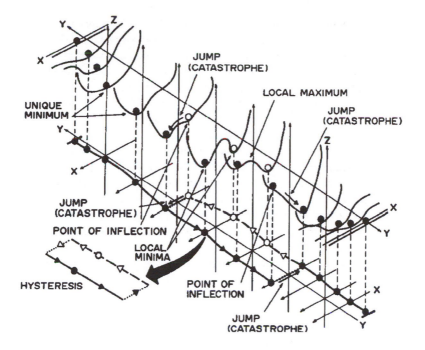

Figure 1.6   **An illustration of an energetic landscape with local catastrophes, discontinuities, and asymmetries noted. From Kugler and Turvey (1987), reproduced with permission**

a snapshot of this 'landscape', although the interaction of environment and observer is not illustrated. Since the present search is to understand how tasks are carried out by goal-oriented humans, we are really interested in representing navigation within this space-time framework. In Figure 1.5 we see a person or system, given by the letter [A], weaving their path through space-time. In the process of completing a task toward a declared goal, there are often perturbations that disturb one's progress toward achieving that goal. Thus, the operator or combined human-machine system must adapt to these various changing circumstances. In the case of an aircraft, for instance, the position and orientation of the craft must be maintained in spite of changes in wind-speed, engine power, fuel load, as well as other impinging factors. Tasks, where a path or goal must be pursued in spite of these perturbations, are fundamentally control tasks. Such tasks may be more or less difficult depending on the tools available and the degree of perturbation and uncertainty in the task environment.

Even when we can anticipate most of the likely sources of disturbance, skill is still required to get the performer to their desired state (Kirlik, 1995, Simon, 1981). Understanding the process of task achievement is difficult but informative. However, even though we might solve the many questions about how tasks are completed, we still face the more vexing question as to the origin of the initial intention or, more generally, why such tasks are undertaken in the first place (Iberall, 1992). In regard to task and goal success and sources of perturbation, a dramatic representation of this problem is given by Robert Louis Stevenson in his classic book *Treasure Island* (first published in 1883). The situation is described from the point of view of Jim Hawkins who is navigating a fragile craft on a difficult sea:

> I found each wave, instead of the big, smooth glossy mountain it looks from shore, or from a vessel's deck, was for all the world like any range of hills on the dry land, full of peaks and smooth places and valleys. The coracle, left to herself, turning from side to side, threaded, so to speak, her way through these lower parts, and avoided the steep slopes and higher, toppling summits of the wave. 'Well now,' I thought to myself, 'It is plain I must remain where I am, and not disturb the balance; but it is plain, also, that I can put the paddle over the side, and from time to time, in smooth places, give her a shove or two towards land'.

(Stevenson, 1946)

Stevenson (in the character of Jim Hawkins) was controlling his coracle (a small round boat) to a degree, and many of the principles that apply in steering such a craft through a rough sea also apply in navigating through the energy distributions in space-time by technological systems. This is not merely an apt analogy because any organism or system needs to establish some semi-stable platform (the equivalent of the coracle) from which to operate. However, an organism, or a human-machine system, faces the momentary demands of an uncertain environment (analogous to the wind and the waves) which acts to modify whatever level of stability can be achieved and to what degree any desired task can be completed. In this sense, navigation (in the fashion that is sought by Jim Hawkins) is the key adaptive capability of all humans. It is this adaptive capacity which is supported by modern technology, and not merely just the extension of senses or actions per se. However, the technological aiding that supports dynamic navigation is a two-edged sword. Technology assists the operator in maintaining control of these systems which expand effectiveness, but again only at the cost of distancing the operator from the site of cause and effect and the moment-to-moment experience of the proximal reality of that action.

When dynamic stability breaks down in such circumstances, it is much more difficult for the human operator to intervene successfully. A well-known example of failure in dynamic aiding occurred in a recorded aircraft incident where a thrust imbalance built up between the engines. The autopilot corrected for the thrust imbalance as long as possible after which the aircraft became unstable and went into a prolonged dive. In this case there were subtle cues as to change in the status of the aircraft and the way the autopilot was adapting to them, but these went unnoticed, largely due to the distancing of the operator from the system under automated operation (Parasuraman, Molloy, and Singh, 1993). Fortunately, the human pilots were able to recover the system and no fatalities were reported. Unfortunately, in other unbalanced systems, fatalities often occur.

The Unaided Individual in Space-Time

The foregoing argument has established that task performance toward a goal consists of events in space-time in which control is attempted in order to achieve desired states of semi-stability. Analysis of tasks that are resolved by human-machine systems is complicated by the interaction among the automated (technological) and human components of the system. Thus it will help in the general argument to first consider how the unaided individual navigates in space-time in order to understand the general principles and problems of such navigation without the added complication of having to consider the interaction between human and machine at the same time.

Human exploration can be viewed as the expansion of the potential paths of progress in the quadrant of the absolute future. As previously noted, this exploration is driven by the disparity between extent of human perception and the reach of human action. The question arises; which specific strategies are used in the exploratory process? It is insufficient simply to state that humans do explore, or simply to affirm that exploration is always going on, all the time, for all individuals. Among other things, this confuses progress with persistence (Russell, 1915). Rather, exploration is a result of goal-oriented decision-making and subsequent task performance in striving to achieve these goals. This form of exploratory strategy can be viewed as a sequence of decisions (cf., Newell, 1986) followed by a sequence of subsequent actions, which themselves trigger the need for following decisions or represent achievement of the goal itself. Figure 1.7 illustrates the contributions to the decision process using an expansion upon Newell's task–environment–organism triad to include the intention for action (the why), and the aiding that technology renders, as included in the process of achievement (the how) (see Jenkins, 1978).

The point of departure in task-oriented navigation is the present location, always at the specious present. The goal is then defined as some *desired state in the absolute future*. Implicit in this concept is the notion of planning. Planning implies the selection of achievable goals based on needs assessments and values (see Hoffman and Yates, 2005; Klein, 2007). It implies the integration of what is known, into a strategy to achieve what is desired. In Holland's (1992) terms it requires the synthesis of feedback with the potential for prediction. In the terms of ecological psychology it requires a blurring of the specious present to include envisioning perception-action effects in the future. This is the memory element that von Neumann noted was required by cybernetic systems. In the present terms it recognizes that dynamic navigation is not merely a reactive response to instantaneously presented conditions. Rather, navigation implies a proactive stance that helps mould the individual and their own personal future. Given

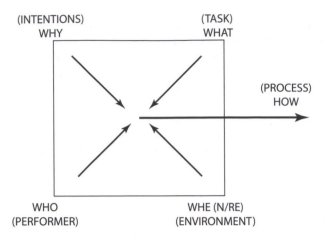

**Figure 1.7   Structure of and constraints on decisions. The outcome of the
decision is dictated by the confluence of constraints from the
four cited elements. The location of intention (why a task is
performed) and the operator (who performed it), as precursors
to action at the left of the diagram is intentional as the time
course of emergence ripples across the left–right arrangement**

that a sequence of actions can be performed based on decisions that are taken,
as illustrated in Figure 1.7, it is anticipated that there may well be significant
periodicities in behaviour that act rather like waves propagating along a channel
(see Iberall, 1992). That is, there are decisions which are then followed by periods
in which planned actions are executed. These in their turn lead to subsequent
decisions as new circumstances emerge to either block or facilitate the planned
path to the desired goal. There are certain intrinsic rhythms to these sequences that
are somewhat independent of the external circumstances.

   In traditional approaches, a goal is most often represented as a single future
location. However, humans and systems frequently seek to achieve multiple goals
at the same time (Rasmussen, 1986). A specific sequence of actions may even
be directed towards the most desirable compromise that exists between two or
more of these competing goals. In the special case of a single goal, the manifest
intention of the operator would be to traverse the region between the present
state and the goal state as efficiently as possible. Constrained by the factors noted
in Figure 1.7, there are a limited number of possible paths which permit this
transition (Shaw and Kinsella-Shaw, 1989). *It is the choice between these paths
which represents the strategies of exploratory behaviour.* Attention is the primary
facet of consciousness which decides on one course of action over its various
alternatives. Indeed, attention may be defined as this very capacity itself. Once a

decision is made, an individual strategy is constructed as the linked sequence of activities directed to attain the prescribed goal.

One of the problems in designing human-machine systems is that they often unintentionally violate this general principle of attaining the desired goal at the least energetic cost. Human goal-directed strategies that work well for the unaided individual in a non-technical environment are sometimes inappropriate in a technologically aided world. For a general example of this maladaptation, consider the role of energy throughout the whole of evolution. The evolutionary imperative on many organisms has been on the need for individual *energy minimization* (Swenson and Turvey, 1991). Those organisms which were inefficient in their uses of energy, most frequently did not survive. However, the advent of technology fractures this strict energetic or 'cost' constraint on actions. Hence, we have an organism (the human operator) with a vestigial strategic imperative (energy minimization), placed in a largely 'manufactured' environment in which such a strategy is frequently no longer necessarily appropriate. Part of the process of designing any form of artefact then is the need to recognize these vestigial imperatives and to amend the perception-action-machine linkages accordingly. Parenthetically, this might be the reason that we often view individuals as 'lazy'. In essence, they are driven by the evolutionary imperative to get as much return for as little investment of energy as possible. This strategy has worked very well when the challenges are framed at the level of the human capacities which have evolved to confront them. That is at levels of unaided human perception and action. The story is very different in worlds which are now largely expanded away from these inherent human limitations.

❖ ❖ ❖

Metaphor, Systems Control, and Ecological Principles

The further any human-machine system operates from the *human-range* in space and time, the more abstract the control representation becomes. The *human-range* is meant to imply some direct perception in terms of object size and event duration. However, it does not necessarily exclude empathy with control spaces that emerge from human-machine interaction. For example, in the origin and development of the Industrial Revolution, we find frequent reference to skilled workers who operate through an intrinsic 'feel' for the process under their control. Thus, anyone who has ever felt for the slot in a screw by moving the handle of a screwdriver will know what I mean. To such individuals, augmented information as to the status of a single variable in the process often meant little more than a distraction. Rather, it was the confluence and emergent properties of multiple interactive factors and the cues that such emergent properties provided upon which their skilled, intuitive or empathic grasp was based. In many cases, measures of absolute level were of limited use compared to these relative values. How many of us have had some 'back-room' person who just seemed to know the system inside-out, while the rest of us struggled with arcane instructions and indistinct symptoms associated with the frustrating, periodic failures?

With the evolution of technology, the ability to grasp intuitively the interactive states of ever more complex systems becomes progressively a more rare skill. This is especially true for new technologies, which themselves do not possess sufficient history such that a skilled cadre of 'masters' can be accessed. Given the learning that is needed, it would seem advisable to make the interface to some of these emerging systems in the form of 'video games'. This is because there always appears to be a following of young people who are ever-willing to learn each of the nuances of such entertainments.

One natural reaction to this reduction in 'process empathy' is the attempt to substitute ever greater amounts of information for former hands-on experience. A specific example of this reduction might be in beer-making, where the brewer in a large facility would know the state of the process by the sounds, the smells and the tastes of an emerging brew. Separating the brewer from this perceptually rich environment and leaving them only in control of a sterile bank of computers in a divorced control room would most likely result in poor beer indeed. Unfortunately, this strategy of substituting ever more representational information for direct experience is based on the supposed principle that embedded within this avalanche of data must be the right 'answer' to the dynamic questions that are currently being posed to the operator. However, the increasing system complexity can and does defeat skilled intuition. This defeat is often exacerbated by the untamed proliferation of physically confusing and ambiguous analogue and digital displays. Such proliferation eventually requires some form of further computer mediation, thus removing the operator even one more step from an empathic grasp of the process itself. The solution to the problem of decreased process empathy does not lie in the first-aid type remediation of poorly conceived displays. Rather, it is founded on a fundamental re-evaluation of the theoretical basis for information displays in the first place. Although metaphor and ecology do not seem to sit well in the same sentence, we should recognize that a profound change in display strategy must be grounded upon knowledge of how the perceiver actually views the world as a display in the first place.

Preliminary attempts at this strategy have generated a class of displays called – 'direct displays'. They are founded upon the critical notion of *affordances* (although there is still no consensus as to what an affordance actually is, see Turvey, 1992). In general, an affordance is a theoretical construct that addresses the perception of meaning in environments and by extension in artificial displays. Gibson (1979, p. 127) explains that:

> The affordances of the environment are what it offers the animal, what it provides or furnishes, either for good or ill. The verb to afford is found in the dictionary, but the noun affordance is not. I have made it up. I mean by it something that refers to both the environment and the animal in a way that no existing term does. It implies the complementarity of the animal and the environment.

He concluded that:

> The possibilities of the environment and the way of life of the animal go together inseparably. The environment constrains what the animal can do, and the concept of a niche in ecology reflects this fact. Within limits, the human animal can alter the affordances of the environment but is still the creature of his or her situation. There is information in stimulation for the physical properties of things, and presumably there is information for the environmental properties. ... Affordances are properties taken with reference to the observer. They are neither physical nor phenomenal.

(Gibson, 1979, p. 143)

Therefore, an affordance is essentially a functional relationship among people, objects, or properties within the environment and the perceptual capabilities of the individual perceiver. The advantage of such a conception is that it obviates the need for translation and representation of the environment on behalf of the observer. Given such an affordance the advantage appears to be that ambiguity is purportedly eliminated, and thus action is uniquely specified. Degrees of degeneration from this 'best of all possible worlds' occur as we introduce individual perceivers, who may or may not assimilate the intended affordances, and for whom the action specified might vary according to their immediate goals or intentions. This degree of degeneration from this pristine version of an affordance resurrects the concept of valence, in which actions are not uniquely specified but probabilistically specified.[1]

The generation of 'direct' displays and its extension into ecological interface design (Bennett and Flach, 1992; Flach and Bennett, 1992; Vicente and Rasmussen, 1990) is an attempt to disambiguate task conditions and, by implication, to make affordances visible. The search for a framework for seeking, validating, and generalizing affordances across multiple conditions is still ongoing. In designing technologies and their displays, we have the advantage of not only benefiting from naturally occurring affordances, but seeking the potential for creating new affordances, or of exploiting culturally defined expectations. Naturally, there is considerable debate over what exactly constitutes a direct display (as there is over

---

1   There are perhaps few concepts as important and contentious as that of affordances. Reed (1988, p. 231) notes that: 'Affordances are the functional properties of objects as, for example, the affordance of a heavy stick or rock for pounding. Any particular object will probably have many affordances. An apple may be eaten, thrown, juiced, or baked to name but a few of its affordances. Yet a given object will also lack many affordances. An apple is no use as a brick or as kindling.' And yet it is. The problem being, it doesn't serve this function very well. It is clear that for an ecological approach to human-machine systems to work, the concept and functional utility of affordances are critical (see Hancock, 1993). It is equally clear that further elucidation is still needed (see Stoffregen, 2000).

affordances themselves), and the extent to which such displays should rely on metaphor in converting displays into a more easily assimilated and understood form. One promising avenue for enhancing directness of displays is the use of virtual reality. However, in spite of problems in defining and implementing directness in displays, it is clear that the evidence against the past approach, where operators are provided with a 'data dump' of undigested information about the system, is considerable and growing. This in turn proves the need for the metamorphosis from data transmission to knowledge apprehension. It is, I believe, primarily through the application of ecological psychology and its principles to this realm of human-machine systems that substantive *near term* gains can be expected in process empathy, and in awareness (Smith and Hancock, 1995) of critical system parameters and states (see Vicente, 2004).

What then is the role of the science of human-machine systems in enhancing process empathy? Clearly it is necessary to implement more direct displays and to implement appropriate metaphors and models where needed. However, there is also a need for a broader view. Technology is driven by forces that require that the boundaries that have been identified are progressively enlarged. Technology is required to become faster, greater in physical size, or at least density per unit volume. When connected with other systems, technology also grows in complexity.

Often such progress can appear relatively 'mindless', or progress for progress's sake. That is, this nominal progress is driven by numerous external forces beyond the control of any one single individual or even coherent group of individuals. Similarly, it can also appear that few individuals are directly concerned whether such progress is 'beneficial' either in a specific or in a more general sense. The latter must nearly always be the case since democratic society specifies no explicit goals other than global assertions such as 'freedom from want', or everyone possessing the right to 'life, liberty, and the pursuit of happiness' as discussed in the final chapter of this book. Thus, while the discipline of Human Factors has frequently been characterized as merely facilitating human interaction with technology, the emergence of a full science of human-machine systems at its most fundamental is essentially a socio-political endeavour, whether or not its practitioners conceive of it as such. In essence, we need to elevate the question 'why' and the fundamental issue of intentionality to its appropriate and pre-eminent position (cf., Iberall, 1992, Nickerson, 1992). Process is all very fine but purpose is the prime mover.

❖ ❖ ❖

Technology and Nature: Symbiosis and Antagonism

The environment in which we live is largely a manufactured one. The adaptations which we now make are to conditions that our forebears created. These previous actions were in turn adaptations to earlier conditions. Scientists may claim to stand on the shoulders of giants, but most human beings stand on the physical foundations fabricated by their forebears. From this general perspective, there is a tendency to contrast the modern conditions of the human built environment with the earlier and supposedly more 'natural' world. This comparison may be moot since there is no obvious metric or scale to measure the naturalness of technology itself (cf., Hoffman and Deffenbacher, 1993, Table 2, p. 320). Horse-drawn transportation is not intrinsically more natural than steam-driven transportation (Pirsig, 1974). The bridle, the saddle, and the wagon-wheel are all technologies of their own time that adapted and changed the environment to suit human tasks and goals. It is not the adaptation of the environment itself which leads to problems, but rather the indirectness and abstraction that has come to characterize such adaptation in today's complex systems. Thus methods of adaptation in complex systems are needed that allow both direct and empathic awareness of system states and parameters. This is what is missing and what some nostalgically yearn for.

The artificial division between 'natural' and unnatural technology finds one of its roots in the origins of science itself. Indeed, one unique facet of human beings themselves is that they are the wielders of science, which is perhaps a stronger distinction of human uniqueness than previous divisions based on the use of tools (Oakley, 1949). Prior to the fourteenth century it was considered both logical and feasible to countenance what we would now view as non-rational explanations of many world characteristics. Indeed, we see that the propensity to invoke such mystical explanations being perpetuated well into the present time. However, the growth of science acted to provide a verifiable account of all experiential phenomena (cf., Bronowski, 1978a). Thus the appeal of science is to the discovery and manipulation of natural laws and not their random suspension or apparent transgression. This observation lies at the very foundation of Francis Bacon's observation on the paradox that 'we cannot command nature except by obeying her'.

Embedded deep in this concept of naturalness is the notion of harmony or symbiosis, which is a face of natural philosophy that has perhaps been tarnished and degraded by the flash and sparkle of technology. From an initial stance of understanding and cooperating with nature, humans have rapidly evolved to an attitude of subjugation of and indeed conflict with nature. This attitude may be explicitly stated, as in the 'unsinkable' epithet applied to the *Titanic*, or implied, as in our confidence in many contemporary processes. In reality, technology has generated a veneer that has fostered in us a self-importance in which we wish only to command. Crucially, we have neglected to understand the critical importance of environmental harmony, although the more recent focus on global climate effects is a welcome contra-indication. Hubris threatens to destroy us. Today, we see in many technologies the characteristics of command and control where 'pressure' in all its physical and metaphorical forms appears as nature is constrained, blocked, and opposed. A particular example of this phenomenon is the US Army Corps of Engineers' permanent battle with the lower reaches of the Mississippi river and its threatened capture by the Atchafalaya river channel. To resolve this we must engage in an explicit search for a symbiosis between nature and technology.

❖ ❖ ❖

Adaptive Systems

We need to develop adaptive systems in which human, machine, and environment operate together harmoniously. The nature of such adaptive human-machine systems has been identified and a strategy as to how such adaptation may occur through the medium of intelligent interfaces has been proposed by Hancock and Chignell (1989). We can extend this argument by considering human-machine symbiosis in a broader context and by projecting such interaction into the future. While the future of machine intelligence and symbiotic co-evolution is necessarily uncertain, we can still expect the general principles of human-machine interaction to apply (see Salvendy, 1987).

Humans and Technology as Co-evolutionary Agents

In a small and increasing way now, but in a much more profound influence in the near future, intelligent technology will assume a major role as an agent in the process of co-evolution. Such growth is contingent upon the degree of nascent intentionality present in technical systems. This issue is very much related to the question of machine intelligence (see Anderson, 1964; Turing, 1950). Since there is no fundamental requirement that an agent which acts to influence evolution in others necessarily possesses intentionality, or even sentience, we are not as yet in direct evolutionary competition with our technology. Yet our dependence on technology already influences who we are and who our progeny will be. It is unclear what our relationship to intelligent systems will eventually be, and how non-biological intelligence will develop in the future (see Moravec, 1988; and Kurzweil, 2005). However, the birth of machine 'intelligence' promises to be a global benchmark that sees us emerge from our present state to a new stage of development of which, as yet, we can only glimpse the dim shadows (Hoffman et al., 2003). Indeed, there are many regions of space-time that cannot be explored by either human or machine alone. I have discussed earlier in this chapter how these regions can be envisaged as energetic 'landscapes' of constraints and opportunities. What we have to appreciate is that humans have evolved specifically to deal with one form of 'landscape' and in doing so have accumulated a wealth of context-specific expertise and capability in order to cope with such conditions. Whether these capabilities will serve as well in a machine-aided world we have yet to fully comprehend. However, it will move our argument forward to consider how resident human expertise has evolved.

The Edge of Chaos[2]

The hallmark of an expert is their ability to operate close to the edge of chaos without falling into chaos itself nor receding to immutability. Like the skilled surfer, the expert occupies preferred regions of operations but never the absolute extremes. A cross-section of such an energetic landscape facing the performer is shown in Figure 1.8. As can be seen, at one end of the continuum we have an absolute minimum. In this situation, the system or person has reached a state in which they are unable to function. Here, adaptation fails. More importantly, exploration has failed and knowledge of one's past and expectations of one's future are of no value unless some exogenous change is enacted (Holland, 1992). The other end of the continuum is pure chaos. Here again adaptation, exploration, feedback and projection are of no value since output is not meaningfully connected to input. Between these extremes we have regions of local minima and regions of incipient chaos (Thompson and Stewart, 1986).

My contention is that experts and by extension 'skilled' or advanced human-machine systems exist in the region of, and need to explore, the edge of chaos. In crossing chaotic thresholds, unintended outcomes frequently result. If the situation is recoverable, we then seek to withdraw to more stable regions and adopt more conservative operational strategies. After a recovery of confidence or trust, we

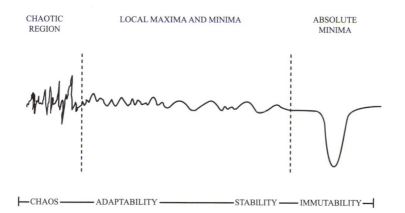

CHAOTIC REGION   LOCAL MAXIMA AND MINIMA   ABSOLUTE MINIMA

├─CHAOS──────ADAPTABILITY──────────────STABILITY───IMMUTABILITY─┤

Figure 1.8   Cross-section of an energetic 'landscape' from pure randomness beyond the chaotic at one extreme to terminal stasis at the other. Adaptation fails at one extreme for lack of stability, it fails at the other extreme for lack of freedom of motility

---

2   The phrase, and an intriguing phrase it is, comes from the Santa Fe Institute group doing work on complexity and self-organization. The originators of the phrase, N. Packard and C. Langton, are those to whom attribution is due (see Kauffman, 1993).

return toward the threshold of chaos, where maximal benefit can be experienced. It is the process of exploring around the edges of chaos that allows people to exploit the operational possibilities that the 'landscape' represents. This is somewhat analogous to the test pilot's task of 'pushing the envelope' (Wolfe, 1979) and can be a design principle for 'direct' displays which seek to make the thresholds in such landscapes visually manifest and operationally obvious (see Hansen, 1995; Vicente, 1995). It has been contended that it was only by exploring these boundaries that life itself developed. By analogy we may expect the edge of chaos to be a breeding ground for the co-evolution of future human-machine systems.

Engineering for success in exploring these unstable regions of operation includes the initial need for exploration, the capacity for error recovery and the explicit recognition of purpose. Such exploration can most readily be accomplished by achieving a simple interchange of knowledge and information between human and machine elements in languages each understand (Hancock and Chignell, 1989). In light of the adaptive and explorative nature of the enterprise, it is clear that these necessities arise for co-evolving human-machine systems that push the envelope of existing technology and knowledge. If we are to safely explore the edges of chaos, we must 'engineer' into these systems the many strategies that originally made humans themselves successful as a species.

It is critically important to recognize that the energetic 'landscape' in which humans have evolved is both *qualitatively* and *quantitatively* different from the 'landscapes' of the absolute future which are encountered when humans work with machines. That is, while humans *were* experts for the vast majority of our species development, technology has radically altered the nature of the opportunities and constraints of the 'landscapes' in which we now operate. It is not merely the outward manifestation of change in the physical environment (for example, the skyscrapers of cityscapes and the 'dark satanic mills' of the Industrial Revolution), but it is the fundamental energetic nature of the operational workspaces that have been altered. Although these latter changes are not as immediately observable as the simple characteristics of our surrounding physical environment, they are nevertheless fundamental elements in the world in which we live.

Some might argue that the 'laws' of nature are immutable and thus the same constraints apply to the actions of collaborative human-machine systems as they do to the actions of humans alone. This argument has a seductive appeal since parsimony and elegance are so prized in the scientific enterprise. Yet such constraints are as much on the mind as on the physical body, and emergent technologies offer realms of exploration in which our hard-won and prized laws no longer apply unequivocally.

An example from modern technology is evident in virtual reality (see Hancock, 2009). Whenever we explore these 'possible worlds' we still take all our resident characteristics with us. Many existing response capabilities simply do not transfer well. Further, in altering the energetic 'landscape', technology introduces any number of novel pitfalls. It is not merely that the steamroller of technology rearranges the landscape, but that it inserts its own (frequently hidden) potentialities for catastrophe. Perrow (1984) and Reason (1990) have discussed at length such forms of system error or 'resident pathogens' which are so easily recognized *post hoc* but frequently so hard to identify *a priori* (Dekker, 2003).

We may be able to gain insight into potential failures of human-machine systems by again referencing recent work on biological organization. Kauffman (1993) has transposed Raup's (1986) data, concerning extinction events in the Phanerozoic geologic era, into a log-log plot and this data is illustrated in Figure 1.9. Here, the event is the living system encountering total failure (extinction). The base axis of time refers to the rate at which such extinction events are encountered 'in the wild'. As can be seen from the graph there are very few, very large extinction events when many species are destroyed at one time. In contrast, there are very many minor extinction events when just one or a few species are destroyed.

In respect of this pattern, Kauffman (1993, p. 268) observed that:

> A first general conclusion is the insight that co-evolutionary avalanches propagate through ecosystems, that such avalanches have characteristic frequency-versus-size distributions which change depending on the parameters of the system. In particular, the distribution of avalanche sizes depends on how solid the frozen state is. If we tentatively accept Raup's data as weak evidence, the frozen state is modestly firm. Using Raup's data and improved evidence, we may ultimately be able to build a theory linking both ecosystems, structure and extent of external perturbations to the size distribution of coevolutionary avalanches and to such phenomena as the distribution of extinction events.

> A second and critical result is this: Perturbations of the same initial size can unleash avalanches on a large variety of length scales. This conclusion is clear and important. In these simulations, the perturbation in each case is a change in the external world of a single randomly chosen species in the ecosystem. If we may tentatively assume that avalanches can be linked to extinction events, then these results strongly suggest that uniform alterations in the external world during evolution can cause a diversity of sizes in extinction events. This possibility stands in contrast to the generally held hypotheses that small and large extinction events are associated with small and cataclysmic changes in the external world. Since the external environment has almost certainly undergone changes on a variety of scales, I do not wish to assert that high variability in extinction sizes does not in part reflect a heterogeneity in intensity of causes. But these results place part of the responsibility for extinction-size diversity on the dynamics of coupled ecosystems and on the ways in which damage propagates.

> But the third conclusion is the most important: Raup's data suggest that ecosystems do coevolve to the edge of chaos. More precisely, the data suggest that ecosystems are slightly within the frozen regime. Thus we ourselves hover on the edge of a new view of coordinated coevolutionary processes among interacting adaptive entities.

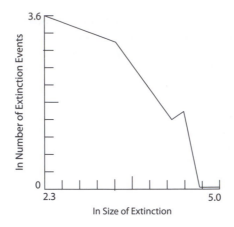

Figure 1.9   **Kauffman's (1993) re-plot of Raup's (1986) data on the log
number of extinction events versus the log size of those events.
If a derived power law relationship held for human-machine
failures also, it would imply a fundamental isomorphism between
biological and technical systems. This is an as yet, empirically
untested proposition which is of particular significance**

If we consider human-machine systems as interacting adaptive agents, which
is a position that I advocate here, then the insights rendered by Kauffman and
Raup have particular pertinence for all human systems engineering. Given the
power law relationship, then an empirically testable proposition would relate the
frequency of failure in complex technical systems to the size of such failures (for
example, disastrous plane crashes are much less frequent than less disastrous
aviation events such as near misses, rejected take-offs, etc.). Confirmation of such
an observation would support the notion that technology is bound by some of the
same constraints as biological systems and hence insights about the latter, their
adaptation, proliferation and failure may be directly extrapolated. Disproof of the
applicability of this power law assertion would question the *qualitative* way in
which human-machine systems resemble 'natural' ecosystems and would imply
the need for additional principles. The present perspective is that there is much in
common but potential differences make the simple assertion of direct equivalence
unwarranted at the present.

❖ ❖ ❖

Summary

Human-machine systems science studies the critical bridge between people and
technology. However, it supersedes this specific constrained role by its supra-

ordinate function as the directed and conscious way in which we manipulate our environment and thus our future selves. James Gibson (1979) himself had much to say about this technical activity. He noted:

> In the last few thousand years, as everybody now realizes, the very face of the earth has been modified by man. The layout of surfaces has been changed, by cutting, clearing, leveling, paving, and building. Natural deserts and mountains, swamps and rivers, forests and plains still exist, but they are being encroached upon and reshaped by man-made layouts. Moreover, the substances of the environment have been partly converted from the natural materials of the earth into various kinds of artificial materials such as bronze, iron, concrete, and bread. Even the medium of the environment – the air for us and the water for fish – is becoming slowly altered despite the restorative cycles that yielded a steady state for millions of years prior to man.
>
> We all fit into the substructures of the environment in our various ways, for we were all, in fact, formed by them. We are created by the world we live in.

> (Gibson, 1979, pp. 129–30)

We were indeed created by the world we live in and the world our forebears grew up in. It is critical at this time to recognize the reciprocal effect in our creation of that world far more explicitly. In his essay on the origins of human-machine studies, Karl Smith (1987) wrote:

> It is the science of fitting the job to the worker and learner as well as fitting machines to people. It transcends limited engineering formulations of the user-machine relationship and deals preeminently with how people have created themselves by systematically human factoring their environment.

In a similar vein, Gregory (1981) argued that:

> The immense importance of technology in molding how we think has implications still only dimly appreciated, … It does, however, imply that any psychology based only on our biological origins is going to be inadequate: what is amazing about man is how far he has escaped his origins. This is through the use of tools, and the effect on us of technology that the tools have created.

It is perhaps appropriate here to give Aristotle the last word. To paraphrase one of his assertions, he noted that:

> We cannot directly will to be different than we are. It is therefore only by changing our environment that we change ourselves.

We can argue over the veracity of this statement. However, we cannot deny that our environment exerts a powerful influence in shaping present and future generations. In contemporary society, there are many forces that conspire to expand the boundaries of exploration through the proliferation of technical capability. In contrast, individuals who act to reconcile these advances with human capacities are relatively few in number. Failures of this reconciliation process are chronicled in the spectacular system failures that almost daily regale the news media. Yet these acute insults to social functioning may be relatively trivial compared with the chronic effects of a continuing maladaptive relationship between people and the technical, manufactured environments in which they live. If it is true that our effective legacy lives through our progeny and the environment that we sculpt for them, then a science of human-machine systems cannot be considered just an appendage to the applied practice of psychology or engineering. Such an endeavour encompasses much more than 'device advice' or a mere 'appliance science'. Rather, it is a pursuit that is central to the success of the human enterprise itself – or its failure.

In what follows in this book, I consider the various descriptive elements discussed in this first chapter and especially, towards the end of this text, the question of morality of human-machine systems and their design and usage. To begin these considerations, I first must turn to the question of intentionality, or more broadly, teleology.

Chapter 2
Teleology for Technology

I have seen
The old gods go
And the new gods come
Day by day
And year by year
The idols rise
Today
I worship the hammer.

(*The Hammer* by Carl Sandburg)

TELEOLOGY: 1. The doctrine of final causes or purposes; 2. the study of the evidence of design or purpose in nature; 3. such design or purpose; 4. the belief that purpose and design are a part of, or are apparent in nature.

TECHNOLOGY: 1. The branch of knowledge that deals with the industrial arts: the sciences of the industrial arts. 2. the terminology of an art, science, etc.; technical nomenclature.

'Lo! Men have become tools of their tools.'

(Henry David Thoreau)

Statement of Purpose

Science and technology have always tried to answer the question 'how?' How does this or that mechanism work? What are the laws and causal properties which underlie this or that phenomenon? In the case of technologies, how can such knowledge be used to develop a useful tool or machine? However, science and technology rarely address the question 'why?' It is often conceived as being outside their respective spheres of discourse. The question is ruled inadmissible or not appropriate for the methods and capabilities at hand. I dismiss this rejection. I believe that the questions how and why are so mutually dependent that they should never be considered independently. Indeed, I attribute much of our present grim circumstances to this unfortunate and unhappy division. Those who know how must always ask why. Those who ask why must always think how.

Overview of the Chapter

With reference to the foregoing thematic statement, I want to examine our collective future by asking questions about our intention with respect to technology. This argument is set against a background of current human-machine systems and particularly the rise of automatic systems. I do this because of my belief that technology cannot and should never be considered in the absence of human intention. Likewise, contemporary societal aims have no meaning without reference to the pervasive technology which powers them. I start off the discussion with a prelude which presents a metaphor to frame the initial considerations. I then define the terms within which the chapter's arguments are framed. This definition of terms leads to an examination of what technology is and to what extent technology is 'natural'. I then examine human-machine symbiosis and potential futures that may be encountered by such a co-evolutionary pairing. I will point to human-centred automation as one stage in this sequence of evolution that will eventually witness the birth of autonomous machine intention about which I express a number of cautions. In noting the stage-setting function of contemporary systems design, I cite earlier warnings concerning previously held principles of human-machine interaction. My hypothesis is that the collective potential future for humans and machines can only be assured by the explicit enactment of mutually beneficial goals. In the immediate future, I caution against the possibility of a society divided by technology against itself. I advocate for a science of human-machine systems as a liberating force in providing technical emancipation, the heart of which is universal education.

❖ ❖ ❖

A Metaphorical Prelude

> It is in this way alone that one comes to grips with a great mystery that life and
> time bear some curious relationship to each other that is not shared by inanimate
> things.

(Loren Eiseley)

Setting the 'Scene'

To start this chapter, I want to put a vision in your head. To do this, I am going to use a familiar icon. This icon is not a single picture but rather, it is a scene from a famous motion picture. The film is Alfred Hitchcock's *North by North-West*, the scene is the coast road. I hope this brief description will let most readers identify the sequence I mean. However, for those who are not familiar with the movie, it is as follows. Our hero, Cary Grant, has been forcibly intoxicated by the henchmen of the evil James Mason on the mistaken assumption that Grant is an investigating government agent. To rid themselves of this menace, the evildoers put the now drunk Grant in a car and start him off on a perilous trip down a steep and winding coast road. Through force of will and no small portion of luck our hero manages to survive both the human and the environmental sources of danger to fight again. Even those who have not seen the film will not be surprised to know that in the end the forces of evil are routed and our hero survives to win the girl.

A Metaphoric Relation

This outcome is all well and good in film plots, but I want to use Grant's vehicular progress as a metaphor for our own uses of technology. I want to suggest that we, like him, are careening down a dangerous path. Like Grant, we have not intentionally put ourselves in this predicament but nevertheless, here we are. We each possess similar goals, in which simple survival has the highest priority. Both we and Grant are painfully aware that the volatile combination of powerful technology and fallible humans in unstable environmental circumstances threaten disaster. While our progress resembles Grant's in many respects, we are radically different in some critical ways. Above all things, we have no director to shout 'cut' when things get too dangerous or script-writer to 'ensure' that the story ends well. Unlike Grant, we also seem to be drinking heavily as we proceed down the mountainside in, apparently, a progressively more chaotic fashion. We do however have a science whose primary purpose seems to be to ensure that we are able to keep a firm grip on the bottle and a lead foot on the accelerator. The science is what has been traditionally known as 'Human Factors'. Also, we have a motive force that seeks to accelerate the rate of our 'progress'. The force is *technology*.

Meta-Technical Purpose

By using this metaphor, I am suggesting that the emerging science of human-machine systems largely fails to address the fundamental purposes of and for technology. Those involved in the facilitation of human-machine interaction rarely question whether technology represents the appropriate avenue through which human society can achieve its necessary goals. The traditional science of Human Factors seems to have accepted the current social assumptions behind technology. In so doing it looks to facilitate human-machine interaction, even if the purpose of the machine is suicide, genocide, or terracide. By this generalization, I do not mean that many individual members of this science do not question such functions; they definitely do (for example, Moray, 1993, 1994; Nickerson, 1992; see also Hancock, 1993). However, as a body, those scientists involved in human-machine interaction have yet to state that it *is* their role to question the very purposes of technology. *I affirm that it is.* Those outside the scientific and technical community frequently protest about their perceived helplessness and the subsequent fallout of technology. However, it is Human Factors scientists and practitioners who shape human interaction with technology that can and should 'direct' from within.

More Than an 'Appliance Science'

Therefore, in what follows I want to question the fundamental tenets of human interaction with technology. I want to question whether the human-machine sciences should *always* facilitate the human-machine linkage, especially when such improvements are clearly antagonistic to the collective good. I want to question whether we should always assume that technological growth, and increased automation in particular, are appropriate. In sum, I want to question where we are going with technology and what our goals and purposes are.

As is clear from the discussion in the first chapter, my conviction is that Human Factors and the emergence of more widespread human-machine sciences are more than just a form of 'appliance science'. I believe that human-machine systems studies can exert a strong influence in what we do with technology and these are beginning to be recognized more and more in that role (Sedgwick, 1993). I believe this science can be a critical voice in determining the goals we collectively set for ourselves. It is the mandate of Human Factors to mediate between humans, technology, and the environment. This mediation requires informed value judgments. I think Human Factors scientists must acknowledge and grasp this social responsibility. The future is too important to be left to the accidental happenstance of time, the pointlessness of financial greed, or the commercial search for something smaller, faster, and less expensive. In essence, the carefree adolescence of humankind is now at an end and this new millennium must hail an age of responsible societal adulthood. If not, it will in all likelihood witness our eventual demise as a species.

I fully realize that the foregoing is largely a series of polemical exhortations. The reader is entitled to enquire not only about the basis for such assertions but the reasons why they should be put forward as important at this time. I think the answer is simple. It is in the final decades of the twentieth century and the first decades of the twenty-first century that we are starting to set the agenda for automated technologies and the stance of humans with respect to such automated systems. In truth, this represents the earliest growth of machine autonomy and independence. Decisions made now constrain what will be possible in our future. I want that future to contain at least sufficient alternatives for one to be our continued survival.

❖ ❖ ❖

A Definition of Terms: Teleology and Technology

> Machines just don't understand humans. They [automobiles] don't understand that they should start even when we do dumb things like leave the lights on or fail to put antifreeze in the radiator. But maybe they understand us too well. Maybe they know we rely on them instead of ourselves and, chuckling evilly in the depths of their carburettors, they use that knowledge against us.

We humans forget how to rely on our own skills. We forget we can survive without machines; we can walk to the grocery store even if it's a mile away. We forget that before the calculator, we used our brains. (Well at least some of us did.) We forget that the Universe doesn't grind to a halt when machines break down. Machines like that. They're waiting for us to get soft and defenseless so they can take over the world.

(Karen Tolkkinen, 'Machines are making us soft', *Minnesota Daily*, Thursday, 27 January 1994)

In what follows, I hope to show some of the fallacies and misunderstandings that underlie Tolkkinen's recidivist position.

Teleology: A Traditional View

I want to define the terms that are central to the arguments which follow. I start with the term 'teleology'. Teleology is a word that has historically been used with respect to the existence of a deity or some form of final cause or purpose for being, although in respect to the Artistotelian interpretation it need not necessarily be so associated. The concept of teleology is founded upon our human observations of order in the universe. The teleological argument postulates that because the universe shows this order there must be some entity behind that order which creates and directs it. Although if the initial act of creation itself served to kill such a god then the process of creation and ongoing direction can be theologically separable. Deism argues for a creator but one that is subsequently uninvolved with what has been created. These assertions concerning a sentient creator has been rebutted by a multiple universe argument which proposes that any order we observe is only present because we, as human beings are here to observe it. That is, many other universes are possible but conditions within them do not give rise to observers who observe them. The latter point is a cornerstone of the Anthropic principle which seeks to shed light on the early conditions of our universe, founded upon the fact that observers such as ourselves do exist. Finally, one can argue that there is no intrinsic order in the universe and that it is we humans ourselves who create such order through our perceptual propensities. Although these argument might not appear to be amenable to empirical resolution, there are opportunities to explore a more scientific approach to theology, an endeavour I hope to be able to undertake.

Teleology: Retrospection versus Prospection

I do not want to use the term teleology in this *retrospective* way to look back to the origins of order, nor to speculate here about the existence of any deity. For me, teleology does not relate to an historic and passive search for ultimate cause. Rather it is an active term concerning our *prospective* search among the potentialities with which we, as human beings, are presented. As a result, I use teleology in the present context to refer to *an active search for unified purpose in human intention*. By using it in this fashion, I am affirming that individuals and society do exhibit intention. That is, regardless of metaphysical arguments as to the reality or illusion of free will, we individually and collectively act in an everyday manner which signifies our belief that our actions are not uniquely pre-determined and that our beliefs do influence ourselves and others. In sum, my use of teleology represents a search for goals and intentions for ourselves and society. In the context of the present chapter, I focus on the role that technology plays in this search.

Technology: Art, Artefact, or Science?

The formal definition of technology that is cited at the start of this chapter is different from that of everyday use. However, it is the term as used in common parlance that I now want to employ here. In these terms, technology is associated with things, objects, and devices, rather than with knowledge as either art or science (see Westrum, 1991). While a concept of information underlies each of these definitions of the word technology, my use of it here very much accords with the common everyday way that we use the term. However, I want to broaden this definition just a little. Technology is often associated with that which is new, modern, and exciting. I want to go beyond thinking of technology in terms of new machines, to expand the definition to include such developments as the domestication of animals and of plants. It might be of some interest to note for example, that carrots were originally white. Their present appearance comes from selective breeding to 'engineer' the vegetable we see today. Likewise, many animals owe their present appearance and sub-serve functions that were 'manufactured' over a considerable period of time. I am grateful to Kara Latorella who pointed out Gary Wilkes' work from the *Mesa Tribune* on an article entitled 'Animal behavior put to task for good – and bad – of humans'. In this he examines birds trained to respond upon seeing the colour yellow being used by air-sea rescue to find downed pilots, the pigeon having much greater visual acuity for yellow than a human observer (and thought to be less affected by the noise and vibration of the rescue helicopter. For a more technical evaluation of this work see Parasuraman, 1986). Also, there is another use in which pigeons were trained to spot defective parts on a production line as a way to relieve human observers of the vigilance burden. Interestingly, this latter project was stopped by protesters who said that enforcing birds to perform this tedious task was 'inhuman'. No one protested for the human workers who were then re-hired to do the same job.

Technology then can be redefined as *the purposive ways in which the environment has been structured to benefit humankind*. Already then, there is teleology in the very basis of technology. (I hope the reader can already see this mutuality such that the chapter may as easily be titled 'Technology for Teleology'.) A wide interpretation of this definition of technology permits the identification and inclusion of rudimentary tools and even forms of communication which are employed by other members of the animal kingdom to structure their own world. Unlike those who seem preoccupied with searching for the absolute unique nature of human beings, I am not unhappy about this wider interpretation of what technology represents.

Humans and Their Technology: A Mutual Shaping

What is demonstrable is that technology has fashioned humans as much as humans have fashioned technology. Elsewhere, I and my colleagues (Flach et al., 1994; Hancock et al., 1994) have argued that our contemporary ecology *is* technology and as such it represents a most powerful influence upon who we are today. Such is the degree of our reliance upon technology that we could not survive in the way that we do without its support. As Arthur Koestler (1978) put it:

> It has to be realized that ever since the first cave dweller wrapped his shivering frame into the hide of a dead animal, man has been, for better or worse, creating for himself an artificial environment and an artificial mode of existence without which he no longer can survive. There is no turning back on housing, clothing, artificial heating, cooked food; nor on spectacles, hearing aids, forceps, artificial limbs, anesthetics, antiseptics, prophylactics, vaccines, and so forth.

While at some very basic level this mutual influence between the conditions of the environment and an individual's actions applies to all living things, the extent to which humans have exploited, and now rely on technology is, I think, sufficiently distinct to provide a watershed differentiation. The central question then is the future for a species that relies so heavily on technological support and what happens to that species as the nature of the support itself co-evolves.

❖ ❖ ❖

Technical versus Human Capabilities

> The servant glides by imperceptible approaches into the master; and we have come to such a pass, that even now, man must suffer terribly on ceasing to benefit [from] machines. If all machines were to be annihilated at one moment, so that not a knife nor lever nor rag of clothing nor anything whatsoever were left to man but his bare body alone that he was born with, and if all knowledge of mechanical laws were taken from him so that he could make no more machines and all machine-made food destroyed so that the race of man should be left as it were naked upon a desert island, we should become extinct in six weeks. A few miserable individuals might linger, but even these in a year or two would become worse than monkeys. Man's very soul is due to the machines; it is a machine-made thing; he thinks as he thinks, and feels as he feels, through the

work that machines have wrought upon him, and their existence is quite as much
as sine qua non for his, as his is for theirs.

(Butler, 1872)

The Direction of Co-evolutionary Changes

I begin my evaluation of our co-evolution through the use of a traditional,
dichotomous comparison of human and machine abilities. This is expressed in
Figure 2.1. I have already indicated that it is critical to find purpose in technology
and to identify purpose at all times. Technology may have been around as long as
human beings have cultivated crops, herded cattle, or created their own tools. What
makes the present different is the change in the respective roles of the machine and
the human operator. A traditional view of this change is illustrated here, where the
horizontal axis is time, on the vertical axis capability.

The curve labelled (b) represents human capabilities. It is perhaps easiest to
conceptualize these abilities first in terms of simple physical achievement. As can
be seen, human capabilities improve over time, but the rate of that improvement
gradually diminishes. These trends can be seen most clearly in world records
for forms of 'locomotion' such as running and swimming. What we know from
experience is borne out in the data, human beings get better but by progressively
smaller amounts. This trend holds for individual learning curves as well as
collective performance, as expressed in world athletic records. Eventually, we will
reach the constraints of physical capability. It is true that unaided by technology
a human can run a mile in four minutes. However, unaided, no human will run
a mile in one minute (at least not a human that we would recognize as such).
The question is: are intrinsic cognitive functions limited in the same way? We
may each improve our cognitive capabilities but eventually, is there a limit upon
sensory resolution, memory capacity, decision-making speed, as well as motor
skills? Assuming there to be such limits, defining where they occur on any ratio
scale of measurement is, of course, much more difficult than for structured physical
pursuits. Parenthetically, this manifest, public measurement of achievement may
be one reason for the attraction of sports in contemporary society, in which the
winner, in most games, is identified unequivocally. It is this pristine and public
way of determining a winner that proves so seductive and hence the outrage which
follows episodes of 'cheating' in major sports which are seen, often naively, as
the one arena of true competition and resolution. For comparison, imagine trying
to have an objective competition to determine which is the best film, scientist,
etc. Regardless of where these latter cognitive limits reside, we can be fairly sure
that unaided by technology, individuals do not possess unbounded, endogenous
cognitive abilities.

The curve labelled (a) represents technology. There are a myriad of examples of
this exponential form of growth (see Card, 1988). For example, the history of the
size, speed, and unit cost of computer memory shows this phenomenal technical

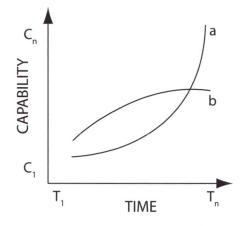

Figure 2.1   Human (b) versus machine (a) capabilities as a function of time

improvement clearly (Moore, 1965) as do similar measures on a greater social scale. Moravec (1988) has also more recently captured this progression in which he also shows how differing forms of technology have supported continued geometric growth. I should note that this approach, which was conceptually developed over a decade ago, was also articulated by Vallee (1982). Before I discuss the significance of this perspective and the point of intersection, I have to examine some of the shortcomings and assumptions of this comparative approach.

Fallacies of Generalization

Of course, each curve is a generalization. We know that technology, like resources in whatever form, cannot sustain geometric growth indefinitely (Malthus, 1798; see also Nickerson, 1992). Indeed, for the function cited in computer memory, and generally known as 'Moore's Law', we seem to be approaching physical limits to the type of capacity for processing and storage (Bennet and Landauer, 1985), although we have not reached it yet. Already, however, futurists are touting quantum leaps to alternative 'technologies' such as photonics and bio-computing in order to fracture what seems to be an intrinsic limit to silicon-based capacities. So, while increase in technical capabilities can appear to be geometric, it is only so for some selected portion of their growth. It is much more likely that the curve for computer processing technologies possesses an inflexion and is shaped more like an ogive. Each kind of processor is, through some intrinsic factor, ultimately self-limited. It is then only by the overlapping of progressively more effective processors *of a different type* that we sustain the illusion of continuous geometric growth. However, this illusion cannot be permanently perpetuated.

With respect to human cognitive capabilities, asserting that we know all about such limits and what constrains human thought at this time is very shortsighted. For every assertion about limits to human intellectual abilities and cognitive capacities, there is an equally powerful assertion about individual variation and strategic skills which counters it (Flach and Hoffman, 2003). Thus, specifying an upper boundary to all cognitive functions is naïve.[1] However, the recognition of some endogenous limits is, in no small part, the stimulus for technology itself. I consider this integrative perspective below. Yet despite these and other simplifications, consideration of the intersection of the curves is of critical importance.

Convergence, Intersection, and Divergence

While the physical abilities of machines superseded the physical abilities of humans some generations ago, I want to suggest that it is in our own era in which the cognitive balance between the human and the machine has begun to invert. Independent of the objections that I have raised earlier, it is within our own generation that certain characteristics of machine intelligence that have outstripped their human equivalents. Pragmatically, what this has meant is that many control functions are now performed more quickly and more accurately by machine. Such is the nature of the technologies we have, and are building, that many are uncontrollable without the use of computer assistance. I hasten to add that the supersession of individual human abilities by machine abilities has happened, ability by ability, at different times. As a result, different sorts of devices have *had* to rely upon some degree of machine control, in an obligatory sense, at different junctures. This progress expressed in systems as complex as nuclear power stations and single-seat fighter aircraft has percolated now to technologies as apparently mundane as washing machines. It has now become a challenge to identify machines that do *not* have some sort of processor in them. Indeed, quite sophisticated processing capabilities can now be seen in smart greetings cards. In the present generation, after holidays and birthdays, it is not unusual to consider these and like items as simply disposable. Indeed, the trash receptacles of many houses this holiday season will contain more computational power than the most powerful systems of only fifty years ago!

It is this transference of superiority in specific areas that generated the birth of *imperative automation*. By imperative automation, I mean automation we cannot do without. That is, the goal of the system at hand cannot ever be achieved by manual action alone. Human beings have always exhibited a fascination with automata and have incorporated governors and other forms of automatic or semi-automatic controllers into devices for almost as long as humans have been making machines themselves. But this was discretionary automation. Humans could exercise control if they had to and in many cases they were found to be the least

---

1   However, as Moray reminds us, we should remember Leacock's dictum that a PhD is a sign that a person's head is completely full and nothing more can be added.

expensive and indeed the preferred way for doing so. However, in our times, we have had to acknowledge that without machine assistance we cannot control some of the things we have built. Many people work better if they have machine support, but some work *only* if they have machine support. Hence the difference is one of acknowledgement that automation is something we *cannot do without*, rather than something we *would prefer to have*.

Why is it important to consider the ascending role of technology now? It is important now since our relationship with technology has changed from discretionary use of automation to mandatory use of automation. With that change has come a more subtle move in which machines are no longer simply mindless slaves but have to be considered more in the sense of a partnership, although anthropocentric views of this partnership are likely to be misleading at best. Any time of change is disturbing. However, we live in an age when non-human and non-animal entities have, by circumstance, been granted perhaps the birth of their emancipation. We have to ask ourselves questions concerning their future, if and when, they will demand the right of franchise.

Summary: Human and Machine Abilities

Human capabilities have progressively been superseded by machine capabilities. In our age, we now build technologies that rely upon these levels of machine ability that cannot be replicated by any human. Consequently, our relationship with machines has changed. They are no longer unquestioning slaves but are becoming active companions. Are they to become more than this?

❖ ❖ ❖

Is Technology 'Natural'?

> One can, of course, argue that the crisis (of technology), too, is 'natural,' because man is part of nature. This echoes the views of the earliest Greek philosophers, who saw no difference between matter and consciousness – nature included everything. The British scientist James Lovelock wrote some years ago that 'our species with its technology is simply an inevitable part of the natural scene,' nothing more than mechanically advanced beavers. In this view, to say we 'ended' nature, or even damaged nature, makes no sense, since we are nature, and nothing we can do is 'unnatural.' This view can be, and is, carried to even greater lengths; Lynn Margulis, for instance, ponders the question of whether robots can be said to be living creatures, since any 'invention of human beings is ultimately based on a variety of processes including that of DNA replication from the invention.'

(McKibben, 1989)

The preceding argument is one which is based on the understanding that humans and machines are to be explicitly contrasted as disparate entities. That is, the perspective is dominated by a view of human versus machine abilities. As we progress, I want to argue that this divisive perspective is itself unhelpful. To do so, I have to first overcome the assertion that technology and nature are in some way 'opposed'. That is, that technology is not 'natural'.

The Importance of the Question

It might seem, at first, that the question of whether technology is natural is either facile, in the sense that technology being 'artificial' cannot be 'natural' or pointless in the sense that the answer makes little difference one way or the other. I suggest that the question is neither facile nor pointless. It is not facile because it forces us to consider what the boundaries of what we call 'natural' are, and what artificial means in this context. It is not pointless since our answer biases the very way in which we think about technology and what the ultimate purposes of technology are. Having considered the nature of technology, let us move to a consideration of the nature of its human operator and to begin I present an examination of how we look to unify and divide any of our descriptions of such individuals.

How Things are the Same, How Things are Different

The term which characterizes individual differentiation is *idiographic*. In contrast, the term for the average patterning of events is *nomothetic*. These twin tendencies form the basis of statistical descriptions since they are reflections of the dispersal and the central tendency of data, respectively. However, the question of grouping or set function goes well beyond this one arena. Indeed, it is a fundamental characteristic of all life that we look for similarities and differences in experience. The use of language represents an explicit recognition of the differentiation or the separating apart of ideas, objects, and things. In contrast, mathematics represents the propensity in the other direction, toward unification. We may start life by distinguishing self from non-self but it is the richness of language that gives voice to the diversity of the world around us and parenthetically it is also language that strikes us dumb with respect to transcendent experience. In essence, we try to name each of the things we can perceive. Before long however, we start to try to categorize these things by grouping similar things together. That is we seek common characteristics through which we can link individual items together. This complementarity between unity and diversity continues throughout life. Essentially, these propensities for differentiation and integration go hand-in-hand in all sequences of perception-action.

In all facets of human life, we rejoice in discovering new ways in which things can be unified so that we can extract pattern from (or impose pattern on) experience. For example, we count the recognition of a 'common' force acting on an apple and the moon at one and the same time, as one of the great insights of science. Indeed, the concept of number in mathematics is an explicit statement that one object is sufficiently of the same characteristic as another object that they can be put in a common class and recognized as two separate occurrences of the same object type. This observation of multiple members of a common set precedes the concept of the set being empty and having no members. This latter state is the formal definition of *zero*. The abstraction of number proceeds from this explicit grouping principle. Elsewhere (Hancock, 2002), I have argued that time is the basis for both this fundamental unification and differentiation and hence stands, as Kant (1781) implied, as an *a priori* psychological and physical construct. However, before this journey proceeds too heavily into the metaphysical, I would like to provide a biological example as a precursor to an examination of technology.

Are Humans the Same as Other Animals?

The example that I would like to examine in detail concerns the difference between humans and the rest of the animal kingdom. We are aware of Descartes' protestation about the soul as the difference between humans and animals (although I suspect that neither Descartes, nor indeed Aristotle before him, were quite the absolutists in this matter that they are now often portrayed to be). It was indeed this barrier between humans and other animals that Darwin, without malevolent intent, so thoroughly ruptured. Contemporary scientific debate does not revolve around the contention of common evolution but one battleground is now established around language. Lurking in the background is the often silent extension into the question of mind and consciousness and the unsaid and now virtually unsayable link to the soul. The arguments centre putatively around the nature of the data but the global agenda of the uniqueness of human creation always hovers in the background.

Why is this? The answer is, I think, understandable. As human beings we have always been, like Cary Grant in the introductory example, the hero of our own story. But our history is a chronicle of our progressive displacement from the centre of the universe. From Aristarchus to Copernicus, from Newton to Einstein, the gradual displacement from the physical centre has progressed (at times stultified) but never ceased (Koestler, 1959). This outfall of science threatens to displace human beings from the spiritual centre of our universe also (Hancock, 2005). It is only in the present century that the concatenation of physical relativity and biological unification has served to shatter some of the foundational pillars upon which the conventional and comfortable world view was perched for so long.

> In 1859, Charles Darwin published the *Origin of Species*. Epic of science though it is, it was a great blow to man. Earlier, man had seen his world displaced from the center of space; he had seen the Empyrean heaven vanish to be replaced by a void filled only with the wandering dust of worlds; he had seen earthly time lengthen until man's duration within it was only a small whisper on the sidereal clock. Finally, now, he was taught that his trail ran backward until in some lost era it faded into the night-world of the beast. Because it is easier to

look backward than to look forward, since the past is written in the rocks, this observation, too, was added to the whirlpool.

(Eiseley, 1960)

Technology and Natural Laws

In the sense I have conveyed, we now have to enquire whether technology and nature are different or whether they are in fact essentially the same. For good or bad, we have come to a situation where strong positive empiricism reigns and technology is the material manifestation of that creed. But is this natural? As I am sure the reader has suspected all along, it all depends upon what one considers 'natural'. That is, are we going to use the term in an inclusive or an exclusive sense? The inclusive, coarse-grained view is that physical entities obey physical laws. Hence, everything is 'natural' by this definition of nature. But this view is biased by a reification and generalization of physical laws. To the strict ecologist, to whom these laws and their application is sacrosanct, technology in general and human-machine systems in particular are *only* extensions of nature. True, they explore more exotic regions that cannot be compassed by any living organism alone, but they are still bound by the same strictures and constraints and are subject to the 'pervasive' laws. But, in conception, they are founded in human imagination which is not bound by any such laws. As Koestler (1972) noted, '*the contents of conscious experience have no spatio-temporal dimensions; in this respect they resemble the non-things of quantum physics which also defy definition in terms of space, time, and substance.*' This unbounding is what makes developments such as virtual worlds so intriguing (Hancock, 2009).

Inevitable Technological Failures?

I have purposefully spent some time considering the general level of the question of 'natural' technology to provide a background for the following and more specific example. We have, in our science, noted and commented on the increasing complexity of technical systems. Indeed, one of the major *raisons d'etres* for automation is this progressive complexity. I shall not argue what I mean by complexity here, since I have done this elsewhere (Hancock and Chignell, 1989). I simply assert that technical systems of today are more 'complex' than those of a century ago. Such growing complexity *compels* comparison with natural ecosystems. Regardless of our eventual determinations on the link between technology and nature, we can look to nature for models of interacting complex systems with biological 'players' as system components. In so doing, we find that there are intriguing models of systems with mutually adapting agents that can provide us with vital information and insight. In particular, we find that the way that failure propagates readily through ecosystems (that is, species destruction) provides a valuable insight. In this sense, they are similar to the tightly coupled technical systems which were discussed in detail by Perrow (1984). However, research on natural ecosystems let us go a little further than the qualitative statements of Perrow. Indeed, there appears to be a lawful relationship between the extent (effect) of any one failure and its frequency. It has been posited as a log-log relationship (see Kauffman, 1993; Raup, 1986), and is illustrated in Figure 2.2 (see also Figure 1.9).

Kauffman has suggested a ln/ln relationship in which the log frequency of failure is linear with the log size of failure events. The crux of the argument is that small perturbations are resident in all complex systems and that in the vast majority of instances these perturbations are damped out in the system. However, from time to time, these same perturbations are magnified through the system resulting in correspondingly larger destruction of the elements of the system. In this chapter, I do not go into all of the nuances of these important observations. For example, what dictates when in the time series of resident perturbations these larger catastrophes occur? For this and other intriguing issues, I would strongly recommend reference to Kauffman's (1993) work. The importance for the science of human-machine systems, of course, is to understand whether this 'law' applies when the entities in the ecosystem are interacting humans and machines. The importance of the general question of the naturalness of technology is now laid

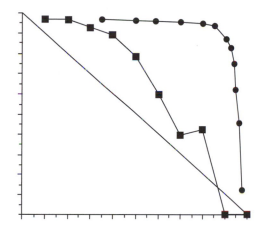

Figure 2.2   Relationships in log/log space. The reason that there are no associated numbers is that the axes refer to two specifically different relationships. In general, the axes represent the frequency of events and size of events respectively. The linear relationship is a hypothetically perfect one, while the two others represent actual data. The circles show human cohort morbidity, the squares show extinction events in the Phanerozoic era. (Conception after Kauffman, 1993; extinction events data after Raup, 1986; morbidity data superimposed here by the present author)

bare. If technology is no more than a logical extension of other natural systems, we must expect human-machine systems to be subject to the same effects. The implication of this conclusion is that there will *always* be failures in such systems and the size and frequency of those failures will be proportional to the complexity of the system. As a result, since there will always be intrinsic perturbations of these systems and as some of these will *always* reach such a disastrous magnitude, there will be catastrophic failures as a function of their very nature. If, on the other hand, we are able to convince ourselves that our technology is not 'natural' then we can return to the comfort of the belief that all engineered systems, however, complex, must be ultimately controllable and therefore catastrophic failure can be circumvented. This latter perspective remains bad news for operators as it argues that human error, in all its forms, will continue to remain the putative 'cause' of such failures in the decades to come.

Rejecting Deterministic Failure

It is almost instinctive in us to reject the assertion of 'inevitable' or 'unavoidable' failure. Indeed, there are several objections which immediately present themselves. Surely technology can be natural without having to fail in this manner. Doesn't such an assertion imply that the safety measures that are put in place are bound to be ineffective? As some reflection will show, it comes back again to the nature of technology and the naturalness of technology. If we believe that human actions supersede the haphazard exploration of potential systems 'spaces' by nature, then we are strong advocates for separation and the positive influence of human intention. In essence, we are optimists (Hancock, 1999). If we view the combinatorial explosion of system complexity with trepidation and have difficulty distinguishing technology from nature then we are liable to favour the more fatalistic view as represented in the latter conception. From the foregoing arguments, metaphysical conundrums such as the mystery of mind, the reality of consciousness, and the power of free will are at the heart of how we conceive possible futures for human-machine systems. If we are to be dedicated human-machine systems scientists, we have to address ourselves to these perennial human mysteries as much as we do the nature of the interface, the character of drop-down menus, or the solution to repetitive strain trauma. For we can never find acceptable solutions to the latter issues unless we have resolved in our own mind our stance toward the former concerns. That is, our science must be mindful, not mindless.

Giving Solipsism the Slip

At this juncture, the morass of radical scepticism and fundamental solipsism may beckon the unwary traveller towards the '*Slough of Despond*'. However, the *pragmatic* solution to this issue is relatively simple (see Kurtz, 1994). As I have noted earlier, regardless of our personal philosophical stance, we all *act* as though we exercise free will. In our discussions of consciousness also, we are mostly willing to attribute consciousness to other human beings, although we are a little less generous with our attribution to animals and positively miserly to other forms of life. Our practical pragmatism means that we use the concept of mind as something that is a shared characteristic of human experience. Therefore, at a practical level we continue to believe that our interventions are important, *whether they are or not* (Kurtz, 1992). Although the position may be advocated as pragmatism, the proposition certainly remains philosophically doubtful. Some would argue that our actions are the clearest evidence of our intentions and on this basis we continue to act as though all events are controllable and failure of control is overwhelmingly a failure in ourselves.

On this basis we will, most probably, continue to exert our best efforts to support the safety of systems as a pragmatic strategy. Of course, as a compromise position, it may well be that safety, being a multidimensional construct, contains some elements which we can influence and others about which we can do nothing. What I advocate here, is that in viewing technology as natural, we have to begin to divorce ourselves from the debilitating concept of blame (see Hancock, Mouloua and Senders, 2008). In a society redolent with litigation, such as the United States, this is difficult. I concede that while there is an element of greed there will always be malfeasance but it is not this form of blame I am seeking to excise. It is the 'blame' directed toward conscientious, dedicated professional operators who may make 'so-called' errors, for which some pay with their lives. To apportion 'blame' in such circumstances is to adhere to a physical model in which Aristotelian 'efficient' cause can be distilled for each and every action. It is also to fall for the tragic 'hindsight' bias, or more accurately, fallacy. As society begins to reject the concept of a personal deity, dealing with fate on a momentary basis, it must also begin to reject this latter physical analogue of complete personal control and thus responsibility as a concept equally impoverished of mind. If we can begin to conceive pluralistically, and through mutual experiences, as facilitated by technologies such as virtual reality, such improved consciousness may be possible. From this vantage point society only indemnifies itself. It would be as if the cells of an organ took out insurance against individual damage while the whole organ ceased to function. This analogy can be continued through the multiple levels of any holarchy (see Koestler, 1978). In consequence, in a technologically replete world, local kinship becomes a vestigial characteristic. Others have argued that the individual in these circumstances is not the correct 'unit of analysis' (Flach and Dominguez, 1995). As much of the science human-machine systems is founded in psychology, this diffusion of the ephasis on the human individual is hard for some to take, but trying to grasp the very conception leads to some most useful insights.

As society matures from the self-centred world of adolescence, our reach must be toward a social consciousness in which the myopia of individuality is replaced with the vision of mutuality. While both secular and religious theorists have advocated similar views, they have, by and large, not been successful in influencing collective behaviour. I suggest that this is because they have attempted to achieve this as a moral crusade independent of the technology to hand during their particular era. True, they have used the existing media of the times, but they have largely ignored or at least failed to embrace the power of technological innovation. It may be that the nascent emancipation of technology will prove an effective catalyst for such change and growth. However, intelligent human leadership will remain a central and crucial requirement.

I claim that technology is evidently natural. But I argue that it can be more. I suggest that we can learn much about complex technological systems by understanding the nature and nuances of complex biological ecosystems. I ask whether catastrophic failure must be an intrinsic characteristic of these linked complex systems and use this as the acid test for the influence of intention. With respect to disaster it may be that humans see more through tears than they do through telescopes. But they have to be looking in the right temporal direction to do so, regardless of any lachrymal barrier.

❖ ❖ ❖

Evolution of Human and Machine

> This is a principal means by which life evolves – exploiting imperfections in copying despite the cost. It is not how we would do it. It does not seem to be how a Deity intent on special creation would do it. The mutations have no plan, no direction behind them; their randomness seems chilling; progress, if any, is agonizingly slow. The process sacrifices all those beings who are now less fit to perform their life tasks because of the new mutation . We want to urge evolution to get where it's going and stop the endless cruelties. But life doesn't know where its going. It has no long-term plan. There's no end in mind. There's no mind to keep an end in mind. The process is the opposite of teleology. Life is profligate, blind, at this level unconcerned with notions of justice. It can afford to waste multitudes.

(Sagan and Druyan, 1992, p. 84)

The foregoing discussion has considered nature and technology almost as though they were static things. However, perhaps the most distinguishing feature of each is their continual change and consequently the next step is an examination of their respective patterns of evolution.

Human Evolution

In considering the respective paths of evolution of human and machine it is important to consider first the disparities of these separate evolutionary processes. With respect to human evolution, we accept a Darwinian-based concept which has been tempered with the continuing discoveries of genetics and molecular biology. In the general run of science, the concept of evolving complexity still holds sway, where the 'survival of the fit' imperative has served as the selective process over the eons of geological time (see Hancock, 2007). However, it is appropriate to ask here, fit with respect to what? It is usual to emphasize the environment of the organism in this respect. However, any environment is a dynamic and multilayered condition. It may be that an organism is perfectly adapted to a specific set of circumstances and then an event, such as a volcanic eruption, over the other side of the world changes these local conditions. Under these conditions the organism may become extinct. In this respect, survival of the fit is actually survival of the survivalists, since excessively specialist adaptations do not pay in the wider order of things (Kauffman, 1993). The best form of adaptation is the ability to adapt and meta-adaptation is the primary human characteristic. It can be argued that this is indeed what the brain has evolved to do (Hancock, Szalma, and Oron-Gilad, 2005). We accept that human evolution has taken several millions of years. We also accept that human evolution proceeds at a slow rate such that differential characteristics propagate slowly through the population. Advantages in one context may be disadvantages in another context, hence with meta-adaptation as the central characteristic it might be expected that human evolution should progress cautiously. In pragmatic terms, evolution proposes and nature disposes. However, what does nature dispose of when technology is the ecology? Under these circumstances, survival of the 'fit' seems a much less pristine selection principle.

The problem, of course, is time. It is perhaps the defining human characteristic that we are painfully aware of our own certain death (Hancock, 2002). However, in our brief flight upon this planet, we remain almost pathologically infirmed with respect to our temporal vision. Again, as the hero of our own story, it is so difficult for each one of us to conceive of a world without us! However, our appreciation of the passage of geological time remains always an intellectual not an empathic exercise. I would like, for a moment, the reader to pause and think on this. The geological year asks us to conceive of time since the origin of the earth (mark this, not the origin of the universe) as a period of one year (a hopelessly embedded temporal structure). Human beings are then said to have been on the planet only during the last seconds of the last day of the year. In such a picture, the difference between human appearance and technical development is obviously negligible. Even with an inkling of the length of duration, it is clear that our species is a newcomer to the world. In a true sense, each species has some hand in 'creating' other species. All partake in the interplay of environment and resources which set the frame of selection. The human 'creation' of technology is distinguished only by the apparent 'intentionality' of the act. It is this intentionality that, I think, provides the difference for contemporary minds. I therefore will appeal to Darwin for armament to help support this view. With respect to intentional selection, Darwin wrote:

> One of the most remarkable features in our domesticated races is that we see in them adaptation, not indeed to the animal's or plant's own good, but to man's use or fancy. Some variations useful to him have probably arisen suddenly,

or by one step. But when we compare the dray-horse and the race-horse, the dromedary and camel, the various breeds of sheep fitted either for cultivated land or mountain pasture, with the wool of one breed good for one purpose, and that of another breed for another purpose; when we compare the many breeds of dogs, each good for man in different ways; when we compare the game-cock, so pertinacious in battle, with other breeds so little quarrelsome, with 'everlasting layers' which never desire to sit, and with the bantam so small and elegant; when we compare the host of agricultural, culinary, orchard, and flower-garden races of plants, most useful to man at different seasons and of different purposes, or so beautiful in his eyes, we must, I think, look further than to mere variability. We cannot suppose that all breeds were suddenly produced as perfect and as useful as we now see them; indeed, in many cases, we know that this has not been their history. The key is man's power of accumulative selection: nature gives successive variations; man adds them up in certain directions useful to him. In this sense he may be said to have made for himself useful breeds.

However, with respect to natural selection Darwin indicated:

This preservation [in Nature] of favorable individual differences and variations, and the destruction of those which are injurious. I have called Natural Selection, or Survival of the Fittest. Variations neither useful nor injurious would not be affected by natural selection.

(quoted in Sagan and Druyan, 1992)

Some of Darwin's critics could never overcome the absence of intention in evolution. Indeed, without intention it is perfectly reasonable to argue that evolution does not represent 'progress' at all, although this is the typical connotation associated with the word. Not progress, but a series of undirected 'accidents.' Consider, for example, the following:

The Darwinian process may be described as a chapter of accidents. As such it seems simple, because you do not at first realize all that it involves. But when its whole significance dawns on you, your heart sinks into a heap of sand within you. There is a hideous fatalism about it, a ghastly and damnable reduction of beauty and intelligence, of strength and purpose, of honor and aspiration, to such casually picturesque changes as an avalanche may make in landscape, or a railway accident in a human figure. To call this Natural Selection is a blasphemy, possible to many for whom Nature is nothing but a casual aggregation of inert and dead matter, but eternally impossible to the spirits and souls of the righteous ... If this sort of selection could turn an antelope into a giraffe, it could conceivably turn a pond full of amoebas into the French Academy.

(G.B. Shaw as also quoted in Sagan and Druyan, 1992)

The original arguments against the Darwinian perspective of natural selection as the intrinsic force of evolution were many-fold. For some, at that time as now, the idea of a descent of human beings was anathema to the notion of original creation. If God truly created 'man in his own image' (women being in biblical terms an afterthought), then evolution transgresses this edict. Essentially, the data took care of this objection, although it is clear that the argument, independent of the data, rolls on today (Wolozin, 2007). In addition to theological disputes, more scientific arguments raised against natural selection invoked the blind and accidental nature of selection. It is the case that an individual of any species might represent the 'fittest' of the group and yet through mere accident or haphazard demise fail to preferentially reproduce. Hence, 'survival of the fittest' as has been noted, can appear to rapidly devolve to 'survival of the survivalists'. As Waddington (1957) observed:

> Survival does not, of course, mean the bodily endurance of a single individual, outliving Methuselah. It implies, in its present-day interpretation, perpetuation as a source for future generations. That individual 'survives' best which leaves most offspring. Again, to speak of an animal as 'fittest' does not necessarily imply that it is the strongest or most healthy or would win a beauty competition. Essentially, it denotes nothing more than leaving most offspring. The general principle of natural selection, in fact, merely amounts to the statement that the individuals which leave most offspring are those which leave most offspring. It is a tautology.

It is insufficient to argue that any preferential trait has a strong statistical chance of persistence and proliferation since mutation, almost by definition, is a rare and even singular event. From this view, natural selection is a process by which life explores its myriad possibilities but with no divine intervention and thus no essential direction. It is this godless and chance nature of evolution which proves to be so upsetting to many who could otherwise accept the observation of progressive change in the expressions of life across the eons of time.

What has always been posed as an alternative, and a proposition that pre-dates Darwin, is the inheritance of learned traits. There is something intrinsically satisfying in this doctrine to those who believe in accountability. Diligence is passed on by the diligent, profligacy by the profligate, skill by the skilful. We still long to see this in operation, hence repeated sports comments about coaches' sons, who by some direct inheritance did not have to put long hours in the gymnasium with their father, but somehow inherited the gene for the 'zone defence'. Sadly, the direct inheritance of only favourable characteristics accumulated by the parent is still very doubtful as a scientific proposition, and what of the children born before their parent accumulated such valuable skills? Direct inheritance does not seem to work for humans. However, the conception of the 'inheritance of acquired characteristics' is rightly associated with Jean-Baptiste de Lamarck, a strategy that Darwin considered important throughout his own lifetime.[2]

Machine Evolution

> Investigation revealed that the landing gear and flap handles were similarly shaped and co-located, and that many pilots were raising the landing gear when trying to raise the flaps after landing (Fitts and Jones, 1961). Since then the flap and gear handles have been separated in the cockpit and are even shaped to emulate their functions: in many airplanes, the gear handle is shaped like a wheel and the flap handle is shaped like a wing. Most other displays and controls that are common to all airplanes have become standardized through trial and error, based on similar errors made over time. But human factors considerations have not been rationally applied to all the devices in the cockpit.

> (Riley, 1994)

If humans take millennia to evolve and apparently do so by haphazard circumstance, what of technology? More particularly for our present purpose, what of machine evolution? In this realm, Lamarck comes now particularly to the forefront. The essence of his 'laws' are that an animal's characteristics and behaviour are shaped by adaptation to its natural environment, that special organs grow and diminish according to their use or disuse, and that the adaptive changes which an animal acquires in its lifetime are inherited by its offspring (see Koestler, 1964). Let us consider machines with respect to these principles. Certainly, a machine's physical characteristics and especially its function seem shaped by its immediate environment, especially if we think in terms of technology such contemporary software. Its special organs certainly grow and diminish according to use.

It has been proposed that evolution proceeds by survival of the fit. However, let us look at this statement with respect to contemporary society. At least in the Western world, we are replete with medical facilities. Many of those who are not 'fit' frequently survive disadvantage and disease. Others, who are in dire economic circumstances and do not have simple access to sophisticated medical facilities may frequently not survive, despite early initial advantages. Of course, the problem, as discussed above, is 'fit' with respect to what? On the machine side, the generalization is that they progress in uniform steps, taking advantage of each previous discovery. However, when we look at technical breakthroughs in more

---

2   I have purposely contrasted two extreme views of human evolution here as stereotyped under Darwinian or Lamarckian banners. Neither view in its unalloyed, pristine condition is held in contemporary times and the questions of evolution have themselves multiplied in complexity. My purpose here is to contrast common views of human evolution with machine evolution. I would note that the equivalence I claim is even more valid when the current views of natural evolution are explained for each realm.

detail, progress is much more serendipitous and haphazard than it might appear at first blush. Indeed, many steps in machine evolution depend directly upon the creative insights of single designers, where design is as much art as it is science. While machines may inherit preferred characteristics, such characteristics might become a liability in succeeding generations, also some forms of technology can become extinct in the same fashion that natural selection proceeds for animal and plant species. One need only think of musical records of the type of 78's vs. 45's in this context (some younger readers will have to look up these forms of early competing types of record on the web to understand the specific example which itself is proof of the extinction principle).

On the surface, it might therefore appear that machines evolve at their observed rapid pace because of the immediate propagation of preferred characteristics. However, it is important to ask where the innovations come from. If human mutations come from haphazard events such as cosmic rays, machine innovations come from the equally haphazard events of human intuition. These events are comparable in all aspects except for their temporal density. Some design innovations in machines are useful for a time and then die out because of supersession of improved abilities, for example, PC's. Other innovations fail because of economic forces in which rival technologies are paired against each other and one essentially 'wins', for example, Betamax vs. VHS, eight-tracks vs. tape's and CD's. What I want to propose is that the processes of evolution for both human and machine asymptote to the common characteristic of exploration. The only fundamental difference is the time scale of the action.

Comparative Evolution

It is worth, just a moment, to pause and to make explicit the differences in evolution between humans and machines as elaborated above. The critical difference is cycle time. The average human life is some decades in length, the average machine life is now in the order of years to months. The machine is replaced as soon as a viable replacement is produced. In contrast, we try to save human beings, at least in general to the degree that we can. Some machines are also 'savable'; for example, second-hand cars. The point being that the landscape of human beings changes slowly compared with that of machines. Also, as human life span itself is increasing, machine 'life span' is diminishing. If this represents the cycle time differences of a single cycle, we should also recognize that the difference in the respective rates of those cycle times is also growing. That is, evolution or change takes place at an increasingly divergent rate. As well as time scale, the respective histories are different in terms of their time. At a surface level it appears that humans and machines evolve in a very different manner. However, there is much in common and only time is the essential distinction. They are so divergent in time scale we see them as more radically different than they are. In reality, these are not separate forms of evolution but go together as we co-evolve.

❖ ❖ ❖

Convergent Evolution and Co-evolution

> It makes no sense to talk about cars and power plants and so on as if they were
> something apart from our lives – they are our lives.

(McKibben, 1989)

Convergent Evolution at the Human-Machine Interface

One characteristic in evolutionary landscape is the convergent evolution of entities
subjected to the same forces. Before considering co-evolution I first illustrate a
case of convergent evolution in the human-machine interface, a topic I return to in
much greater detail in the following chapter.

The computer is now the dominant and preferred system which mediates
between human and machine. Frequently, of course, the computer itself is the
machine of concern. However, for both large-scale complex systems and
small appliances, some form of computational medium has become ever more
pervasive in our society. This trend toward ubiquity has had distinct effects on
human-machine interaction. The generation of a common communication and
control medium fosters convergent evolution. In essence, as we tailor interfaces
for human capacities, it becomes progressively less clear as to which specific
device is being controlled. The critical difference between different sorts of
devices lies in their distinct response characteristics. However, the computer as
the intermediary between human and system can 'hide' or 'buffer' many of these
differences so that what specifically is controlled can surprisingly, become less of
an issue. Eventually, if this buffering process were carried to its logical extreme,
the differences between controlling an aircraft traffic sector, a nuclear power
station, or a household washing machine could become virtually opaque to the
operator sitting at a generic control panel viewing a generic display. Would this
line of progress be an advisable strategy? Is there any unfathomable rule which
demands that there be complex interfaces for complex systems? Indeed, as all
have to be 'navigated' through some complex phase space of operation, it may
be that the metaphor of a boat on an ocean is one which captures many common
elements of all systems operation (see Chapter 1). The task of the interface
designer would then be to bring the critical variables to the forefront and allow
their 'emergent' properties to become the sea-lane that the controller has to 'pilot'
their craft through. That this could be done most easily using the four-dimensional
wraparound world of virtual reality is an intriguing proposition and one which
offers useful vistas for future exploitation. Such convergence of evolution is a
strong reason for adopting such virtual interface which takes advantage of intrinsic
human visuo-motor capabilities. But the question remains. Although this is one

possible path of human-machine evolution, is it a safe, effective, and reliable one? And more to the point, who decides on these questions?

Mutual Co-evolution

If one basis for a unifying theme of the present chapter is the consideration of technology as a facet of the natural environment, we should take the step of recognizing technology as a nascent co-species with ourselves. Indeed, it is not a species the like of which we have seen before. We have to abandon the perspective that technology will remain merely a human appendage. We have to acknowledge our complete dependence upon technology and recognize that we could not be who we are without technological support (see also Hoffman et al., 2003). We have to free ourselves from the conception that technology is merely *just* one of the many shaping facets of the environment and contemplate its own future, potentially as an independent entity (Moravec, 1988).

We have denied 'souls' to animals, and still cling hopefully to this supposed difference. Not to do so would be to deny not only our 'special' place in creation (Hancock, 2005), but our very individual separateness. This separateness is daily and continually sustained in each of us by our existence as a unified individual conscious entity (Hancock, 2002). With the growth of technology, we are having progressively more trouble sustaining this world-view. In an age of virtual reality, of email, of fax, of teaming, of telecommuting, of collaboration, what is it to be 'separate' any more? Which individual under 30 does not have a cell phone permanently in their ear? As our physical dependence on technology grows, so does our sense of cognitive dependence. Perhaps this is why there is an ever greater collective clamour for the different, the unique, the outré in experience since it supports our vestigial and comfortable view of ourselves as strong independent entities (the myth of the hero dies hard, *Die Hard* being a good name for a film, or *Last Action Hero*). We can no longer claim to be simple differentiated entities.

Nutritionists have always known that 'you are what you eat' and organ replacement at least shows that spare part grafting is feasible and useful. The cells of the body are all replaced cyclically at a different rate over a period of a short number of years. Hence what is left of any individual after one of these full cycles is a remembered informational pattern. But modern computer technology is wonderful at detecting, storing, and replicating patterns. We are now enticed with the vision that our own personal pattern could be extracted, replicated, stored, and perpetuated, offering the dissolution of that pattern in time and in space and the hope of immortality. Moravec (1988) desperately grasped at the idea of individual downloading as a preservation of the self, but at best it seeks to replicate our present state of consciousness. Perhaps it is consciousness which is the problem?

What I suggest here is that the status of individualism is slowly dissolving. The divisions that are eroding are not simply between ourselves and technology but between ourselves as distinct individuals. The two antagonistic tendencies of *self-assertion* and *integration* have always been locked in some form of battle (see Koestler, 1978); however, technology has joined that fight, not merely as a weapon but as an active combatant. The success of technology is evident in the way that it has insinuated itself into society so completely and so unobtrusively into our very consciousness. One well-illustrated example is that of the telephone (Fischer, 1994). It has recently been argued that video games change brains in certain predictable ways (Wilce, 2006). I was tempted to quote Orwell's last paragraph in *Animal Farm* where the farm animals looked 'from man to pig, and from pig back to man and saw no difference', and to replace the word 'pig' with the word 'machine' (fundamentally a form of the Turing test). However, this still retains the divisive or divided perspective which I want to challenge and fosters the unfortunate arguments about machine 'replication' of human abilities. Co-evolution is much more than this simple re-creation of ourselves in a technical surrogate or operational avatar. It is more dynamic, more elusive, and intellectually much more interesting. That co-evolutionary results may initially be crude does not militate against the possibility of a progressively more sophisticated symbiotic interaction.

The disparity in human versus machine evolution is one of cycle time. Convergent evolution is seen in conditions where comparable constraints dictate common processes. Co-evolution, the mutual shaping of constituent members of an ecosystem, is dynamic and explorative. The spice of intention adds novelty to human-machine symbiosis. The possibility of 'emergent' machine intention promises a new form of overall mutual evolution which in its embryonic stages is likely to be seen with respect to contemporary developments in human-centred automation.

❖ ❖ ❖

Human-Machine Symbiosis

> Either the machine has a meaning to life that we have not yet been able to interpret in a rational manner, or it is itself a manifestation of life and therefore mysterious.

> (Garet Garrett, 1925)

Mutual Dependence

Could contemporary human beings survive without technology? If we take technology to mean more than just machines and include animal and plant domestication, I am fairly sure that the answer is no. At least not in the way we understand human beings at present. In these terms, we have shaped the environment that now shapes the individuals and society we are. We have come so far down that evolutionary path, that there is no going back. Could contemporary human beings survive without computational machines? Perhaps they may be able to do so. In one of the following chapters I consider this possibility with respect to a specific example in the early 1800s. But such a society would be radically different from that which we experience today in the developed and developing nations of the world. Pragmatically, we will not give up our technology and practically, its influence continues to spread daily. We must therefore conclude that there is already one elementary form of human-machine symbiosis. Machines cannot exist (or at least cannot be created as original structures) without humans; but, by the same token, humans do not exist without machines. It may be more comfortable to look upon this symbiosis as an elaboration of what it means to belong to the species *Homo Sapiens Sapiens*. For example, no longer are we restricted to storing information and energy endogenously. The immediate and portable availability of information and energy frees individuals in time and space to an extent that is enormously greater than the rest of the animal world. However, this nascent level of symbiosis is only one stage in the developmental sequence linking humans and machines. True symbiosis results when one entity progresses from total dependence to the status of a full partner. The stage after mutual interdependence is some degree of the beginnings of independence. For the machine, that is *automation* and *autonomy* of function.

Automation: The Birth of Machine Intention

There are, of course, multiple levels and multiple forms of automation. These levels have been discussed extensively by others (see Parasuraman and Mouloua, 1995). Yet, however autonomous a system might appear at present, there are still human beings involved. This involvement might be at the conception or design stage or it may be at the care and maintenance end but at some juncture human operators still enter the picture. I take this human participation even further. That is, even if we can think of a device that has no maintenance, a device that was designed by a software program so divorced from its programmer that it no longer appears to be based upon human action, even then it still subsumes human goals. Up until the present time, the motive force for the origin of any machine remains essentially human. All machines work to achieve human goals and rather than goals of their own. No machine has created another machine in order to satisfy its own needs or desires yet. In fact, to the present, no machine really expresses or articulates an external need or desire and perhaps that is what is missing in the effort to create surrogate, self-motivating intelligences?

Does this always have to be the case? Can we conceive of machines that are not predicated upon human intentionality? Indeed we can for they surround us in nature. The insect world knows essentially nothing of human intentionality and continues its activity relatively unmolested or polluted by our goals. Of course we all have to exist on the same global platform but insects are rarely *of* technology in the same way that domesticated animals are (always remembering their adaptation to human products such as pesticides, etc). Can we then conceive of machines as having their own intention, at least at a level that say an ant has intention? We can certainly conceive of it but with the result of proliferation of interactions in systems, are we now beginning to witness it in some of the machines we have created?

I do not advance this as a 'strong AI' position which would protest that machines can 'think'. I appreciate Searle's (1984) argument concerning syntactic versus semantic content but would suggest it misses the mark. Each such argument is based on the question of whether machines can 'think' like humans 'think'. I find this a very constricting approach. Frankly, I would prefer that machines *not* 'think' like humans 'think' since we already appear to have thoughtful humans (an empirical statement open to much dispute). Rather, I would hope that if mind is the emergent property of brain function, then machine intention could be an 'emergent property' of machine function. As I have argued earlier in this book, it is indeed an exercise in imagination to understand what characteristics such emergent properties possess. It is desperately to be hoped that they do not merely mimic that which already exists.

Design: The Balance of Constraint and Opportunity

> May we not fancy that if, in the remotest geological period, some early form of vegetable life has been endowed with the power of reflecting upon the dawning life of animals which was coming into existence alongside of its own, it would have thought itself exceedingly acute if it had surmised that animals would one day become real vegetables? Yet would this be more mistaken than it would be on our part to imagine that because the life of machines is a very different one to our own, there is therefore no higher possible development of life than ours; or that because mechanical life is a very different thing from ours, therefore that it is not life at all?

> But I have heard it said, 'granted that this is so, and that the vapor-engine has a strength of his own, surely no one will say that it has a will of its own?' Alas! if we look more closely, we shall find that this does not make against the supposition that the vapor-engine is one of the germs of a new phase of life. What is there in this whole world, or in the worlds beyond it, which has a will of its own? The Unknown and Unknowable only!'

(Butler, 1872, p. 215)

One of the central questions we face in specifying goals at a societal level is plurality. Individuality is a central pillar of the democratic system. While pure individuality, like the comparable notion of freedom, is a myth; in the United States at least there is a strong mandate to protect 'the rights of the individual'. This position is in contrast with collectivist societies in which the needs of the individual are sublimated to the greater needs of society. As a consequence, societal aims are frequently expressed as generalities that provide constraint and threat to no one, such as 'life, liberty, and the pursuit of happiness'. The question to be addressed here is twofold. First, can we continue with such vague social goals in the face of technology which demands specification? Second, do we want to accept societal goals if they override our valued individuality?

I think the answers to these questions lie in seeing how technology has addressed human needs as expressed in Maslow's hierarchy shown in Figure 2.3 (see Maslow, 1964). Clearly, technology looks to serve to free society and individuals from the want of the basic physiological needs. It is of course more than ironic that there are many individuals with more than sufficient monetary resources for several lifetimes who are unable to attain other levels in the noted hierarchy. However, technology rarely expresses explicit goals with respect to other levels of the hierarchy, I submit that this is a reflection of the separation of the ideal from the actual, or more prosaically, the why from the how – the propositional divorce of purpose and process. My central protestation is that technology, cognizant of the

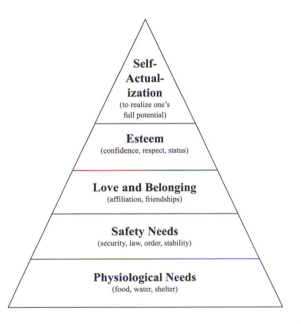

Figure 2.3   The classic hierarchy of human needs as proposed by Maslow (1954)

Note: That this is a descriptive structure, where the individually specified levels bear only a nominal relationship to each other and the 'hierarchy' is a weak descriptor at best. Putatively, there is an order dependence such that one level is founded upon another. The implication is that, for example, friendship is predicated upon law. Clearly, these intrinsic relationships need not be dependent. It is clear, that technology acts to support the base of the pyramid. That is, technology underlies the availability of food, water, and shelter in contemporary society. Unfortunately, the contemporary function of technology attempts to expand the certainty of basic needs and does not foster vertical transition.

fact or not, shapes the why as much as the how. *And in this it has failed.* The science of human-machine systems has largely failed to attack the question of purpose in a scientific manner. The issue of purpose has been conveniently finessed by science and left to elected legislators as though purpose cannot be studied by science and specific goals, expressed in terms understandable and achievable by technological systems. I argue here that one approach to this lacuna of scientific responsibility lies in the use of advanced technology for enhanced education. The fact that our basic educational delivery systems are essentially indistinguishable from those of over a century ago is an indictment indeed (Hancock, 2000a).

I am acutely aware that the determination of purpose remains inherently a political decision. I do not have room to discuss the role of technology in the political process itself, although it is a matter to which considerable thought needs be directed (Woods and Hancock, 2000). Rather, I acknowledge political power and assert that any proposed innovations unsupported by such power are liable to have a restricted impact. The quintessential bottom line is that technology must be used to enfranchise not to enslave (Illich, 1973) and that the political system, however, formed, should be directed to support this goal.

❖ ❖ ❖

Our Mutual Future

Helena: What did you do to him [Radius the Robot]?

Dr. Gall: H'm nothing. There's reaction of the pupils, increase in sensitiveness, and so on. Oh, it wasn't an attack peculiar to the robots.

Helena: What was it then?

Dr. Gall: Heaven alone knows. Stubbornness, fury or revolt – I don't know. And his heart, too.

Helena: How do you mean?

Dr. Gall: It was beating with nervousness like a human heart. Do you know what? I don't believe the rascal is a robot at all now.

Helena: Doctor, has Radius got a soul?

Dr. Gall: I don't know. He's got something nasty.

(Capek, 1923)

The Love-Hate Relationship

We often express a literal love-hate relationship with the machines we create. On the one hand, we extol their virtues as labour-saving devices and more generally as mechanisms for freeing humans from the bondage of manual work. On the other hand we decry the loss of employment and human dignity that comes with progressive automation. This relationship is, of course, culturally contingent. The countries of the East and those of the developing nations each have differing perspectives on the advantages and dangers of technology. We in the Western world express this ambivalence toward technology in many differing ways. For example, our fiction is redolent with visions of technical systems that turn against their human masters. From Samuel Butler's *Erewhon* through Capek's *Rossum's Universal Robots*, now to Schwarzenegger's *Terminator* and Reeve's *Matrix*, we have a collective and seemingly pathological fear of the machine as master. Yet at the same time, nothing alters the headlong rush toward ever more 'automation' as the solution to a growing spectrum of societal problems.

One suspects that one's position with respect to technical innovation is very much influenced by the threat that technology appears to pose to you as a person versus the potential individual gain that is to be had from such developments. Scientists can always study it, professors can always pontificate about it, and businessmen can always seek a profit factor. Hence, I would expect most who would be inclined to read this text would certainly view technology as a valuable enterprise. However, should we pose the idea of the development of an automatic research machine that can also teach and do away with capitalistic profit, there might be some dissent, even in the present readership? But even with such a machine, I still suspect that scientists could always study it, certainly professors will always be able to talk about it, and I would be most surprised if someone could not find a profit in it. I think, for the present reader, automation holds little terror. However, if your skills are limited, your circumstances straitened, or more directly your job position recently replaced by a machine, I think your perspective might be somewhat different. There again, I suspect the vast majority of the individuals in the latter group will be too busy trying to make ends meet to purchase and read a book such as the present one. Such are the vagaries of power.

Beyond Anthropomorphism

At present, human society shares a comfortable delusion. The delusion is anthropomorphic in nature and relies upon biological assumptions. The assumptions are that because machines are not self-replicating in the way biological systems are self-replicating, then the proliferation of technical systems is controllable. The anthropomorphic delusion is that because machines do not possess intelligence and therefore intention, or at least possess them in the same way that humans possess intelligence and intention, then the absence of machine intention will persist. Despite our best and desperate efforts at machine intelligence as a surrogate of human intelligence, we still do not have any substantive evidence of machine cognition, largely because such evidence is constrained to take a form that mimics human intelligence. This is the central fallacy of the Turing test, which requires that evidence of any 'intelligence' is had only through reference to human abilities. This naïve, anthropomorphic, and impoverished perspective (see Akins, 1993; Nagel, 1974) is that which provides a cloak to foster our present 'warm feeling'. To some it is a much 'colder' feeling. In his radical and interesting work, Illich (1973) deplores the contemporary direction of technology for precisely this reason when he noted:

> The re-establishment of an ecological balance depends on the ability of society to counteract the progressive materialization of values. Otherwise man will find himself totally enclosed within his artificial creation, with no exit. Enveloped in a physical, social, and psychological milieu of his own making, he will be a prisoner in a shell of technology, unable to find again the ancient milieu to which he was adapted for hundreds of thousands of years. The ecological balance cannot be re-established unless we recognize again that only persons have ends and that only persons can work toward them. Machines only operate ruthlessly to reduce people to the role of impotent allies in their destructive progress.

(Illich, 1973)

In disputing the later contention, it is still important to recognize the validity of the initial premise concerning the reification of material values. Further, given the present treatise on teleology and intention beyond the individual human, Illich's latter points must also be given careful consideration as a condition in which diversification of intention fails.

The societal ambivalence toward machines is then, never far below the surface as for example, the Luddite attacks of the Midlands of England demonstrated. Indeed, the theme of the machine as an enemy runs deep. It is noteworthy that Asimov tried artistically to concoct 'Laws of Robotics' each of which was sequentially broken within the first few years of robotics research and operations (Hamilton and Hancock, 1986). Are we destined for the dark ruins of twenty-first-century cities firing hopeful lasers at Skynet's malevolent hench-machines? I should note that this is largely a Western, developed-world preoccupation. Technology is not universally seen in this manner by any stretch of imagination. In addition, differing cultures have widely divergent goals and world views which do not accord with the main themes of our society. Such pluralism must be considered in the aims of global technology (see Moray, 1994).

In its own way, this view of the machine as threatening master is as sterile as the 'mindless' path we progress along in reality. Moravec (1988) has postulated that silicon-based intelligence will soon tire of our terrestrial confines and will seek its fulfilment in the celestial spaces, unfettered by the constraints of biological needs. With the exception of the latter vision, these futuristic perspectives are largely linear extrapolations of polarized facets of contemporary development. What is clear is that the uncertainty of future developments depends precisely upon non-linear effects. Prediction of these sudden quirks of changes in history is problematic at best.

Back to Arcadia?

Have I, by these remarks, allied myself with the recidivists who seek a return to a happy but mythical 'golden-age?' Am I a committed utopian or even 'autopian'? (Hancock and Diaz, 1991; Sidney, 1593). I think not. Rather, I seek to put the development of automation and the role of the human in some perspective. Our decisions at the present, nascent stage of machine independence will constrain our possible decisions at subsequent and potentially more volatile stages of human-machine interaction. I do not advocate a giant 'OFF' button, since as we have seen, we have already built globally complex networks and the interconnections of those systems refute the possibility of such a simple strategy. Rather, I advocate that we keep to the forefront of systems design the thought of Francis Bacon, who opined that science was designed 'for the uses of life'. In the same way, we must design technology 'for the uses of human life.' For without such a teleology for technology we are lost indeed.

❖ ❖ ❖

Two Cultures: A Technical Society Divided by Technology

> Tools are intrinsic to social relationships. An individual relates himself in action to his society through the use of tools that he actively masters, or by which he is passively acted upon. To the degree that he masters his tools, he can invest the world with his meaning; to the degree that he is mastered by his tools, the shape of the tool determines his own self-image. Convivial tools are those which give each person who uses them the greatest opportunity to enrich the environment with the fruits of his or her vision. Industrial tools deny this possibility to those who use them and they allow their designers to determine the meaning and expectations of others. Most tools today cannot be used in a convivial fashion.

(Illich, 1973)

Bifurcations of Society

I have discussed the proposition that our ecology is technology and I have advocated a manifest purpose for that technology. I have given considerable space to reflections on the impact of technology in particular as a positive force. However, it is important to give considerations to the downside of technology.

I base this argument on the original observation of C.P. Snow (1964) concerning the two 'cultures' of society. Briefly, Snow observed that:

> I christened [it] to myself as the 'two cultures.' For constantly I felt I was moving among two groups – comparable in intelligence, identical in race, not grossly different in social origin, earning about the same incomes, who had almost ceased to communicate at all, who in intellectual, moral and psychological climate had so little in common.

However, the bifurcation of society that I contemplate is one that is much more radical. It does not concern the divergent 'world views' of the educational aristocracy. Rather, it represents the very division of society itself between those empowered by technology and those subjugated by that self-same technology.

Bifurcations in society are based upon the differential control of resources. The obvious manifestation of those resources are physical wealth expressed as goods, lands, or currency (more generally 'capital'). However, control need not be direct ownership per se but may be more indirectly expressed. The classic example is the control exercised by European medieval clergy over the nobility of those time. The ecclesiasts mediated between man and God largely through their exclusive access to and understanding of written forms of knowledge. It was not unusual for many powerful landowners to actually be illiterate. Our development of technology promises to institute an alarmingly similar form of division. Some will understand the arcane esoterica of technology and will consequently rule over its blessings. Most, however, will not. They will suffer under either its benevolence or its malevolent oppression. For those who dismiss this as pure fantasy, I only ask them to recall the early days of computing when programmers wrote almost only for other programmers, or even worse, themselves alone (see also Vallee, 1982). Others of us mere users, albeit intelligent and well-educated scientists, struggled mightily to understand indecipherable error codes founded themselves on alpha-numeric ciphers. Who then exercised control? It is an almost inevitable rule of human existence that power follows money and vice versa. The power over technology will, in the near term, prove to be the ultimate power.

Access Denied

It is comforting to believe that applied psychology in general and human-machine systems science in particular had much to do with improving computer interaction and making communication with machines more facile and accessible. However, the truth lies nearer to the financial drive to sell technology to ever-wider markets which mandates more open, easy interaction. In these circumstances, the science of Human Factors of the past has acted in a remedial rather than proactive role. It might now be assumed that computer interaction is open to all. But I require the reader to consider the disadvantages of the illiterate in our society, many of the older members who have not grown up with technology and who are not facile with its manipulation. The physically and mentally challenged, the uneducated and the poor for whom education itself and access to technology is not seen as a priority. What of these members of society? This does not even consider many of the world's population also to whom access is denied. These individuals are not in the information super-highway slow lane, they have yet to come within a country mile of the on-ramp. As yet, many such individuals have neither a vehicle nor a driver's licence.

If I have talked here in general evolutionary terms, then it is these latter individuals who are threatened with the ultimate in adaptive failure. For they will have failed to adapt to the current ecology, that being technology. Thoughts of this extinction raise critical moral dilemmas in themselves. I further suggest that the bifurcation between technically literate and technically illiterate rapidly grows into rich and poor, privileged and oppressed. This distinction may divide society in a more profound manner than any of our presently perceived divisions. At one time, I believed that the only solution to this tragedy was education; after the events of 9-11 I am not so sure. Education should be the right of each member of an enlightened society. A world that promotes an arcane brotherhood wielding disproportionate power by their secretion of knowledge is doomed to failure (McConica, 1991). Or as one wit put it in political terms: '*today's pork is tomorrow's bacon*'.

❖ ❖ ❖

The Actual and the Ideal

> Dichotomized science claims that it deals only with the actual and the existent and that it has nothing to do with the ideal, that is to say, with the ends, the goals, the purposes of life, i.e., with end-values.

> (Maslow, 1964)

The present chapter started with a statement of a basic paradox in technology. On the one hand, the explicit aim of technology is to improve the lot of humankind. In actuality, the unintended by-product of contemporary technology seems to be the threat of global destruction, through either its acute or chronic effects. 'Arcadians' look to advocate for the dismantling of technology and then somehow living in a world of sylvan beauty. This vision features peace, harmony, and tranquillity as the central theme. Their hopes are laudable, their aspirations naïve. Peace, harmony, and tranquillity are not the hallmarks of a world without technology. Such a world is one of hard physical labour and the ever-present threat of famine at the behest of an uncertain environment or war at the behest of equally unpredictable neighbours. Humankind has fought for many centuries to rid itself of these uncertainties and the dogma that attends them.

Our ecology is technology. If we are to achieve our individual and collective societal goals it will be through technology. I have argued here that we must actively guide technical innovation and be wary of the possible alternative facets of machine intention which in no way resembles our own. We must state explicit purpose for the machines we create and these purposes must be expressed at the level of a global society, not that of an individual or even single nation. When expressed at this higher level, we can expose the antagonistic nature of some of the systems we create to an overall good. I further argue that we cannot view ourselves socially, or even individually, as separated from technology. The birth of machine intention will pose questions whose answers will become the central force that shape our future. How we interact with machines, the degree of autonomy we permit them, the rate of comparative evolution, and the approach to mutual co-evolution form the manifesto of our potential future. That the ground rules are being set in our time makes the current work on human-centred automation all the more important. I point to our past failure in setting such constraints and ask how we propose to do better in the future?

Human Factors professionals have long clamoured to be involved early in the design process. That is in *how* an object is designed. However, it is now time to step forward and become involved in that process even earlier. That is, those in human-machine systems design must have a hand in determining *why* an object, artefact, or machine is designed in the first place. Human Factors has been a bastard discipline which sits astride so many 'divisions'. It has linked art (or design) with science. It has dealt with the social (human) and the technical (machine). It has looked to integrate the subjective (psychological) aspects of behaviour with the most concrete, objective (engineering) realms of existence. Therefore, it is imperative that in this unique pursuit we must also encompass both the Actual (what is) and the Ideal (what should be). It is why the Human Factors of old must evolve into the human-machine sciences of the future.

> After all then it comes to this, that the difference between the life of a man and that of a machine is one rather of degree than of kind, though differences in kind are not wanting. An animal has more provision for emergency than a machine. The machine is less versatile; its range of action is narrow; its strength and accuracy in its own sphere are superhuman, but it shows badly in a dilemma; sometimes when its normal action is disturbed, it will lose its head, and go from bad to worse like a lunatic in a raging frenzy; but here, again, we are met by the same consideration as before, namely, that machines are still in their infancy; they are mere skeletons without muscle and flesh.
>
> (Butler, 1872)

Conclusion

Superna Quaerite: Enquire After Higher Things.

Earlier, I suggested that the turn of a millennium was an appropriate juncture for human society to turn from its adolescence to a mature adulthood. This is a comfortable homily in that it sounds most impressive but in actuality signifies almost nothing. I want to elaborate this statement in my final comments for this chapter, so that it means something substantive and, I hope, significant. I claim that for the childhood and adolescence of humankind we have acted as passive victims of an omnipotent environment. Our various names for events that happen to us – 'Act of God', 'fate', 'Kismet', 'accident', 'happenstance', 'luck' – all connote a conception that life simply *happens to us* directed by forces outside our control. I do not claim all natural forces are within human control. I do claim that the passive and victim-laden attitude that we adopt with respect to external forces is within human control. For much of our existence we have had to label such forces as benevolent or malevolent 'deities' which evolved in some incarnations as a single deity which arbitrates all earthly and cosmic events. While not wishing to trespass too egregiously upon personal beliefs, I do reject the idea of an individual deity who follows us around to continually control, test, and evaluate. In the absence of a personalized deity, our society still desperately seeks an entity to 'blame' for untoward events which happen.

Earlier, I mentioned the 'as if' pragmatic approach and postulated that much of society adopts this positive pragmatism. I propose that this form of pragmatism be adopted as a basis for the teleology of technology. That is, while we may continue to argue over the existence and role of an omnipotent deity, we assume this mantle of maturity upon a local scale and become *responsible* for our collective future.

I started this chapter with, and have made it a theme, that our ecology is technology. I end it in a similar manner by affirming that technology is also fast becoming our contemporary theology. I propose the term *teleologics*, to cover the concept of intention in technology and its comparative theological referent. If we do not knit together the explicit scientific co-consideration of purpose and process, the division will destroy us. I can only countenance this alternative in the words as voiced by Shakespeare's *Macbeth*:

> Tomorrow, and tomorrow, and tomorrow,
> Creeps in this petty pace from day to day,
> To the last syllable of recorded time;
> And all our yesterdays have lighted fools
> The way to dusty death. Out, out, brief candle!
> Life's but a walking shadow, a poor player
> That struts and frets his hour upon the stage
> And then is heard no more: it is a tale
> Told by an idiot, full of sound and fury,
> Signifying nothing.

(Act V, scene v)

Chapter 3
Convergent Technological Evolution

Introduction

The interface is the element which connects the human to the machine in any human-machine system. The following chapter is primarily about this crucial bridge, how it is created by design and how the common evolutionary forces on it act to converge its fundamental form.

Design is directed evolution. It is the manifest presence and intention of the designer that differentiates technical evolution from evolution in the rest of nature. As a consequence of this difference, evolution in technology can appear to proceed with great rapidity while evolution in nature is in comparison, most often represented as imperceptibly slow. However different these respective processes might at first appear, as I have argued in the foregoing chapter, the processes of natural and technical evolution have a great deal in common. In each circumstance, the entities that are created must adapt to the environmental demands which they encounter while trying to pass on the advantages with which they may have been conferred. What is passed on and how it is passed on remains a topic of extensive investigation in the study of natural evolution. In technology, of course, designers often specifically seek to incorporate improvements that have been shown to be useful, although in an information-overloaded age this is not always feasible. In general though, we see change in technology taking place now on almost a daily basis. In contrast, most individuals rarely see natural 'evolution' occurring. Although we may recognize evolution as a logical inference from assembled remnants and remains reflecting vast epochs of development, we do not have the 'direct' experience of human evolution happening at first hand. It is the recognition of this vast time scale of change which arguably engendered Darwin's original insight on evolution in the first place (Hancock, 2007) and it is this fundamentally 'personal' time scale of experience that encourages us to separate out technical from natural evolution.

Designers look to take advantage of past experience whilst they still frequently have to build upon existing designs with all the constraints that this process of revision entails. However, on occasion they can start from scratch and throw away everything that has gone before. While the latter opportunity appears to be one of many differences between natural and technical evolution, it is in fact a parallel of the mass extinction events and the subsequent sudden growth of species which are also hallmarks of the natural evolutionary process (see Raup, 1991). In reality, it is only the difference in rate of change which represents the fundamental *descriptive* distinction between each of the respectively identified evolutionary process.

From this and other evidence, and because technology is actually as 'natural' as other evolutionary processes it is subject to predominantly the same influences that occur in nature. This equivalence of process is helpful for our understanding since the evolution and extinction of naturally occurring ecosystems provide important models for understanding the behaviour and potential failure of complex human-machine systems. This understanding promises to be a cornerstone for future design of such systems. The characteristic of evolution that I want to consider and illustrate here is the process of 'convergence' of form in systems experiencing common evolutionary 'forces'. With respect to natural evolution and convergence, Gould (1980) observed that:

> Separate development of similar features is very common in evolution; we refer to it as parallelism, or convergence. We anticipate convergence in a few relatively simple and clearly adaptive structures when two groups share the same mode of life.

The technical realm in which I wish to present convergence is that of the human-machine (computer) interface. My argument is founded on the following premises that:

1. complex human-machine systems show evidence of evolution and to a large extent they evolve in similar ways to natural ecosystems;
2. the design of complex human-machine systems can be informed by the parallel between natural and technological evolution so that the catastrophic failures that regale the history of natural ecosystems can be avoided in such technological systems;
3. species of human-machine system asymptote to a common functional form given their subjugation to common 'forces'.

If this latter evolutionary characteristic can be confirmed, it would provide an important rationale for direct ecological influence on the technical design of human-machine systems. This would not be a metaphorical link but rather a common representation of the self-same process. Thus the question extends beyond design considerations alone to the fundamental role and nature of theory in science of human-machine systems itself.

❖ ❖ ❖

Forces for Convergent Evolution

There are two primary forces which, I claim, dictate convergent evolution at the human-machine interface. I characterize the first force as the 'push' of computer technology and the second force as the 'pull' of inherent human information-processing capabilities. While it is useful to dichotomize these for the purpose of discussion, their mutual presence and their mutual interaction are critical for the process of convergence to occur.

I do not claim that these are the only forces involved. There are, of course, clear economic and market forces which, through monopolies or other influences, may either sustain a poor design or suppress a superior one. A manipulated market can control price and availability, for that is its purpose. Indeed, the economic purpose of a product is to dominate its market by extinguishing all of its competition (for example, VHS vs. Betamax). But, competition lies at the very heart of evolution and I would claim that few designers purposefully sub-optimize their design, relying on marketing personnel for its subsequent success. Further, I would claim that any such sub-optimization would actually represent a specific opportunity for competitors to exploit. My direct concern here is for the factors that drive progress in the longer term (see for comparison Petroski's 1992 arguments on the functional evolution of objects). Evolution in technology then is only partially a result of market forces. However, the source of causation is not totally due to this factor since evolution itself is anathema to that which any monopoly seeks to achieve.

❖ ❖ ❖

The Push of Computer Technology

The first 'force' I want to consider is the 'push' of computer technology. The effects of computer technology on society are obvious, profound, and still growing. The computer is the dominant and preferred tool that mediates between human and machine and of course, it is itself often the machine element as well. In developed societies, in both large-scale complex systems and within small stand-alone appliances, some form of computational component is virtually mandated. This ubiquity of a common control medium shapes and constrains possible human-machine communication. As computers penetrate further into everyday existence, into realms as diverse as driving and shopping, this force gains power (cf., Hancock, Dewing, and Parasuraman, 1993).

This power has a side effect and that side effect is that the proliferation of computer systems fosters a combinatorial explosion of available data. This explosion becomes a conflagration when computers are linked so as to readily communicate with each other. However, without context and without cognition, these data are sterile. But cognition and context can be overwhelmed by the scale of such a data avalanche. Thus data overload is a particular problem, especially in the sequence of extracting information from data, and directing actions based upon knowledge derived from such information. The question arises then as to how to structure the interface between the machine (the data element) and the human (the cognitive element) in order to deal with this information overload problem. It is here that the second force exerts a critical influence.

❖ ❖ ❖

The Pull of Information Processing Capabilities

The force which 'pulls' interfaces towards a common representational form resides in the inherent constraints on human cognitive processing capabilities. Humans are basically visual creatures and operate well in navigating dynamic, complex four-dimensional worlds. Individuals have ready developed perception-action skills and do well in conditions which present such challenges. Comparatively, humans are not so skilled in representational decision-making environments that require transformation of problems and formulations of answers through formal or logical expressions of things, objects, or concepts. It has been suggested (Hutchins, 1994) that the transformation of problems from this representational decision-making domain to the perceptual-motor domain make them eminently more amenable to efficient resolution. Indeed, this transformation is a cornerstone of the ecological interface design movement (Vicente and Rasmussen, 1992). Thus computations that can be rendered into four-dimensional perception-action challenges are much simpler to resolve than, for example, complex mathematical representations of the same problem (see illustrations in Gleick, 1988; and conceptions in object-oriented design, Booch, 1991).

Human beings are highly visually oriented and this characteristic is reflected in, among other things, the processing capacity of the cortex given over to vision. The critical link between perception and action has been emphasized by Gibson (1979) among others. However, it is the explicit recognition that our understanding of complex cognitive functioning *must* be based upon this perception-action framework that represents an insight into our evolutionary development. Capabilities such as language are latecomers on the human scene. For the vast majority of our existence, we have been solving complex four-dimensional, perceptual-motor problems by muscular resolution not by linguistic deliberations. Such is our facility with these forms of problem that we often fail to consider such capabilities an explicit skill or even an asset at all. However, it is the case that the ability to walk and chew gum at the same time is indeed a valuable capacity. Indeed, it is often the case that the problem of seeing is seeing the problem. Our familiarity with these skills has bred such contempt that we are hardly aware that our visuo-motor capabilities *are* skills at all. That is, unless we are among those who directly study them or until we lose them or try to replicate them in an artificial surrogate. Upon the explicit acknowledgement of this fact, we recognize that human beings can process vast amounts of visual information and when formatted as perceptual-motor problems, resolve such questions with an ease and speed that connote both desired and superior performance. Little wonder that there is a fast-growing focus on graphical problem representations via visual graphics.

❖ ❖ ❖

Convergence of the Physical Interface

Contemporary Directions

What has become rapidly obvious to designers, especially given the observations of the disaster and error literature (for example, Goldberg, 1984), is that ever-increasing information cannot be satisfactorily represented on endless, single function analogue and alpha-numeric displays. The practice of adding a new display each time a new system component is developed simply does not work, since this leads to an unbound exponential growth in displays as illustrated in the observation of Card (1988), and shown in Figure 3.1. While at some point one simply runs out of real estate for the physical displays themselves, the real concern is that critical information is resident as much in the interaction between individual displays from each sub-system as it is in the singular effects shown on each uni-representational display. Therefore, what has happened in physical display space is that the multiple layers of virtual material are now contained within video-display terminals (VDT). These alternative display forms have replaced individual, physically discrete displays at the surface (physical) level of the system.

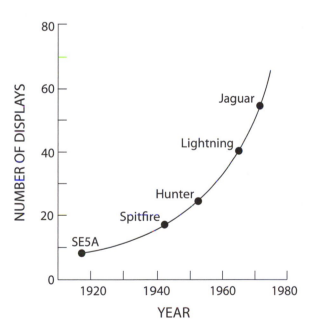

Figure 3.1 **Exponential increase in the number of displays in high performance aircraft versus the year of development. Reproduced from Card (1988)**

It is possible that with menuing and multiple display pages, there may be a continuing exponential growth in the amount of information that is available. However, in the electronic interface this proliferation has been hidden. As physical screens themselves are only visible in a limited number of locations, we find that the configuration of workstations have begun to evolve in the same direction for systems designed to control widely different types of processes. In Figure 3.2 I have shown an illustration of a physical workstation arrangement that has been developed, showing this convergent characteristic. I have chosen this simply as one example of the much more comprehensive convergence process. However, there is a plethora of other examples which support my contention. Indeed as time has gone by this trend has only continued to increase. My case is made stronger each day as this trend persists. For example, in only one Proceedings of the Human Factors and Ergonomics Society, there are comparable cases shown by Segal (1994), Thomas and McClelland (1994), and Winsch, Atwood and Quinkert (1994). Since this first observation, I find that the convergence has accelerated and has become ever more evident in more modern systems.

Figure 3.2   **View of a modern-day cockpit showing the distal display space (the out-of-the-window view), with the proximal display spaces as represented by the series of panels of VDTs in front of the two pilots**

The Future in Virtual Environments

There is much then that is common between different workstations despite their widely differing functions. However, there remain some important differences. While the illustration (Figure 3.2) shows interaction via numerous VDTs, their arrangement is largely in a single plane of display. The more recent control room environments feature displays that surround and are projected in a number of different planes and angles. Before I am inundated with criticisms that previous control rooms also use this form of display arrangement, let me emphasize that my point is general and is not restricted to any single system. That is, individual devices will have differing evolutionary approaches toward a common representation, and if they 'discover' certain characteristics in differing orders it does not invalidate the general argument of convergence. So, in essence, in modern systems, the individual is being 'surrounded' with information. In some contexts, these surrounding displays have little interlinkage, so that almost an endless sequence of displays is presented upon four walls of the control room (see Figure 3.3). Note here also that software manipulations such as 'windowing' techniques elaborate upon this display strategy to overlay multiple representations of additional 'virtual' physical space on a constricted actual physical space.

Figure 3.3   **Modern control room configuration replicates the cockpit displays. Here, the out-of-the-window view is replaced as a distal display space by large-scale viewing screens. The proximal display space remains the VDTs associated in this case with several operators as compared to the two pilot spaces shown in Figure 3.2**

What I want to emphasize is the tendency to place the individual operator, or team of operators, in an 'information bubble', where all of the distal space (in the case of large operational control centres these are the walls of the room) are used as displays. This selfsame conception has been used to construct some virtual environments in which the 'world' appears, displayed via back-projection upon the four walls of the room, sometimes labelled the 'virtual cave' (Defanti, Sandin, and Cruz-Neira, 1993; and see Hancock, 2009). I suggest that each of these respective stages of progress represent the tacit and sometimes explicit recognition that the physical interface for human-machine interaction is moving toward immersive representation which may be either complete (as in the case of virtual reality) or a hybrid form of organization (as in the case of augmented reality; Goldiez, Ahmad and Hancock, 2007).

There are several ways to present such virtual and augmented environments. Advanced simulation capabilities often including actual vehicles, with associated motion dynamics, have been embedded in a virtual display world. These simulation facilities can get very close to passing the Turing test for reality. The stereotypical virtual reality system is represented by head-mounted display and data gloves in which the individual literally 'wears' the surrogate world. Recent attempts have been directed toward the improvement of display resolution in such systems including advances in boom-mounted technologies in which virtual worlds are seen through moveable, counter-balanced binoculars. What is clear is that some form of virtual and/or augmented environment is the next step along the path of the evolution of the physical interface. Needless to say, many commercial efforts are currently directed to this goal. Some form of virtual reality type technology will represent the machine interface of the future. But, what these interfaces will present and whether the format of information presented will also converge in the same manner are matters as yet not fully resolved.

❖ ❖ ❖

Convergence of the Information Format

The Nature of Information Displayed

If physical displays, in diverse work systems, now resemble each other, what of the information itself and how is it structured for display? Convergent evolution is not simply the widespread use of the same computer system or display type, since this might occur as function of availability, compatibility, general affective response, or simply from a common procurement procedure or some artificialities of market dominance. In terms of information display, there has been progress toward some consensus. Alpha-numeric line commands have been replaced with icon-based approaches (Shneiderman, 1983), although, as with all evolution, residual and vestigial characteristics frequently remain a part of the technology. Some of this progress can be seen in the comparison of differing forms of data display as presented for example by Jacob, Egeth, and Bevon (1976; see also Jacob, 1989) and discussed in detail in Wickens (1984, p. 170).

Over the decades there has been, and continues to be, a vast spread of graphic user interfaces. It is no coincidence that there has also been an explosive increase in the development of graphics computational power and a substantive increase in the percentage of each computer's operational capability devoted solely to interface operations. Hence, the nature of the method of information display has itself changed to emphasize graphics capability. It therefore seems a logical step to propose that wraparound, four-dimensional representative worlds, or virtual environments, promise to become the interface structure of the future. Indeed, conceptions such as *Star Trek*'s 'holodeck' provide four-dimensional surrogate worlds in which immersion is achieved inside a manipulable physical space. It is an unfortunate impoverishment that such immersion is predominantly shown as only replicating veridical physical spaces and not more advanced emergent properties such as complex data fields. This is especially unfortunate, since *what* is displayed is not independent of *how* it is displayed.

The Metaphors of Representation

Displays represent systems. The important differences between systems lie in their individual and distinctive response characteristics. However, as the intermediary between human and machine, the computer can 'buffer' or hide many of these differences. In consequence, *what* is controlled might become less of an issue, compared to *how* such control is effected. Eventually, it could be the case that, for example, the differences between air-traffic control and the control of a nuclear power station could become virtually opaque to the operator sitting at their generic control panel viewing their generic displays. But would this strategy be advisable? Is there any unfathomable rule which demands that there be complex displays for complex systems? There is a considerable effort to seek displays that present the 'emergent properties' of complex systems (for one example see, Moray et al., 1994; for a more comprehensive perspective see Vicente and Rasmussen, 1992). One question that is constantly asked is; what is the best metaphor that can be used for representation? As all systems have to be 'navigated' through some multidimensional phase space of operation, I return to the metaphor of a boat on an ocean as the one which captures many common elements of widespread systems operation. It bears repeating that this metaphor is perhaps the most apt and can best be envisioned through art and literature. Here, I explicitly re-iterate the passage from Robert Louis Stevenson's classic *Treasure Island*:

> I found each wave instead of the big, smooth, glossy mountain it looks from shore, or from a vessel's deck, was for all the world like any range of hills on the dry land, full of peaks and smooth places and valleys. The coracle, left to herself, turning from side to side, threaded, so to speak, her way through these lower parts, and avoided the steep slopes and higher, toppling summits of the wave.

Well now, I thought to myself, It is plain I must remain where I am and not disturb the balance; but it is plain also, that I can put the paddle over the side and from time to time, in smooth places, give her a shove or two towards land.

(Stevenson, 1946)

Here, the inherent uncertainties of the world are given by the state of the ocean and the system itself is the boat (in this case a coracle which is a form of a boat that is notoriously difficult to control). The individual looks to steer the boat with a limited repertoire of controls, in the present metaphor this is the paddle but it could well be the sails and rudder of more elaborate ships. The operational phase space is represented by the state of the ocean and the origin and destination of the boat are specified by the individual controller. There is evidence of the power of such a metaphor. Indeed, the self-same picture is shown on the front of the classic book on 'naturalistic decision making' by Klein et al. (1993) (Figure 3.4).

Figure 3.4   The front illustration of the text by Klein, Orasanu, Calderwood and Zsambok (1993). Reproduced with permission

It is also intrinsic to some observations made by Brian Arthur as quoted by Waldrop (1992) and reproduced below:

> The alternative [to the Newtonian clockwork metaphor] – the complex approach – is total Taoist. In Taoism there is no inherent order. 'The world started with one, and one became two, and the two became many, and the many led to myriad things.' The universe in Taoism is perceived as vast, amorphous, and ever changing. You can never nail it down. The elements always stay the same, yet they're always rearranging themselves. So it's like a kaleidoscope: the world is a matter of patterns that change, that partly repeat, but never quite repeat, that are always different.
>
> What is our relation to a world like that? Well, we are made of the same elemental compositions. So we are part of this thing that is never changing and always changing. If you think that you're a steamboat and can go up the river, you are kidding yourself. Actually, you're the captain of a paper boat drifting down the river. If you try to resist, you're not going to get anywhere. On the other hand, if you quietly observe the flow, realizing you are part of it, realizing the flow is ever changing and always leads to new complexities, then every so often you can stick an oar into the river and punt yourself from one eddy to another.

The progress of individuals through the complexities of an environment when that environment is expressed metaphorically as a rolling ocean is not confined only to the scientific realm. The idea of the person as a storm-tossed entity is often expressed in the arts as shown, for example, among others by Magritte (1965) in his 'Second Nature' (Torczyner, 1979) as illustrated in Figure 3.5. The artist contrasts the dynamics of the fluid medium with the conventionalities of its human occupants (see Mutter, 1993). Indeed, such contrast is central to the artistic impact. However, any interface metaphor needs to emphasize the complementarity of the circumstances over its contrast (Jordan, 1963). The underlying theme of these representations, as it is in the systems themselves, is the retention of stability in the face of uncertainty and the emergent characteristic of adaptability which indeed is the leitmotif of life itself.

❖ ❖ ❖

An Example of Process Convergence

One interesting contemporary example of convergence of process as opposed to interface display structure concerns transportation control. While many technologies are involved in these developments, one critical source of information comes from Global Positioning Systems (GPS) and its derivative Differential GPS. The latter system is capable of establishing a suitably equipped object's terrestrial location within a few centimetres given a short period of time with the capture of sufficient

Figure 3.5   'Second Nature' 1965: René Magritte. © 1998, C. Herscorici, London/Artists Rights Society (ARS), New York

positioning signals. As a consequence, it is possible to track the precise location of all so-equipped entities given the widespread use of such technology.

The introduction of this GPS capability has had vastly different influences on two forms of transportation. In commercial aviation, the ability to accurately track one's own aircraft and that of other aircraft has, among other influences, generated advocates for the 'free-flight' conception. In 'free flight' the pilot is responsible for the path of their own aircraft and for avoiding other aircraft in their local airspace. The presence of GPS (and other technologies) has gradually permitted this goal to be achieved. As a consequence, 'free flight' is an initiative that seeks to change the control structure from a highly centralized ATC system to a highly-distributed system. This evolution is based on the principle that distribution allows the best use of resources and negates the problem of information and control overload at one central location.

The impact of GPS and DGPS has also found its way into ground transportation systems. Given the current and increasing accuracy of DGPS systems, there are even expectations that are rapidly being fulfilled that, in tandem with other technologies, it can provide real-time guidance. However, the issue here is that information from such locating systems also allows for the dynamic tracking of vehicles from origin to destination. In direct, contrast to aviation, the proposal in ground vehicle transport, as embodied in Intelligent Transportation Systems (ITS) initiatives, is toward ever-greater centralized control. As illustrated in

Figure 3.6, we have a common technical stimulus that on the one hand has generated advocates for more distributed control in one current, highly centralized system (air traffic control), and yet on the other hand has generated an equivalent but opposite interest in another system (road traffic) for centralized control in driving activities, which have traditionally been of a highly distributed nature. Two caveats are important. I am indeed aware of the number of companion technologies which accompany position-location and positive control in both realms and have emphasized the role of GPS in the present example above some of these others. Also, I am aware that such technology does not affect transport vehicles only. Indeed, the role of the future infantry soldier is a good example of similar effects upon control structure given the dissemination of information and the sharing of control (National Research Council, 1995).

The main point of these observations is my contention that in each of these respective systems, which are subject to common comparable technical innovations, the same general form of hybrid control is emerging. This hybrid control is a two-level approach in which normal, everyday operations are accomplished under distributed control. Here, local operators exercise immediate decisions over their own immediate sphere of influence. Higher centres are occupied in supervisory roles and it is only under transient or unusual conditions (for example, bad weather, or a road-traffic incident) that exception processing is handled in these higher-level, more centralized facilities. The ability of these latter centres to 'see the big picture' enables them to deal efficiently with such unusual or exceptional circumstances. We should not be surprised to find such forms of control already in operation and indeed, one can also follow the development of theories of advanced brain function which have also led to precisely this same hybrid control

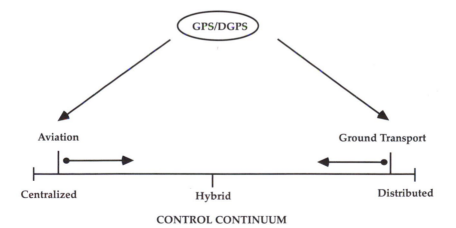

Figure 3.6   Convergence of control structure in different systems under the influence of common technology

conception. My point is that convergence does not have to solely be represented in physical things, entities, and objects but can also be seen also in the very processes of control themselves.

❖ ❖ ❖

Summary

What I have proposed here is the following. Technology is, to a large extent, 'natural'. As such, technologies are subjected to many of the same forces that impinge upon other complex systems in nature. When they are subjected to these selective forces technologies tend to asymptote toward common structure and function. This process is known more generally in biology as convergent evolution. It is only the periodic injection of required variability that acts against this powerful tendency. The inherent necessity to include direct consideration of common human user capacities pushes technology toward a common form. It is, of course, one of the ironies of evolution that convergence often provides the basis for subsequent divergence. Consider the following quotation from Gould (1980):

> Two organisms may maintain the same feature because both inherited it from a common ancestor. These are homologous similarities, and they indicate 'propinquity of descent,' to use Darwin's words. Forelimbs of people, porpoises, bats and horses provide the classic example of homology in most textbooks. They look different, and do different things, but are built from the same bones. No engineer, starting from scratch each time, would have built such disparate structures from the same parts. Therefore, the parts existed before the particular set of structures now housing them: they were, in short, inherited from a common ancestor.

Of course, this and the main theme of the present chapter are direct examples of unity in diversity and diversity in unity, which are central characters in how we structure our world view.

Technical evolution happens much more quickly and manifestly than it does in nature because of the intent of the designer. In adopting preferential characteristics I suggest that convergent evolution is observable in the human-machine interface. I propose that this happens not only for the physical structure of the workstation but the very way in which resident information is displayed and processed. I have provided one metaphor that I believe might prove useful for common representation across many divergent systems.

Are these observations helpful for the scientists and the designer? I think they are. For those involved in designing physical interfaces, I think the projected development toward a wraparound information 'cocoon' suggests a good, hard look at virtual and augmented reality approaches to represent the physical interface of the future. For the software designer, the task is to bring the critical system variables to the forefront and allow their 'emergent' properties to become constraints and contexts for the 'sea-lane' that the controller 'pilots' their craft (system) through. This conversion or transformation of complex alpha-numeric and analogue information into unified graphic distillations represents the software design challenge of the twenty-first century. While it is expected that training will still be important in developmental stages (Walker et al., 1994), eventually, the interface might achieve a level of transparency such that the problem becomes 'self-obvious' and the solution to the demands posed by such problems is then immediately apparent also (see Bennett and Flach, 1992; Flach and Vicente, 1989). In such circumstances the operator will directly 'see' the solution. More formally, if displays are homeomorphically and veridically mapped to the task domain, then the task solution becomes self-evident. If displays are only isomorphically mapped from the task domain, solutions may also be evident but the operator need not *know* what specific system they are controlling. This latter circumstance may or may not be a good thing. While we are still some way from such representations, I think it is important to articulate such a specific goal. For as William of Orange said, 'No wind can be favorable for one who knows not where he's going' (Servan-Schreiber, 1988).

Chapter 4
The Future of Function Allocation

THE BLACK RIDERS

Many workman
Built a huge ball of masonry
Upon a mountain top.
Then they went to the valley below
And turned to behold their work.
'It is grand,' they said.
They loved the thing.
Of a sudden it moved:
It came upon them swiftly,
It crushed them all to blood
But some had opportunity to squeal.

(Stephan Crane)

Preamble

The allocation of tasks to humans and machines lies at the very heart of all human-machine systems science. It is absolutely critical for the successful design of any socio-technical system. Indeed, who does what, when, where and how are the central factors in the design of any human-machine system for the conceivable future. However, persistent criticisms have proposed that the traditional conception of function allocation is itself flawed, or perhaps worse, totally inoperable in practice (Fuld, 1993). If this critique were true, where does such a conclusion lead? Is the traditional science of Human Factors then just a haphazard collection of ad hoc heuristics? Are there no function allocation principles other than the apocryphal 'common sense?' What is the future of such a science if such a conclusion is accepted? Although not the first such observation on the problem of function allocation, Fuld's critique is especially disturbing. This chapter does not seek directly to refute the arguments made by Fuld (1993) and his intellectual forebears, since there are many of his points with which I am in agreement. Rather, it seeks to illustrate why 'static task allocation' has failed as a design process and, further, what contemporary developments have been made in 'dynamic task allocation' which can answer such concerns. It is one of the bases of the evolution of Human Factors into a philosophically founded science of human-machine systems.

❖❖❖

The Foundation of Function Allocation

Any discussion of the concept of function allocation has to start with the classic report of Fitts (1951). Unfortunately, like many other 'classics' in science, this one is far more often cited than it is read. This is a great pity, since a detailed reading of the Fitts report reveals many interesting and telling observations. For example, although Fitts' name is directly associated with the work, it was actually authored by ten researchers, including the likes of Alphonse Chapanis, Walter Grether, and Alexander C. Williams, Jr. who are recognized alongside Fitts as some of the founding fathers of Human Factors. If there has been a lack of recognition of the latter contributors, there has also been a lack of acknowledgement of the actual content. The goal of the report was to improve air-navigation systems and to guide future interdisciplinary research in the area. Issues such as technical feasibility, economy, and manpower and personnel were considered only briefly while dynamic human issues such as selection, morale, motivation, fatigue and monotony were indicated as important future issues, but, were not considered in any detail in the final report. This latter point has an enormous impact when considering what was extracted and subsequently highlighted.

What caught the eyes and imagination of early readers considering human design recommendations was the now 'famous' Fitts' list. For completeness, these original lists are reproduced with their original illustrations here in Figures 4.1 and 4.2. Past and contemporary citations of the Fitts (1951) report are associated almost exclusively with these lists as though they were the central product of the report. But these comparative lists were only a small portion of the report and then only provided in order to develop research objectives. Without an understanding of the context of their presentation, these lists have been interpreted as a basis for design recommendations for function allocation. As a result, if static or traditional function allocation has failed as a design process; one reason may be that such comparative descriptions were never meant to serve as a basis for design in the first place! Consequently, some of the subsequent criticisms of the descriptive comparisons of human and machine abilities as a basis for design cannot be laid at the door of the authors of this landmark report since their purposes did not include such an aim. Regardless of the interpretation issue, it is the case that the descriptive comparisons were taken as a basis for function allocation and it is the failure of such interpretations with which we must now concern ourselves.

❖ ❖ ❖

The Failure of Function Allocation

The failures of what has been called traditional or 'static' task allocation have been explored in detail by a number of thoughtful commentators (see Chapanis, 1965; Fuld, 1993; Swain and Wohl, 1961). As a basis for understanding the future evolution of function allocation such failures are instructive since, as Petroski

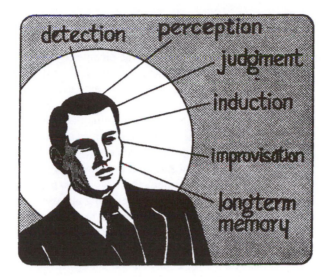

Figure 4.1   The listing of abilities in which human capability exceeds machine capability. List and illustration from the original Fitts (1951) report

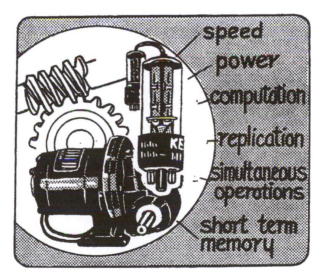

Figure 4.2   The listing of abilities in which machine capability exceeds human capability. List and illustration from the original Fitts (1951) report

(1992) observed, often it is a case of 'form follows failure'. An intrinsic failure of the static approach is found in its essential form, that of a descriptive listing. Lists are comparative and divisive by nature. Hence the dichotomy implied in the listing fosters a mindset for design in which tasks themselves are similarly divided. This discrete division negates the very idea of mutual sharing or 'complementarity' which is, I believe, essential for evolving, dynamic systems (see Jordan, 1963). Descriptive lists also require the semantic specification of abilities. The nature of the actual language which is used to describe such abilities is critical. Following the Fitts description, most lists use an information-theoretic-based description, that is itself a product of the information processing era in which the list was developed. This inevitably leads to problems, since abilities are expressed in machine favourable terms and it frequently appears that selecting the machine alternative is thus the preferred one, especially for future development. The ramifications of this point have been elegantly expressed by Hopkin (1988) who noted that:

> As technology advances, more functions can be considered for automation. Measures taken of manual and automated forms of the same task often introduce a bias: if functions are fulfilled better by the human, strenuous efforts are made to make the machine reach or surpass that performance. But, if the machine is superior to the human, comparable effort is not devoted to trying to raise the human's performance to the machine's level. The allocation of functions to person or machine depends more on measures of system and task efficiency than on satisfying the needs of people at work.

(p. 552)

The point concerning description can be most effectively made if we consider a comparative listing that favours human qualities such as 'the ability to experience remorse', or more provocatively, 'the ability to evaluate trust' (see also Lee and Moray, 1992; Riley, 1994). In circumstances with these specified requirements, we can quickly regain our appreciation for the superiority of the human operator in a number of dimensions. The fundamental argument is one that revolves around which human abilities can be replicated by a machine and which cannot. It is clear from the whole literature on artificial intelligence that some surprising cognitive activities can be mimicked through machine capabilities, such as the capacity for exhaustive search. However, other human abilities relating to the emotive or energetic aspects of behaviour are far less amenable to machine instantiation. As a consequence, the omission of the energetic aspects of performance in the original Fitts work (for example, learning) turns out to be a critical omission when translated into a human-machine design recommendation.

❖ ❖ ❖

As this is not meant simply to be a critique of static allocation I shall mention only one other major problem since it is critical to my subsequent argument. This is the question of operational context. In research on human activity, we seek descriptions of human response that hold over the widest possible range of conditions. When we find such relationships, we occasionally elevate them to the status of 'laws'. Indeed, Paul Fitts himself is rightly famous for his 'Fitts' Law of movement control which relates the speed of a movement to its accuracy (Fitts, 1954). Such laws are not acontextual expressions of behavior, rather they are multi-contextual expressions, and indeed such is their ubiquity that we become concerned only in those circumstances in which they fail to apply. At first sight, the Fitts 'list' promises to possess this 'law-like' property by expressing what machines are good at and what humans are good at. However, the flaw is that the lists themselves are expressed in an acontextual framework. When designers attempt to apply them in context, they fail and frustration is the result. Why is this?

In respect of human-machine systems, the answer is that the context is always critical for the performance outcome (see Flach et al., 1995; Hancock et al., 1995). More tritely, 'static' allocation is not dynamic. Thus, the sterile listing of capabilities fails to capture the essence of socio-technical systems operation which is that they change over time. This change is especially true of the human component whose expressions of non-stationarity include learning, boredom, and fatigue, as well as a plethora of other characteristics that defy a one time, unchanging attribution (see also Chapanis, 1965). When we try to ignore change, it is small wonder that it leads to the state of affairs so cogently described by Fuld (1993). And there is one more subtle but crucial effect of the static allocation approach. As observed by Hopkin, the outcome of such comparisons in machine terms fosters the development of devices with greater and greater degrees of function given over to the machine. In contemporary design, this is seen in the expansion of automation in many processes and work systems. The potentially catastrophic result is that the human operator is then relegated to 'the subsystem of last resort' (Kantowitz and Sorkin, 1987). In such work systems, operators are required to engage, almost exclusively, in the prolonged monitoring of computer performance; 'a job for which they are magnificently disqualified' (Hancock, 1991). Finally, operators are required to immediately take over in emergency conditions and recover the system flawlessly in circumstances in which the machine has found this impossible and has failed in its function. Of course, when this recovery process is unsuccessful we have operator 'error', with which our news media are all too ready to regale us.

Despite its attendant frustrations, static function allocation at one level is a relatively simple procedure. At some point in the process of design, construction, prototyping, shakedown, or operations, someone has to decide whether a task is to be performed by a human or a machine. It is certainly the case, and something that is not disputed, that humans and machines have different capabilities. However, the fundamental problem remains that at all points in the design process, the static allocation problem is chronically *underspecified*. That is, there is never sufficient knowledge of the situation so that all tasks can be described in Fitts-like terms and apportioned respectively. It is thus the indeterminacy of the real world that defeats the determinacy intrinsic to the static allocation strategy. An additional temporal problem I have emphasized and do so again is that no element remains constant. The machine breaks down or wears out. The human learns skills over the years but gets fatigued and bored on a daily basis. Even if these basic functions stay relatively constant, the environment against which system performance is set, is itself often changing. Little wonder that the single specification of static allocation fails abysmally in the face of this constant fluctuation.

There have been many recent efforts to change the fundamental approach to automation from a machine-centred to a human-centred one (Billings, 1989). It is clear that for this metamorphosis to succeed, that we have to re-cast and re-evaluate our whole view of the allocation of tasks. It is the present argument that such re-evaluation is in progress and this emerging conceptual basis is now examined.

❖ ❖ ❖

The Future of Function Allocation

If traditional static allocation is frustrating to the designer, ineffective for operations, and incomplete as a descriptive structure, must it also follow that task allocation, in general, is a vacuous construct? I argue that the future of task allocation is much brighter if we shift the focus from static allocation to a dynamic allocation. But given our criticisms regarding the under-specification of static allocation, does dynamic allocation mean that all tasks are apportioned on a moment-by-moment basis depending upon the whims and vagaries of immediate demand? Certainly not! To deny we know that humans and machines have respective strengths and weaknesses is to throw away valuable and hard-won knowledge. It is the knowing of both *how* and *when* to make such allocation changes that represent the promise of dynamic allocation.

One particular facet of dynamic allocation that has been the focus of much recent research is adaptive allocation. In this form, a change in allocation is triggered by some change in, for example, the performance level of the human operator. Particular concern is given over to the prevention of task overload (or conversely underload) imposed upon the human. Hence this process becomes a significant element of the human-centred automation philosophy (see Scerbo, 1995; Hancock and Chignell, 1987). The conceptions of dynamic and adaptive allocation do not deny the differences in human and machine abilities. Rather, they seek to take extensive and effective advantage of these differences through a strategy which allows the momentary, daily, monthly, or even yearly changes in task allocation to occur. The strategy can also be responsive to the knowledge of the context of current performance and the momentary and long term abilities of both the human and machine. In contrast, static allocation simply states who does what. It is unchanging in a world of change. Dynamic allocation seeks to circumvent the problem of under-specification by adapting to a world of change. It not only addresses 'who?' (humans or machines) but many other questions as well. I have couched these questions in a list (ironically) of if-then relations:

IF: Operators perform within a pre-determined criteria. (WHO?)
THEN: Operators shall keep task control, otherwise the task is allocated to machine control.
IF: Only parts of tasks are being performed poorly.(WHAT?)
THEN: Only these parts shall become available for dynamic allocation.
IF: Certain intervals are associated with increased demand or error. (WHEN?)
THEN: These periods will become available for dynamic allocation.
IF: Particular environments or combinations of environmental variables are associated with increased task demand or error. (WHERE?)
THEN: Encountering these environments triggers dynamic allocation.
IF: Extended periods of allocation have detrimental effects (objective or subjective). (WHY?)
THEN: Allocation shall both remove and return control.
IF: Operator performance, environmental attributes, and psycho-physiological indexes are paramount for successful human-machine interaction. (HOW?)
THEN: Each of these are inputs for allocation shift.

I do not claim that the advances in adaptive allocation solve all the problems of system design. Neither do I claim that many of the major research problems associated with dynamic change in human and machine function have been completely solved. However, such innovative strategies do provide an avenue of progress. It also implies that the enterprise of Human Factors is more than a collection of common-sense heuristics, it is evolving into a principled science of human-machine systems. Consequently, dynamic function allocation represents a central pillar of human-systems science, even if the shape of that pillar has evolved somewhat in the face of changing technologies and changing design demands.

❖ ❖ ❖

Design and Meta-Design

There is another benefit of dynamic allocation which extends beyond the scope of the individual human-machine systems themselves. This is the benefit to the designer. Earlier I noted that design is directed evolution. The designer has the opportunity and privilege of creation and can be the inspirational source behind artefacts which may last years, centuries, or even millennia. Much of what we understand of ourselves is bound up in the thought that is made material by designers and artisans of the past. However satisfying this achievement, design is never complete. One frustration of design is that there comes a point in the process when it must be considered 'good enough' and pass beyond the designer's hand to those who manufacture and fabricate what was once just imagined.

The dynamic and adaptive approach to function allocation discussed here goes one step further beyond this moment of parting. For the first time, design itself can become dynamic. That is, the very nature of what is created can change as a function of circumstance. This is a most exciting development for those who now have to turn their minds not merely to optimizing a human-machine system in a state of being but rather how to optimize such a system in a state of becoming. Consequently our concern is not interfaces per se, but interface processes and the evolution of those processes. Now, the designer never has to be divorced from their design, but can watch it grow, self-correct, and evolve, perhaps in ways never initially conceived. With the cost and reliance we have invested and placed in many of our world-wide systems, can we afford to have less?

Chapter 5
The Sheepdog and the Japanese Garden

Our species is the only creative species, and it has only one creative instrument, the individual mind and spirit of a man. Nothing was ever created by two men. There are no good collaborations, whether in music, in art, in poetry, in mathematics, in philosophy. Once the miracle of creation has taken place, the group can build and extend it, but the group never invents anything. The preciousness lies in the lonely mind of a man.

(John Steinbeck)

A Statement of Purpose

What is the future of human-machine systems? In this chapter I focus on human-machine systems in which the human and the machine engage in some form of collaborative action in order to achieve their defined goal. I examine the contemporary status of this human-machine interaction against the background of a paradigmatic evolution that is occurring in how such complex technical interaction can be understood. I point to the impact that innovations in both theoretical approach and technological instantiation may have on the design and use of future technology. I begin by examining the global forces that drive such technical developments and illustrate potential and actual roles that humans currently play with respect to machines. I posit that the evolution of human-machine interaction explains how a prescription based solely on an understanding of human cognition is unlikely to succeed, at least to the degree which is desired. I point to the reciprocity of complexity between the evolution of contemporary understanding of both the human and the machine and turn to the critical issue of intention in systems design and operation. I then use two metaphors for contemporary systems, being the way in which humans and machine are expected to interact in the near future and how systems can successfully interact within their operational environment. The metaphors are (i) the sheepdog and (ii) the Japanese garden. I use these metaphors as a basis for understanding the development, evolution, and future for human-machine interaction. I analyze the utility of considering the human-system-environment as the useful unit of analysis (see also Hoffman, Hancock, Ford and Hayes, 2002). I seek to integrate aspects of this construct, with the proven utility of the best elements of traditional approaches to the question of system development. Having embraced the more theoretical aspects of integration I conclude this chapter by looking at the innovation in recent technology and again consider the use of virtual reality as the modal interface of the future. I attempt to indicate how the tenets of ecological psychology can be employed in using virtual interfaces for system control.

❖ ❖ ❖

The Winds of Change

Man masters nature, not by force but by understanding. That is why science
has succeeded where magic failed: because it has looked for no spell to cast on
nature.

(Jacob Bronowski)

How we interact with any machine depends directly upon our individual view of
our relationship with that machine (Norman, 1988, 1991). Historically, humans
recognize themselves as the master of the interaction and in our contemporary
society, the technologically literate individual (including all who read this) views
human-machine interaction from this perspective. However, for the majority of
individuals who work on a day-by-day basis with computers, their role as master
is not so clear. In operating repetitive, machine-paced processes, it can become
painfully apparent that it is the machine which largely is dictating the rate and
nature of events. At some level, in repetitive production processes, humans can
eventually become the slave of the machine in that they act to mindlessly service
the needs and demands of a system whose benefit they only very indirectly reap.
Contemporary technologies are considered still 'mindless'. Therefore such roles
adopted by said machines may not be viewed as intentional or malevolent, as they
would be with a human dictator. Nevertheless, the way in which we perceive our
relationship with the machine can often dictate the boundaries and constraints on
the interactions in which we might engage. Consequently, any consideration of
the future of hybrid human-machine systems must examine the impact of these
differing respective roles.

❖ ❖ ❖

The Human as Master

At a time when the world is seeing dramatic political change, there is a comparable,
albeit less obvious, change in how we view human interaction with machines.
At one level, humans act as creators. In this capacity, humans can transmute the
fantasy of imagination to the realm of reality. Designers and fabricators look to
create our future selves through the manufacture of such devices and entities
which match or even exceed our own abilities. Whether these acts of creation also
reflect a fundamental need of humans to 're-create' themselves remains uncertain.
However, on a pragmatic level the development and instantiation of technological
innovation has generated our unprecedented ability to manipulate natural forces.
Putatively, we retain control over these machines that have been designed to serve
us. In contemporary society, it is human intention which still provides the well-

spring for action and in the vast majority of interactions, contemporary machines remain subservient. Not only do we still view humans as the masters, in some ways we will always be constrained to view ourselves in this manner. This is because in an historical sense we will always be able to point to the original act of creation. But true mastery implies a level of control and understanding that is now rarely the case for operators of present day complex systems.

❖ ❖ ❖

The Human as Servant

In contrast to the position as master, we have to consider another role for the human operator which reflects upon ourselves less glamorously. In this role, the human acts to service and maintain machines and the growing nature of our dependence can lead to a sinister view of the human-machine relationship. Perhaps nowhere has this been more cogently expressed than in the insightful work of Samuel Butler (1872), who expressed such a concern now over a century ago. I make no apology for quoting at length:

> We are misled by considering any complicated machine as a single thing; in truth it is a city or society, each member of which was bred truly after its kind. We see a machine as a whole, we call it by a name and individualize it; we look at our own limbs, and know that the combination forms an individual which springs from a single center of reproductive actions; we therefore assume that there can be no reproductive action which does not arise from a single center; but this assumption is unscientific, and the bare fact that no engine was ever made entirely by another, or two others, of its own kind, is not sufficient to warrant us in saying that engines have no reproductive system. The truth is that each part of every engine is bred by its own special breeders, whose function it is to breed that part, and that only, while the combination of the parts into a whole forms another department of the mechanical reproductive system, which is at present exceedingly complex and difficult to see in its entirety.

> Complex now, but how much simpler and more intelligibly organized may it not become in another hundred thousand years? or in twenty thousand? For man at present believes that his interest lies in that direction; he spends an incalculable amount of labor and time and thought in making machines breed always better and better; he has already succeeded in effecting much that at one time appeared impossible, and there seem no limits to the results of accumulated improvements if they are allowed to descend with modification from generation to generation. It must always be remembered that man's body is what it is through having been molded into its present shape by the chances and changes of many millions of years, but that his organization never advanced with anything like the rapidity

> with which that of the machines is advancing. This is the most alarming feature
> in the case, and I must be pardoned for insisting on it so frequently.

Butler's view is one of progressive machine superiority. However, do not let us depart too hastily from the examination of the contemporary role of the human as a servant.

In the foregoing discussion, it was emphasized that much of the impetus for action came from human intention, and indeed this is true. But whose intention is this precisely? In many if not most contemporary complex systems, the intention was imparted, albeit imperfectly, in the initial design, test, and evaluation phases of development. However, after such endeavours have reached their respective fruition, the actions of the average operator are, more often than not, those of a servant in servicing and maintaining the momentary and longer term needs of the device itself. We have a group of servants whose expressed function is maintenance, yet it is also the case that many operator functions are those which also act to service the machine. As the acknowledged role of the human operator as a system monitor increases in automated and semi-automated machines (Hancock, 1991), this servicing and caring function has come to predominate. The question becomes to what degree individual human operators are then controllers or servants of machines? Even at this stage I continue to protest that the machine still works for human good and so is still at a global level 'our' servant.

One most controversial question in considering the perspective of the human as a servant is whether this vision of the human condition is appropriate for many individuals in society. Certainly Henry Ford (Ford and Crowther, 1922) thought so when he observed:

> We have to recognize the unevenness in human mental equipment ... The
> vast majority of men want to stay put. They want to be led. They want to have
> everything done for them and have no responsibility. (This) thought is terrifying
> to me. I could not do the same thing day in and day out, but to other minds,
> perhaps the majority of minds, repetitive operations hold no terrors ... the
> average worker ... wants a job in which he does not have to put forth much
> physical exertion – above all, he wants a job in which he does not have to think
> ... for most purposes and most people, it is necessary to establish something in
> the way of routine and to make most motions purely repetitive – otherwise the
> individual will not get enough done to live off his exertions.

While I disagree with this paternalistic view of the nature of human aspirations, I believe that it is easy for some to fall into this trap. It is then equally easy for someone of Ford's drive and individuality to believe this is a natural tendency for the mass of humanity. However, it comes down to our view of basic human nature and mine still remains a little more optimistic than Ford's, although I do acknowledge and later discuss the idea that humans are themselves biologically designed to try to get as great a return as they can for as little effort as possible.

Indeed, the nature and direction of the future of technology and technical systems in general is actually predicated upon the view that one holds of human nature. Certainly Ford would appear happy with a human-as-servant perspective, but would anyone be happy with the condition of human as the absolute slave of machines?

❖ ❖ ❖

The Human as Slave

In contemporary Western society, we have an evident repugnance of slavery. In our past, humans have been slaves, but we now look back upon such times with an increasing degree of revulsion. Indeed, it is a commonly held belief that such practice was barbaric and that the abolition of slavery was a clear step forward for human society. (However, we must remember that individuals at different times did not hold this view and this did not, of necessity, make each and every one of them completely immoral, either by their own or our standards.) Today we still retain a form of slavery in the evident practice of economic indenture. The idea of financial debt may seem much less oppressive than physical slavery. However, the individual who is in debt remains, at least to a degree, under the control of the person or institution to which they are indebted. Modern economic conditions appear to be generating circumstances in which we enslave ourselves not only in financial terms but with respect to our own technology also. If we are seeing the growth of symbiosis between human and machine, the vector of that evolution eventually promises to see machines exceed humans. At that juncture, we will not be the dominant species.

No species on our planet has ever exercised direct control over a more 'advanced' species. Rather, it is a truism of nature that dominance is held in an hierarchic fashion in which the superior blend of physical and cognitive skills gives ascendancy. Today, the battles between humans and evolving technical systems are played out only in science fiction. Unlike the scenarios in these stories, however, it seems much more likely that humans will go out with a sudden bang rather than a valiantly fought whimper. However, it is critical to recognize that the seeds of such potential conflict are embedded in the groundwork of today's technology.

Much depends upon whether one takes an optimistic or pessimistic view of our future, and here the keyword is 'enfranchisement'. Technology should act to expand the freedom of human exploration and discovery, yet like knowledge through the ages, technology holds the potential to disenfranchise much of society. As technology grows, it is in danger of becoming progressively more impenetrable to the everyday citizen. I must reinforce my earlier observation that we are in distinct danger of creating a bifurcation in society between the technologically competent and those to whom technology remains a closed book. The parallel here is to early Christian religious practice between the clergy (who controlled access to God) and the laity (who were intimidated and manipulated by such power). As indicated by Bronowski (1978b), such division is counter to the very nature of science itself as an endeavor and may intrinsically contain the seeds of its own, and also society's eventual destruction. A science of human-machine systems labours to achieve the aim of making technology amenable to use, and open to any individual who chooses to use it. Thus, like Humpty Dumpty, who dictated that words could mean whatever he chose them to mean, technology can still, at the present stage of development, be anything we choose it to be. That choice is with us now and we must 'choose wisely'. If we do not, our progeny may have no such choice to make. Having taken this brief glimpse at the global forces that drive us toward different potential futures for hybrid human-machine systems, it is important to embark upon the specifics of what we should do now about our contemporary and evolving interaction.

❖ ❖ ❖

The Seven Ages of Human-Machine Interaction

> And one man in his time plays many parts, His acts being seven ages. At first the infant, mewling and puking …

(William Shakespeare, *As You Like It*)

In examining the way in which humans interact with technology, particularly computer-based entities, we pursue a dynamic search in which the nature of the relationship is in a state of continual flux. A principal driver of this change is the progressively indeterminate character of computer operations. Set in contrast with this, stand the improvements in our knowledge concerning the capabilities of the human operator. It is against this background that I coined the term *hybrid systems* (Rahimi and Hancock, 1986). Such hybrid systems are defined as: *systems in which both human and machine interact, each as a 'cooperative intelligent entity'*. The three key elements of this definition are the terms 'interaction', 'cooperation', and 'intelligence'. It specifies collaborative actions directed toward a common goal of perceived or implied utility. As such, the definition was focused on the emancipation and partial autonomy of the machine element as a cooperative partner in a shared enterprise. The underlying question of intelligence is a difficult one. For most people, intelligence implies at least a partial representation of the goals and constituent tasks at hand but leaves unresolved the all important question of machine intentionality and self-recognition or self-awareness.

In contemporary human-computer interaction, the operator and the system work essentially as independent entities. The motive force for activity comes from the operator (or designer) whose path towards a goal is smoothed or hindered by the largely determinate actions of the software at hand. While such software may be either poorly or richly designed, its actions still do relatively little to accommodate the subtleties and nuances of each individual user. We recognize that such a static, deterministic approach is inappropriate for many shared activities and look toward a more dynamic interaction predicated, at least initially, upon the notion of a third mediating entity. This intermediary is an 'intelligent interface' which is *an intelligent entity mediating between two or more interacting agents who possess an incomplete understanding of each other's knowledge and/or form of communication* (see Hancock and Chignell, 1989). Here the emphasis is on the development of an interpreter that can act as an honest broker between the two still separate yet cooperative entities. While they can continue to operate in their own particular manner, they are assured that their issuance and acceptance of commands and their overall communication will be enacted through a third purpose-built member of the team. Within the operation of such a triad, we expect that the common representation of goals and actions will lead to their shared fulfilment, yet the emphasis on initiation and motivation still remains with the human operator.

In the future, full symbiosis will be recognized by the shared integration of both representation and intention. Our basic questions will, at that time, be centred as much on the goals and intentions of the machine system. At present, we have few ways to conceptually capture the manner in which initial and emergent intentions may grow into our independent autonomous computer colleague. Essentially, we will be forced into the recognition of the computer system as a parallel living entity, worthy of the true partnership that symbiosis implies. The manner in which such a partnership is founded and subsequently evolves is in our hands, even at this moment.

❖ ❖ ❖

Who Does What?

In light of the above observations about the future of the human-machine partnership, it is important to revisit the question of function allocation. It is perhaps the quintessential question of human-machine interaction and as such has been the focus of discussion for many decades (Birmingham and Taylor, 1954; Corkindale, 1971; Licklider, 1960; Whitfield, 1971). Indeed, the Greek word for law (*nomos*) is derived from the verb (*nemein*) meaning 'to allocate'. Thus the *nomos* of Ergonomics is preceded by the *nemein* of allocation. However, the allocation problem only arises when the human and machine can perform the same function. Recognizing the current capabilities of the human and machine and the time frame of their respective evolution, we can clearly see that function allocation represents the slow but consistent usurpation of various human functions by the machine. In the realm of physical action, this transition has proceeded toward ever greater completion, since machines first proved themselves capable of superhuman physical response many centuries ago. The problem faced in our age is the equivalent integration of nascent 'intellectual' machine capabilities.

Despite the formal recognition of this problem for some considerable time (see for example Craik, 1947a, 1947b; and my previous chapter in the present book on this issue), we have yet to provide an answer that extends beyond a fundamentally descriptive one. The prototypical approach to formal description is embodied, as I have noted, in the Fitts list (Fitts, 1951). In this approach, the attempt is made to identify which comparable capabilities of the human are 'best' and which of the machines are likewise 'best,' and then attempt in both design and actuality to 'match' those best capabilities with aspects of the overall task at hand. While this tactic has evolved though a sequence of different incarnations, the fundamental approach itself does not vary (cf., Bekey, 1970; Fitts, 1951; McCormick and Sanders, 1982; Meister, 1985). For a variety of reasons, although this endeavour is well intentioned, this bipartite approach is unlikely to succeed either in principle or in practice. In principal it is a fallacious approach since it acts to dichotomize human and machine in the very instances where the human-machine linkage should be the unit of concern. In practical applications, the same limitation applies, since the necessary interchange between human and machine militates against ever being able to deterministically assign one task component of a complete assembly to one element and then expect that such sub-task resolution can proceed independently.

Jordan (1963) sought to resolve this impasse by appealing for an understanding of human-machine task allocation on the basis of *complementarity*. This approach came from a recognition that the descriptive structures essentially try to represent the human and the machine in the same language. Almost inevitably, this language is expressed in the quantitative terms that favour the machine. When stated in this fashion the conclusion is the predicate. So, these forms of comparisons will always find the machine quicker and more reliable but relatively inflexible, while the human will be flexible but unreliable (see also Kantowitz and Sorkin, 1987). The logical outcome of this form of comparison would be to give as many jobs as possible to the machine (see Chapanis, 1970).

To illustrate further the fallacy of direct comparison, it is instructive to again reconsider the listing of capabilities from a human perspective. One can easily imagine comparing capabilities on the grounds of pity, sensibility, love, hate, anger, altruism, etc. In these 'affective' capabilities, the machine would have a very limited scope for contribution indeed. Many would then indicate that this is an unfair comparison, which is of course exactly the point for, as Jordan (1963) has indicated that '*Man is not a machine, at least not a machine like the machines men make.*'

Thus the comparative approach is on one hand divisive where it should unify, in that it considers and contrasts the separate properties of human and machine. On the other hand, it seeks unity of description at the point where it should be discriminatory, such that it tries to compare using the same (machine) terms when acknowledgment need be given to the fundamental qualitative and quantitative differences. Little wonder that descriptive listings prove so frustrating and impractical for the designer (Fuld, 1993; Kantowitz and Sorkin, 1987). More recently, Hollnagel (1993) offered an extension of the descriptive comparison, but here the emphasis is not on the comparison of capability based on common, machine-oriented scales. Rather, the effort is directed toward describing differences on more global scales of comparison that do not appear, at least at first blush, to favour specifically either human or machine. There is a recognition, albeit implicit, that indeed, the human is a machine but not like the machines that we make, and further presumably machines are growing in affect, but not affect in the way that we conceive of human affect (see also Turing, 1950). Whatever the future of affect with respect to machine systems, we can still consider the notion of collaboration of prime importance.

Kantowitz and Sorkin (1987) indicated that:

> Instead of thinking about whether a task should be performed by a person or by a machine, we should instead realize that functions are performed by people and machine together. Activities must be shared between people and machines and not just allocated to one or to the other.

This is an important observation in that it serves to swing the argument away from the notion of exclusive and divided actions into the notion of shared and collaborative actions. This, of course, is a reflection of what Jordan (1963) tried to articulate in the concept of 'complementarity'. This selfsame debate still causes much contention into recent times (cf., Dekker and Woods, 2002; Parasuraman, Sheridan and Wickens, 2008).

If the trend is from discrete function allocation to load sharing, then the emphasis changes from progressive automation to user-centred operations. Predicated upon this perspective, it appears advisable to allow the user to dictate the profile of task sharing. Indeed, Kantowitz and Sorkin (1987) indicated that the end product of such a sequence might be that dynamic allocation requires no conscious effort on behalf of the user. However, if we consider the question of load sharing in more detail, we have to consider whether the shared load pertains to the objective demands of the task, or the 'effort' or 'resources' that human and machine have to employ to resolve specific demands (see Figure 5.1). As one major characteristic of this process is non-stationarity, it is vital to consider the dynamics of such a process at the same time as we consider the nature of mutual sharing.

❖ ❖ ❖

Adaptive Allocation in Automated Systems

A resolution of the dynamic task allocation problem lies in the implementation of computer-aided adaptive allocation strategies in which both static and dynamic representations of operator and system capacity are presented for continual

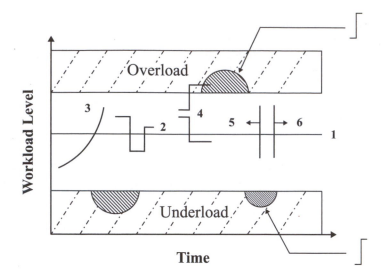

Figure 5.1   **Identification of factors influencing potential strategy changes
in response to workload variation. Hatched regions of overload
and underload are identified, while stable state (1), direction of
change (2), rate of change (3), recovery level (4), history (5), and
future expectation (6) are also identified (after Hancock and
Meshkati, 1988). Each of these have the potential to be used
as signal sources for input into an adaptive allocation strategy
enacted through an intelligent interface**

evaluation and manipulation. Achievement of such allocation strategies promises
benefits from the best abilities of both human and machine while providing neither
with incompatible task demands or excessive task loadings. The realization of such
a conception promises the next substantive step in human-machine interaction and
has been the topic of a number of recent major research programmes. However,
the attendant problems still to be solved are both diverse and complex. These
problems range from basic questions about human and machine capabilities
to fundamental issues in emergent interface design. The question of adaptive
automation allocation remains central to control of complex systems.

In terms of the development of adaptive allocation, the greatest benefits promise
to accrue in high workload, high demand conditions. Under such circumstances,
it should be anticipated that such level of demand will have a significant impact
on the overall capabilities of the human partner. For example, the experimental
literature indicates a phenomenon of 'narrowing' as operator stress increases
(Easterbrook, 1959). The nature of this phenomenon was initially assumed to relate
to effects on visual sensory capacity. More recently, the narrowing phenomenon
has been shown as a facet of attention, where individuals are able to 'narrow' on

to cues of high salience regardless of spatial location (see Beringer and Hancock, 1989; Dirkin and Hancock, 1984). Typically, salience co-varies largely with display conspicuity which itself is composed of factors such as size, intensity, and relationship to other background displays together with the perceived relationship of the information to task goals. These observations on cognitive 'narrowing' provide a strong rationale for further consideration of the physical characteristics of display design as pertinent to automation adaptation.

❖ ❖ ❖

The Sheepdog and the Japanese Garden

> All is well with a tool, instrument, or utensil when it serves the use for which it was made, though in this case its maker is not present. But with things formed by Nature, the power that fashioned them is still within them, and remains in them. All the more, then, should you have it in reverence, and be assured that if only you live and act according to its will, you have all things to your liking. That is the way in which the Universe, too, has all things to its liking.

> (Marcus Aurelius)

We often find it helpful to understand the nature of any complex concept through the use of metaphor. As I find such a device most useful in my own thinking, I take the liberty here of advancing two such metaphors. The first metaphor is presented as a basis for the understanding of human interaction with progressively more intelligent machines. The second metaphor relates to human goals and aspirations with respect to the actions and achievements of complex technical systems set against a background of environmental opportunities. As represented in the title of the chapter, the two metaphors I wish to employ are the sheepdog and the Japanese garden.

Man's Best Friend

There is a clear evolutionary sequence with respect to human interaction with the tools they have created. At the most primitive level we recognize that tools are possible, in order that the environment can be manipulated in some manner via objects beyond one's own physical structure (Oakley, 1949). This is indeed the most rudimentary level since it is clear that numerous other animals have also discovered the utility of naturally occurring tools. The idea of this as the first step is also represented in our own individual development from earliest childhood. Unlike human children who mature and expand their interactive repertoire, with notable exceptions very few animals have taken the subsequent step of modifying these natural objects in order to better achieve their desired goals. At this stage of development, all the motive force and intention behind the tool are essentially properties of the user themselves. In humankind, there grew a proliferation of tools in the broad sense, including mental constructs such as language and mathematics which are reasonably described as non-physical tools designed to achieve desired aims. Certainly in one sense, we can see that the 'tool' of science itself is a global recognition of general laws and a parallel understanding that these laws enable consistent manipulation of the environment on a global scale.

As humans, our step of harnessing and redirecting exogenous sources of energy provides a unique fracture to an age-old constraint on the individual search for food. For most other organisms, a vast amount of time *must* be given over to the search for sufficient energy for their continued existence. One need only picture the hummingbird to understand what a terrible time burden this search for sustenance imposes. It is a further, arguable proposition that it is the highly visual nature of human beings that makes night time so relatively disadvantageous, turning humans from predator into prey. It is this enforced restraint on human physical activity which permitted an increased time for contemplation. What one sees at night are the stars and, as I have noted earlier, it well may be that the origin of conceptual thought started with this period of contemplative time.

Of course, one of the major sources of energy that humans have harnessed is the power of other animals, and it is this relation that provides us with our first metaphoric representation. In the first step of the sequence of animal (machine) domestication, humans essentially had to take what was on offer. The position on the phylogenetic scale of the animals 'targeted' for domestication seemed to dictate the chance of success. Here the nemesis of individual 'intelligence' raises its pervasive and most disturbing head. One may ask apparently bizarre questions such as why didn't man domesticate the ant? Ants can get into many differing environments not open to man, are purportedly tireless workers and would seem, within their own system of operations, to be exceptionally well organized. As such, domesticated ants as human servants would seem to be very useful. Yet, we do not appear to have even the rudimentary beginnings of a channel of communication with ants, hence their work cannot be 'directed' in the sense that human intentions can be translated into ant action. It appears absurd to even suggest such an attempt at domestication. Dogs, on the other hand, are a very different proposition (Budiansky, 2000).

However, we must go beyond the simple act of domestication, as most of the animals with which humans interact actually represent captive sources of food also. For those whose function is more than simply as a source of human food we can distinguish between draft animals, whose primary function is to provide motive power for operations that exceed the energetic capabilities of human operators, and those which represent more of a collaborative function. In the case of the horse, we can see that such lines of demarcation blur, and indeed those individuals who work with draft animals on a daily basis, for example, a mahout, would justifiably claim a greater degree of collaboration. But *Harper's Weekly* (1899) pointed out:

a good many folks to whom every horse is a wild beast feel much safer on a machine than [on] a quadruped, who has a mind of his own, and emotions which may not always be forestalled or controlled.

For birds, we can distinguish some similar uses. For example, the carrier pigeon is used simply to exceed the velocity of unaided human communication and we rely on our exploitation of its homing capacity for our own purposes. Birds of prey used in falconry operate in a more direct manner, but again each are employed in directed uses of their natural instincts. It is this sculpting of somewhat malleable instinctive behaviour that brings us to our main example: the sheepdog.

One of the more fascinating sights in human existence is the collaborative action of shepherd and sheepdog. Typified by those shown on the BBC's programme *One Man and His Dog*, sheep-dog trials require the combined efforts of human and canine. Necessarily, the communication between shepherd and dog is of a very limited bandwidth and must occur over relatively large distances. As might be expected, training a sheepdog to perform in this manner can take a considerable time and learning from example is a frequent tactic for shepherds to use. During the performance of a trial then, the dog certainly has some prior experience and some global notion of the overall task goal, for example, to drive the sheep together as a herd. Also, the dog needs no help or assistance in the rudiments of navigation or control of their limbs; such things are considered 'automatic' and essentially do not swim up into the conscious concern of either shepherd or dog. What is essential is a limited lexicon of unequivocal commands in which a small degree of actual performance latitude is retained by the dog in terms of exactly how the high level commands are to be interpreted and accomplished. In this way, the dog may have an intimate knowledge about the skittish nature of sheep and yet need not have, and may indeed not have, any precise idea of the high-level goals that the shepherd is attempting to accomplish.

Let us now examine how this type of symbiosis can be applied analogically to human-machine interaction in the context of large scale systems. If this analogy is appropriate, it should already be apparent as to how this application can be made. Obviously, the human operator sets the higher-level goals and some of the actual methods and sub-routines to accomplish such action are not only opaque to him or her, they may be equally opaque to the animal (computer) itself. Second, for collaborative action, the computer needs some degree of biddable intelligence, however one wishes to define the latter construct. It is of course, the absence of the emotive (affective, energetic) instinctual facet of computer systems that currently inhibit the realization of this latter capability. However, even with contemporary capabilities, we can well imagine simple task elements being performed without the active involvement and direction of the human. While the contemporary vocabulary for interaction is relatively restricted and the physical interaction remains cumbersome, the shepherd/sheepdog relationship between human and machine can certainly be envisaged as a viable near-term development for partnering human-machine systems. This partnership is one which may then subsequently control the vagaries and deviations of environmental demands (in the analogical sense this represents the unpredictable behaviour of the herd of sheep). Note here I am drawing a conscious and explicit distinction between the interactive elements (that is, the proximal human-machine [computer] entity), and the overall environment in which control is to be achieved. It is the latter interaction which is served by the following, second metaphor.

Oriental Horticulture

In the immediate past decades, we have begun to see a renaissance of the attitude to nature intrinsic to the concept of the 'unsinkable' *Titanic*. This attitude serves to emphasize the notion that nature must be tamed and then mastered (see for example, McPhee, 1989; Porter, 1988). In some ways this is a clear extension of the same thinking that sought to domesticate members of the animal kingdom in the first place. The words that are used in this endeavour typify what must be considered an occidental philosophy, namely constraining, taming, mastering, and controlling. The problem lies in the fundamental foundation of this thought, the idea of mastery and not collaboration. The idea of mastery retains a powerful attraction to human beings. Indeed, how can we direct nature except through conscious control? The answer is to be found, I believe, in considering the metaphor of the Japanese garden.

Having had the opportunity to visit Japan, I find that it is their approach to ornamental horticulture that strikes the present empathic note. In this we can see the explicit contrast with many occidental cases of human interaction with nature. For example, the central thesis of McPhee's (1989) book is an examination of engineering case studies in which heroic efforts have been generated to 'battle' nature. Pre-eminent among these is his story of the Army 'Corps of Engineers' and their ongoing attempts to confound the bid by the Atchafalaya river to overtake the main channel of the Mississippi. A second example of this notion of opposition and control comes from the Icelanders' effort to slow the onslaught of a threatening lava flow. In essence each of these efforts are representative of the Western approach to technology, that seeks to tame or at least subdue nature. This perspective is nowhere better expressed than in the confidence of the White Star Line in their new flagship *Titanic*. Little wonder there were not enough lifeboats for an emergency; what need of lifeboats for a ship that could not sink? Their advertising literature was redolent with this purported triumph over nature. Despite this painful lesson in humility that the *Titanic* rendered, we still continue to oppose nature. Indeed, the idea of mastering nature is still intrinsic to much contemporary thinking.

What I wish to propose here is the suggestion that our technologies should be designed not to oppose nature, but to complement the actions of nature and thus I turn to the metaphor of the Japanese garden. In the evident search for harmony within such gardens, the Japanese gardener seeks to comprehend and, where possible, enhance the natural trends already present. The key word is harmony. Harmony is not achieved by imposition or opposition but by cooperation.

Consequently, if the sheepdog typifies the nascent cooperation between human and proto-intelligent machines, the Japanese garden represents a similar need for cooperation on a macroscopic level between technology and environment. Thus we must seek to more fully specify cooperative aims and by implication establish long-term goals of mutual evolution and progress, not simply identify 'selfish' goals with respect to human action alone. At this juncture, I wish to depart from a general argument concerning the future of hybrid systems and focus on a more near-term issue which specifically concerns the potential for a paradigmatic evolution in some basic perspectives concerning human-machine integration. The adoption of this emerging perspective would, I believe, facilitate the achievement of some of the general goals laid out above.

❖ ❖ ❖

The Unit of Analysis

One of the central questions of evolving human-machine systems involves the paradigm conflict between traditional information-processing approaches intrinsic to the extant Human Factors enterprise and the ecological psychology approach to the identification of the relevant unit of analysis (Gibson, 1966, 1979). For the purpose of illustration and argument, it is perhaps easiest to polarize these respective positions and to examine the extremes of their implication rather than focus on the more subtle and murky differences of the middle ground. Information processing has a central focus on the human. In this view, it is of critical importance to understand the nature and limitations of human perceptual, cognitive, and motor capabilities which are brought by any individual to the operation of a particular machine system. In essence, the human is face to face with a device and the Human Factors scientist stands with the human. Thus information-processing oriented Human Factors has sought solutions for problems based upon our respective knowledge of each separate component of the human-machine dyad. For the ecological approach in contrast, the meaningful unit of analysis is the 'human-machine-system-environment' itself. I have framed the latter in quotation marks in order to emphasize that this collective *is* the unit of analysis (Hoffman, Hancock, Ford and Hayes, 2002). To seek to fracture this unit into its component parts is to eliminate the very essence of what is meant by the ecological perspective. In this latter view, we can now ask critical questions about the constraints that are imposed on this higher-order unit and to visualize and predict the way in which it will react as a totality, not just as a group of individual parts. One outcome of this latter approach is that such an analysis can reveal that behaviours which were previously thought to be the result of complex human cognitive operations alone are actually more parsimoniously expressed as simple functions of the assembly as a unit in itself (Kirlik, 1995; Nagge, 1932; Simon, 1981).

It is encouraging to note that these brief observations allow us to suggest that these two apparently contrasting approaches are not necessarily mutually exclusive (see Hancock and Diaz, 2001), but indeed may be complementary in attempts to understand complex system operation. As Kirlik (1995) so trenchantly noted:

> Due to their roots in either economic theory or artificial intelligence, rational action models ... are more concerned with sufficiency considerations than they are with necessity considerations. The great appeal of such models is their ability [to examine] and often prescribe behavior in a huge variety of situations. Nearly any, and perhaps all, behavior can be rationalized as being the result of some cognitively-intensive process such as search through a problem space, hypothetico-deductive inference, or the comparative evaluation of options with respect to a goal structure or utility function. No empirical evidence could ever be brought to bear on limiting the *sufficiency* of these rational methods for action selection. However, identifying when these sorts of complex cognitive activities will actually be *necessary* for successful performance requires models capable of indicating when such activities are *not* necessary.

It is important to first discuss what an ecological approach to cognitive engineering does *not* require. First, it does not require that we conceive of all human-environment interaction as purely perceptually guided activity. Direct perceptual guidance of action, as discussed by Gibson, might surely be possible although it is likely that it is specific to those information-rich environments in which perception evolved or to artifactual environments designed to mimic such environments. There is no reason to expect that evolution anticipated the modern aircraft cockpit or the word processor. In such environments the need for post-perceptual processes such as problem solving and decision making is quite likely. The ecological and information processing approaches need not always be considered to be at odds, but may instead both contribute to a more complete understanding of human-environment interaction.

❖ ❖ ❖

Interfacing Through Virtual Reality

The next level of human-machine interaction as mediated by computer systems is clearly going to lie in the realm of an area that has come to be referred to as 'virtual reality' or 'virtual environments.' This technology immerses an individual within a computer-generated graphics world and allows that individual to make manipulations therein (Weiser, 1991). My suggestion, as articulated in a preceding chapter, is that graphics surrounds should be used to provide 'direct' control of complex system operations. There is an obvious linkage between this form of immersion as such and the notion of 'direct' interface as postulated by Flach and his colleagues (see also Naimark, 1990; Sheridan, 1990) as well as the notion of ecological interface design championed by Vicente and his colleagues (Vicente and Rasmussen, 1990). At the present time, 'virtual' interfaces are still in a strong growth phase and the fundamental developments are focused on existence proofs of the feasibility and nascent, novelty value of this innovation rather than focusing on the nature of facilitation of user interaction per se. In many ways this development bears much similarity to early interface progress in two-dimensional worlds.

For virtual interfaces, perhaps the critical current question concerns the appropriate metaphor for control in virtual space. While desktop metaphors are useful for two-dimensional interface structures, any parallel metaphors have yet to be unequivocally distinguished for a four-dimensional environment. Contemporary efforts at bodily representations (that is, the representation of a personal avatar within the virtual world) provide one limited, yet intuitive, manner in which interaction may occur. However, for the typical data-glove type configuration, the interactive process must combine the natural actions of the hand, for example, reaching, grasping, etc., together with functions such as bodily locomotion. This limitation detracts from the 'direct' experience that is sought in such virtual environments. While approximation to 'real' four-dimensional objects and body elements represent one way that such a metaphor may be constructed, the challenge of virtual worlds is to imagine and create alternatives in an environment that presents much greater exploratory opportunity than the limited two-dimensional interfaces of common VDTs. Like many other aspects of interface design, such innovations are as much a matter of innovative artistic creation as they are of logical scientific progress.

In addition to identifying a general metaphor for four-dimensional interaction, a fundamental question is also raised as to how to represent a complex system in a virtual environment. Current 'virtual' worlds, including videogames, look to re-create terrestrial environments with all the attributes and characteristics of those types of environment. However, it would be of limited use if a virtual interface to a complex system just replicated that system *in toto*. Indeed, such a representation would in essence 'be' the system but would provide no fundamental advantage in doing so. Hence, some level of abstraction is implied by any four-dimensional interface structure. Therefore, how the operational phase space, as well as the physical structure, of the complex system could be represented is a considerable challenge for interface design. An additional question is to what degree do we want to completely immerse an operator in a virtual world? For example, an operator can be fully immersed using head-mounted displays and control devices, whereas lesser degrees of immersion may include a virtual window, where a display is coupled to head movements such as occurs in augmented reality (AR). Indeed, these AR systems are now rapidly emerging (see Goldiez et al., 2007). If virtual worlds and augmented realities can eventually pass the Turing test (1950), the operator would not be able to distinguish real from computer-based events. This is fine for the developer who would be overjoyed to be able to sustain such a comparison (see Dennett, 1991; Loomis, 1992). However, such full immersion might not be appropriate when the operator is required to control a real system like an automobile (but see Hancock and Sheridan, 2008). However, AR may be most inappropriate when an individual is doing a task such as maintenance when frequent comparison is needed between the real world and its virtual comparator.

Virtual Addiction and Virtual Boredom

One issue that may well beset virtual interfaces in the future, and which is only now beginning to get the attention that it deserves, is the question of virtual addiction and virtual boredom. Boredom can easily emerge for an experienced user in a simple virtual world, where all possibilities of exploration are quickly exhausted. This is the trap that faces many electronic game developers. Boredom is also of particular concern for real-world operations where an experienced operator might rapidly become so familiar with the boundaries and interactive properties of their operational world that they are trapped into an insidious complacency (Parasuraman et al., 1993). At the other end of the spectrum, we encounter virtual addiction, where the alternative reality proves so seductive that an individual is tempted not to return to the real world. Examples, of this form of addiction (if it can be termed as such) are being reported daily in the mass media. Of course this issue also begs the 'many worlds' question. It starts to make us ask what we mean by 'reality' anyway. Clearly, there are some individuals that we class as insane who have 'created' their own personal reality from which they have not and do not wish to return to our 'normality'. Many purportedly 'normal' individuals day-dream about being in other situations or other locations, sometimes to be dragged only unwillingly back to the world of 'mundane' reality. Can we say that someone who is a 'king' in their own, social, interactive world is 'addicted' to that world, or are they making a reasonable, rational choice? This, of course, assumes they return to the real world for essentials such as health and nutrition. These are important questions that need to be resolved if we are to move the control of complex systems closer to the 'games' worlds we have created as yet only for entertainment.

What is clear is that virtual environments are going to have a profound impact on how future complex systems are controlled. We need only think of the challenge of air-traffic control to realize what a tremendous advantages wraparound four-dimensional interfaces can provide, especially when compared to present-day flat-panel displays. However, the inherent problems, both theoretical and technical, pose considerable challenge to the human-systems scientists (for example, Kozak et al., 1993). Although many recent developmental projects have been undertaken, much work remains. The intrinsic appeals of virtual worlds are aspects such as their novelty and their manipulability. These issues again bring interface sciences to the forefront of development if such technologies are to have the hoped for impact.

❖ ❖ ❖

Summary

May not man himself become a sort of parasite upon the machines? An affectionate machine-tickling aphid?

(Samuel Butler)

What then is the future of human-machine systems? Too often we ask the question of how to develop this future, too rarely do we ask the question *why* such development? As Flink (1975) said in his text on the influence of what he calls 'automobility':

> Americans have historically had unbounded faith in technological progress. They have accepted an essential aspect of American democracy that the marketplace and the profit motive should determine the fate of technological innovations defined as consumer-goods items. And they have assumed that any adverse unanticipated consequences would be corrected in time by the market or by other technological innovations.

In human-machine symbiosis then lie the hopes for our future but also the potential seeds of our own destruction. If destruction is the more likely outcome then the science of human-machine integration might be regarded as a misguided and indeed vestigial attempt to bridge a gap between two evolving races of differing evolutionary paths. It may be that its pursuit positively *mis-serves* humankind by implying that there will always be ultimate human control over machines. Can we be as sanguine as Moravec (1988) in asserting that our silicon progeny will be so interested in outer space that they will not remain on earth for the few nanoseconds it will take to exterminate the pesky carbon-based vermin? Or, will they treat us like gods, permanently adhering to Asimov's 'Laws of Robotics' to protect and serve. The latter seems like an unlikely eventuality since robots have already broken these laws (Hamilton and Hancock, 1986).

Critics may claim that events around human-machine competition and symbiosis are far into the distant future and do not need immediate consideration except by the more macabre futurists and members of the science fiction communities. Unfortunately however, for good or bad, the seeds of this future are sown at this time. As any gardener knows, which seeds are sown and the way they are cultivated dictate the nature of the crop. Let us ensure that we do not sow the seeds of discontent, and reap the whirlwind of a harvest of sorrows.

As is clear from the present remarks, the design, test, evaluation, operation and improvement of complex technical systems does not occur in a social, temporal or moral vacuum. Whether acknowledged or not, Human Factors and ergonomic practices have an inherent social manifesto, whether such implications are explicitly considered by the designer and operator or not. As agents of change, those in the human-machine sciences wield influence over the future nature of human society. It is incumbent upon its practitioners to use their influence wisely. Our choices not only dictate what is possible in the future they also create the very individuals who are to make such decisions. By engineering technology and our environment, we engineer the future generations either directly or indirectly. How many future generations this represents is still up to us, although the window of that opportunity is closing in a fearsomely fast manner.

Chapter 6
On the Future of Work

'We have to pursue the subject of fun very seriously if we want to stay competitive in the twenty-first century' (George Yeo, Singapore Minister of State for Finance and World Affairs, quoted in R. Petras and K. Petras (1993) *The 776 Stupidest Things Ever Said*, New York: Doubleday). In this case perhaps George Yeo was not as stupid as the authors intimate as they failed to look below the surface of the remark for the deeper meaning. It is this deeper meaning which is explored here.

Introduction

Ergonomics concerns the laws of work. Therefore, to understand the role of ergonomics in the design of technology we must be very sure that we know what work is. But isn't this obvious? I believe that the answer is that it is not really as obvious as it first seems and that our conception of what work is now, and what work can or will be in the future, has itself to evolve. Ergonomics has been overwhelmed by references to the change in the composition of work from a largely physical to a largely cognitive pursuit. Hence, we have seen in more recent years that growth and dissemination of terms such as 'cognitive ergonomics'. However, this transition represents a change in the *form* of the demand imposed upon the worker, not in the fundamental conception of work itself as a form of demand. I want here to propose that in the near future that the division between what we now think of as work and what we now think of as leisure will dissolve. Further, I want to propose that this dissolution should be an explicit aim of technological design. As a consequence, future human-machine interaction that is not intrinsically enjoyable will, by definition, be poorly designed. How, and in what fashion, the dissolution of our concept of work will occur depends upon both future innovation but also societal attitudes predicated upon these emerging designs.

❖ ❖ ❖

Work and Leisure

It was not many centuries ago that leisure was the privilege of the very few. For most individuals, work totally dominated their life and time away from the everyday grind of hard physical work was spent in other obligatory duties such as religious devotion. We even retain epithets to encourage the supposed righteousness of this view of existence as one of eternal, unmitigated toil, for example, the devil makes work for idle hands! In Judeo-Christian cultures, idleness (or more pejoratively sloth) was not considered a blessing but, as the semantic overtones still imply, a sin. For the labourer, prestige and standing were frequently associated with prowess at work, where physical strength was valued alongside the skills of the artisan. (We still see the persistence of this idea into recent times as when people admire Lenny in Steinbeck's *Of Mice and Men*.) Much of our present-day attitude towards work is a residue of these societal values, although different cultures certainly vary in their views (see Gladwell, 2008). Although the world has changed radically, even since Steinbeck's time, the permeating Occidental attitudes toward work have changed little. Work is still an arduous and demanding endeavour and it is a duty to perform it as such. Indeed, it is possible that the etymological basis for the word task is the word tax!

Older members of the scientific and technologically active society have each experienced the metamorphosis in the content of work that has accompanied the information age. Within two generations, the currency of modern work has gone from joules to bytes and it promises no future return. Certain facets of this change have been examined in exhaustive, not to say exhausting detail. In complex socio-technical systems, the transfer of task demands from the physical to the cognitive and the associated role change from active controller, through passive monitor, to strategic systems manager has been the topic of extensive discussion (for example, Sheridan, 2002). However, the possibility of the affective changes that could accompany this transition has clearly not been explored to the same degree. In particular, the assumptions about our attitude toward work in relation to how tasks are designed and implemented have clearly not evolved at the same rate as the technology itself.

Why is it that a child can sit quietly and watch cartoons for an extensive interval and yet be viewed as having 'attentional' (ADHD) problems in school? How can a data-entry clerk sit in front of a VDU all day and experience severe visual fatigue, yet arrive home and be perfectly happy watching TV for several hours? The dichotomy here is not between active and passive behaviour, since many people embrace the active challenge of videogames, while other individuals watch screens for a living. The differentiation is in *attitude* toward the specific activity. This attitude difference is intertwined with the nature of the way that the activity itself is presented and consequently how tasks are designed and associated information is displayed.

It is clear that the individuals who are regarded as having the most fulfilling existence have incorporated their passion with their work. Csikszentmihalyi (1990) refers to these individuals as 'autotelic' workers, who seek and generate their own personal challenge frequently *despite* the way in which their work is organized. Indeed, Csiksentmihalyi is of the opinion that 'whether a job has variety or not ultimately depends more on a person's approach to it than on actual working conditions'. For example, professional athletes frequently protest that they would play the game for free if they were not paid. An example is the wonderful comment by the boxer Marlon Starling, the WBA Welterweight, talking about a contest with title holder Lloyd Honeyghan, when he said: 'I'll fight him for nothing if the price is right.' Pilots get out of cockpits of 747s only to go and fly in their own personal aircraft. For these and like individuals their work and their lives are one and the same thing. Indeed, I suspect that most professionals gain considerable satisfaction from their job, although they might protest that some components are less enjoyable than others. For us, therefore, it may well be a step of empathy to see that the vast majority of individuals do not enjoy their work in almost any way at all. We even have names associated with this antipathy (for example, Monday morning blues, TGIF, etc).

Why should it be the privilege of the few to enjoy their work? I suggest that this is partly because of our vestigial and now very definitely outmoded attitude toward what work should be. I suggest that these attitudes come from the era when physical effort dominated work and theological mores and indeed religious dogma dominated attitudes. But these influences are fading and do not dominate as they once did, especially in an information age. We should now assert that work will be enjoyable not just by accident, a twist of circumstance, or individual idiosyncratic attitude but should be *enjoyable by design* (Hancock, Pepe and Murphy, 2005). Consequently, designers should seek to redesign the hedonic aspects of work; it should be one of their explicit goals. In what follows, I would like to illustrate why I think this should be so and the manifest benefits that accrue from applying such a design imperative.

❖ ❖ ❖

Autonomy at Work

How is the goal of enjoyable work to be achieved? One of the first steps concerns the question of autonomy or control over one's own working conditions. Control is a vital factor in how work is viewed and thus how the individual responds to it. Traditionally, industrial workers have had little or no control over their own activities. In the past, extrinsic control was a central characteristic of the manufacturing process since the constraints on the production sequence require that parts and assembly be completed according to a centralized time schedule. This is just one example of how human beings have also traditionally been made slaves to time (Servan-Schreiber, 1988). However, the injection of some degree of freedom into an individual's control of their activities accrues very important benefits, especially in reducing problems such as work-related stress issues, health problems and absenteeism (Karasek, 1979). These benefits extend well beyond any momentary changes in attitude alone. They have clear and beneficial influences on long-term productivity and in Hendrick's well-known phrase they illustrate a case of 'good Ergonomics being good Economics', of which more later.

One obvious example of the opportunity to increase an operator's control of work scheduling is in telecommuting. In such pursuits, the worker is minimally constrained in time or space. Typically, work is performed at home and piecework

rates are paid for productivity. Flexibility is currently reflected in the spatial
location of work and to a lesser degree the temporal scheduling of work. I propose
that there should be a comparable flexibility in the *structuring* of the very work
itself – by design. That is, the individual should be able to decide not only when
the work is done and where the work is done, but *how* the goals are to be achieved.
These avenues increase the levels of flexibility which are then directly reflected
in how, for example, any machine interface is to be configured to accomplish this.
When information is both the medium of the work and the content of the work,
and the computer systems are the platforms upon which such work is erected, then
choice as to the structure of the form of the work itself should be both a feasible
and indeed supported opportunity.

❖ ❖ ❖

Designing Enjoyable Work

Advocating that enjoyment should be a design imperative is all very well, but
how is this statement made more than a simple assertion? After all, some human
beings sit quietly in a corner with a good book and call it enjoyment while others
use the same term for jumping out of low-flying aircraft on glorified elastic bands!
Obviously defining enjoyment presents the challenge here. The challenge is similar
to, and I want to relate it directly to, the concept of an 'affordance' as expressed
in ecological psychology (see Flach et al., 1995; Stoffregen, 2000). As we have
seen, there remains great controversy over the exact nature of the concept of an
affordance, even between those who strongly espouse the use of this. In general,
an affordance is expressed as a relational opportunity between an individual and
their surrounding environment. In a similar manner, enjoyment is an interactive
property, although some early philosophers claimed it is subjugated almost totally
to human control (Aurelius, 120).

Moray (1994) has advocated the exploitation of affordances to design artefacts
which encourage the behaviour patterns of least resistance (the latter being my
interpretation and not his phraseology) with respect for example, to critical global
problems such as energy and water conservation (see Sanquist, 2008). Thus
designs are created to minimize wastage by channelling behaviour patterns toward
preferred activities as, for example, in the use of the low-volume flush toilet. In
essence, design becomes the design of affordances. I would suggest, however, that
one characteristic of this 'affordance of least resistance' is that the designer should
promote an individual's engagement in the desired activity not simply in a passive,
accepting, and almost unconscious manner but in an active, enjoyment-seeking
form. The critic might well attack this approach as exploiting human frailties;
the pragmatist might well ask whether there is any alternative? Any declared
attempt to manipulate behaviour is always viewed with great concern. However, if
technology is to bless rather than curse society, changes in the patterns of human
behaviour must be re-acknowledged as a clear and explicit goal of design.

In some ways, enjoyment is like art, we might not understand it very well, but we each know what we like when we personally see it. It is in this observation that we find one approach to a solution. In this and other areas of human behaviour a common impasse arises. We recognize that all individuals are different but we still want to make general assertions about how they are the same in some fashion. To accommodate this demand for both general and individual satisfaction, systems themselves are becoming progressively more customizable and adaptive (Hancock and Chignell, 1987, 1988). To achieve this aim, interfaces between humans and systems must themselves possess a degree of intrinsic 'intelligence' (see Kantowitz, 1989). With intelligent interfaces, individuals can customize their own physical workstations *and* also the structure of their work to accommodate their own particular, idiographic interests. Also flexibility of operation should itself evolve over time as operator's capabilities and desires also evolve. The central pillars of this form of work organization are variety and challenge, which present to the designer explicit design goals with a clear channel of feedback about how well this aim has been accomplished. However, as Moray rightly points out, interfaces should not be infinitely adaptable as it can be the case that continual reconfiguration will ultimately prove not simply confusing but also error-promoting. Further, adaptive capability must be carefully crafted if the interface is to be used by groups, teams, or several individuals at differing times. Under such circumstances it may well be the case that: 'one operator's interface can become another operator's nightmare!' Ultimately, we will all carry our own personal computational avatar, who will act as our advocate when we interact with any new system. The avatar will be our personal, electronic guardian angel whose sole purpose will be to ease our passage though an ever more complex technological environment. We will come to love them more than they will ever come to love us.

Since design is the confluence of art and science, design innovations cannot simply be prescribed by some interface development algorithm. Hence, good ideas need frequently to be highlighted in the form of instructive case studies. One of the more novel of such instructive examples comes from the work of Sweeley, Holland, and their colleagues (for example, Holland, Leary and Sweeley, 1986; Sweeley et al., 1987). It would be reasonable to say that these individuals are not formally related to any aspect of Human Factors science. However, it would be equally reasonable to say that their work is a shining beacon of the aspirations of such a science. The original goal of these researchers was to evaluate urine samples for potential irregularities in the normal metabolic profile. Traditionally, this had been accomplished using an oscilloscope display. Under the monitoring conditions presented on the oscilloscope, minor irregularities were very rarely detected. As a result of this ongoing performance efficiency problem, the task was re-designed. The 'peaks' on the oscilloscope, which represented the metabolites present in the urine, were converted to an auditory display featuring a sequence of musical notes. When the profile was normal, the system played a popular and very recognizable tune. Any anomalies were expressed as very jarring notes that then very much 'stood out' in the ears of the monitoring individual. This simple translation of the display changed the detection rate from near chance to virtually 100 per cent. The tune itself, which by the way was 'Yankee Doodle Dandy', was immaterial to the conception. The point being that the transformed display boosted performance significantly. But now comes an even more interesting dimension of the findings. After the initial gains which were experienced, the observers asked whether the system could play any other tunes, since listening to one tune repeatedly can quickly become de-motivating. Of course, in principle one could use any snippet of any tune as long as it was immediately recognizable by the listener. Indeed, many individuals would be happy to listen to music all day, even if occasionally a jarring note did come up! The displays were re-transformed to other tunes and enjoyment was added to the benefit of efficiency.

However, such transformed displays need not be limited to musical notes, in other contexts, they could be represented by touch, by a visual scene, by an olfactory sequence of stimuli. Indeed, the mapping between the task domain and the display configuration offers a whole cornucopia of possibilities. There is no necessary requirement for the work domain to be unvaryingly mapped to the display domain. One could be doing very productive work just watching movies! The opportunities for design should be clear and evident.

The ability to control one's time is also a very important attribute of job design. Ron Westrum (1991) categorized technologies upon a continuum from technotonic to technostressful depending upon the degree of control available, the skill demands, the aesthetic pleasure and the affective associations which any device invokes. This follows on earlier work which identified characteristics that make work either attractive or aversive (Herzberg, 1966). Understanding the dimensions of design which make work either pleasant or unpleasant is of considerable value and underlies many contemporary design recommendations. However, the radical change in what currently composes information-mediated work demands a modern re-appraisal. This re-appraisal certainly relates to the form of work itself, but more critically it questions whether our fundamental conception of what work is can or will hold in the future. Computer-based operations mean that tasks, their display, and their allocation can be flexible when intelligent interfaces are components of system design (Hancock and Scallen, 1996). *Adaptive task design* then is a facet of software flexibility. All of these elements are able to be manipulated and are critical in the generation of enjoyable and challenging pursuits. However, we must never lose sight of the fundamental basis of worker attitude since it seems, at present, that the attitude of the individual is the prime driver of this situation.

An instructive example of the primacy of attitude comes from recent research on vigilance and workload. Enforced monitoring is a stressful pursuit, resulting in a high level of perceived load generated from the 'apparently' passive task of sitting watching display screens (Hancock and Warm, 1989). Sawin and Scerbo (1993) questioned these assumptions. They asked their participants to watch a screen of uniform colour for thirty minutes looking for occasional 'flickers'. Half the individuals were given traditional instructions for a vigilance task that is to monitor carefully and report all 'critical' signals. The other half were simply told to relax and watch the screen and if some flicker occurred it would be nice if they reported it. The outcome of this ingenious experiment showed that there were no significant difference in the detection performance between the two groups, although both groups experienced the expected decline in hit rate over time, the so-called 'vigilance decrement function'. However, there was a substantive difference in the level of perceived workload. The relaxation group reported significantly less workload (particularly on the frustration scale) than their peers in the traditional detection paradigm. The clear inference is that it was the *attitude* of the participants that had a direct effect on their perception of the workload of the task without adversely influencing their actual response efficiency.

Would we be justified in suggesting that the long-term adverse effects of high workload could be reduced with this simple manipulation? Indeed, the freely chosen rate at which we work is frequently close to an individual's long-term optimal rate (Sparrow, 1985). Thus, individuals are themselves adaptive and, if permitted, seek optimal solutions to imposed physical demands. The suggestion here is that this intrinsic strategy extends into an individual's search for optimal solutions to cognitive demands also. This can only occur in jobs that are *designed* to provide such freedom and flexibility. I propose that enjoyment of work is one hallmark of success in that search for cognitive optimality. In respect of the findings of Scerbo and his colleagues, the lesson seems to be that the nature of the authority which imposes the imperatives of the work has a crucial effect on how that work itself is perceived and subsequently accomplished. As the computer begins to be perceived more and more as the arbiter that sets the work and monitors the worker's response, the requirement of worker control is not simply a matter of preference; finally it will be a matter of performance. Finding out what an individual likes and then transforming their work into that format will not be simply a cute hack, it will be central to our whole aspiration for achievement.

❖ ❖ ❖

Design Recommendations

How is the designer to make jobs enjoyable? What practical advice can be distilled from the present set of observations and the associated literature? The following provides initial guidelines, although at the present stage they cannot be considered incontrovertible rules:

1. The provision of autonomy and choice are critical design characteristics of tasks.
2. Work should be paced by operators not machines.
3. Interfaces should be adaptive. Both the physical workstation and the information interface should permit and promote individual customization.

4. Tasks should present challenges and permit safe exploration of possible operational states.
5. Repetitive operations are primary candidates for automation.
6. Work should be designed such that the desired goals provide intrinsic satisfaction in their achievement.
7. The operator should be involved in the design of tasks themselves and especially how the system functions are mapped to interface characteristics.
8. Variety, rhythm, challenge and exploration are key dimensions in the design of enjoyable work.

As such goals are achieved, it may well become progressively more difficult to distinguish what we now characterize as computer-based work from what we now think of as computer-based games. When this threshold is crossed, we will have to redefine what we class as work. It may well be that we begin to design goals and processes and allow individuals to match their aspirations and preferences to such processes and goals directly. The machine system will not be merely an intermediary but more an insightful companion concerned with how goals are achieved as much as the safety and efficiency with which they are achieved.

❖❖❖

Concluding Remarks

The way we view work, especially information-based work, is now rapidly becoming outmoded. While we have reaped many of the benefits of the electronic age, we do not yet seem to have exploited fully the affective change in the fundamental nature of work that is enabled by the software and the computer systems we have created. In our 'charge' for the high-ground of automation and semi-automation we have rarely stopped to ask whether the individuals involved might *want* these changes. Given that we do ask these questions (for example, Hancock, 1996), it is even rarer that we have stopped to ask ourselves how such work might be made enjoyable (but see Helander and Tham, 2003).

Work has always been juxtaposed to leisure and there is the disturbing and antithetical proposition that human beings might *need* it that way! Definitions of leisure include reference to discretionary time not spent at work. Leisure has been defined as *my* time, while work, in contrast, is viewed as *company* time. In an information age, such a view is outdated, recidivist, and ultimately self-defeating. However, we can argue against but never ignore the counter-proposition that the differentiation in activity that work provides represents a form of requisite variety that human beings cannot do without! Thus, for mental health purposes, human beings might need work to be different from leisure, although whether that difference should be in the way that work is aversive and obligatory is certainly open to debate!

Work is an important and indeed serious business. However, it should never be mind-numbingly boring, or soul-destroyingly repetitive (Hoffman and Hayes, 2004). Serious does not always mean joyless and importance does not always exclude pleasure. If individuals work better on tasks they enjoy, then enjoyment is directly related to both productivity and safety. Long faces are not always efficient nor smiling ones idle. Societal attitude toward work must change. While changing human nature might be a well nigh insuperable problem, changing the work environment to 'afford' enjoyment and therefore influence behaviour is a feasible design objective. I echo Csikszentmihalyi's exhortation that 'The sooner we realize that the quality of work experience can be transformed at will, the sooner we can improve this enormously important dimension of life'. Yet most people still believe that work is forever destined to remain 'the curse of Adam'. In the future, it need not necessarily be so.

Chapter 7
Men Without Machines

Now scientists are too often genetically infected optimists. We believe that problems, even seemingly intractable ones, can be addressed and solved. In any case, it is too late to retreat the world is stuck with science and technology. The problem will be to design a strategy that maximizes the possibilities of using science and technology for the advancement of humankind.

(L.M. Lederman)

Preamble

In our technologically replete world it is easy to be seduced by the novelty and excitement of the latest innovation. Advocates of 'human-centred' automation can easily become enraptured by the seditious attraction of viewing the machine as the 'problem' to be solved. Just as for the designer and engineer, the human can easily be envisioned as representing the critical problem or fundamental sticking point. Perspectives can be quickly narrowed to the immediate present and attitudes oriented toward addressing the downside of machines. Here, I want to redress that balance somewhat by considering an historical example of men without machines. To do this, I first want to distinguish tools from machines, since these individuals certainly did not exist without tools. Similarly, I want to later distinguish machines from Self-Intentioned Systems (SIS) which I believe represent their next stage of development and evolution. This latter distinction is important. While the topic of the present chapter concerns the explicit removal of machines but not tools, at the chapter's end I want to consider the possibility of the explicit excision of self-intentioned systems while we try to retain machines. Perhaps the present story will give us some guide in this latter circumstance. From the bleak conditions of the story I describe, it is clear that machines render great human benefit and that there is no machine-free, natural Arcadia for future generations to aspire to. Therefore, when we point to the costs of machine failures, it is necessary to consider the antithesis in examining what conditions would be like in their absence. This enforced absence will also guide us to our future.

❖❖❖

Introduction

In advocating for human-centred automation, those in the human-machine sciences seek ways in which advanced technologies can be made responsive to and consistent with human capabilities. Frequently, this means pointing out the problems and failures with existing designs, prototypes, or actual operational software and hardware. Champions of the human operator are, in consequence, often perceived as being somehow 'against' the machine, or more realistically, against the design of insensitive systems. Such critics stand in danger of being considered simply negative in nature and the continual highlighting of problems over time can lead to the perception that it is always the machines themselves that are the problems to be 'solved'. We might, under such stimulation, be in danger of losing sight of the many manifest benefits that machines continually bring to us. Earlier in this book, I suggested that technology is a dangerous enterprise and that human-machine systems sciences should help steer the course of technology toward safer waters. In this welter of concern and criticism we can loose sight of these advantages machines bring and consequently ignore their central and symbiotic role in current and future human development. The following chapter is a caution that we do not lose sight of such benefits.

❖ ❖ ❖

Distinguishing Tools from Machines

It is problematic to distinguish accurately when in time human beings first appeared as a separate species. It is almost as problematic to distinguish when such human beings first began to use tools. Although we are not so familiar with the work now, Kenneth Oakley's book *Man the Tool Maker* was a well-known scientific text of its time which protested that the primary distinguishing characteristic of human beings was their creation and use of tools (Oakley, 1949). Although there are some examples of tool use in the animal kingdom, the degree to which tools extend human abilities is qualitatively distinct from any other organism. Here, I take *tools* to be direct extensions of the organism's capabilities but restrict them to *that class of objects that require immediate intention and energy to effect their action*. Even in the case study that I describe below, the individuals involved did not live without such tools and it can be asserted that modern society could not survive without such tools.

Tools require not only the presence of the individual to guide them, but rely solely upon that individual for their motive power. *Machines* I define as *that class of objects which are directed by an organisms intention and which use sources of power not derived solely from the organisms own energy*. The difference between machines and tools then lies directly in the source of power. If the source is some hybrid form of both human power and that of some other agency, the object is a machine by default. The step from tool to machine was a step from human to other sources of power. This step occurred early in human development as early machines such as the windmill and the watermill were established in early antiquity.

❖ ❖ ❖

Distinguishing Machines from SIMs

If machines evolved from tools, today we stand at the birth of the next generation. Now, not only has the source of power changed from solely that generated by the human, but we see systems in which the source of intention is migrating solely from the human through various hybrid stages, toward one of solely machine intention. The full achievement of this latter transition will create a new entity that is not tool and is not machine. I propose that the name of such entities be Self-Intentional Systems (SIS). In their earliest stage of development, the intention of such systems will inevitably be closely bound to human intention. The next developmental stage will blur intention across many individuals and there will be the birth of some elemental form of 'emergent' machine intention. This is the hybrid stage and it is this stage of development that we are now entering. The occurrence of fully autonomous SIS's will be a state as significant as would be the discovery of other life in our universe. However, since that development will happen in gradual stages and before our own eyes, we may not recognize it as a comparable watershed event. Although human beings will continue to use tools and machines, there is no reason to believe that SIS will stand in the same dependent relationship. All this however is in the future. Here I want to emphasize the value of machines by illustrating specific examples of men without machines. No society, having developed a technology goes back. Consequently, it is only under very unusual circumstances that we can see the activities of an institution which has knowledge of machines but does not use that knowledge. Perhaps the only unequivocal examples are formal penal colonies.

❖ ❖ ❖

Sarah Island, MacQuarie Harbor, Van Diemen's Land

One of the harshest penal colonies ever constructed was the settlement of Sarah Island, Macquarie Harbor. This was in Van Diemen's Land, which is now the island of Tasmania off the south coast of Australia (Julen, 1976). Although in existence for only eleven years, from 1822–33, Sarah Island had one of the blackest reputations of all prisons and easily matched London's Newgate in its harshness. It was conceived of as a last resort and housed individuals who had been initially transported from England to Australia and had then subsequently committed further offences following their transportation (Brand, 1990). In this there is a parallel with Norfolk Island (Hughes, 1987) but the present chapter is confined to Sarah Island. While some of these offenses appear trivial in nature, convicts assigned to Sarah Island were regarded as incorrigible (Butler, 1975). In providing a mandate for the institution, Governor Arthur insisted upon 'continuous and unremitting physical labour'. The first act of settlement was to clear the island of virtually all vegetation and to build a thirty-foot high fence on the western shore of the island to protect against the more savage effects of the winds known as the 'roaring forties'. No pack animals were allowed on Sarah Island. The only sources of motive power were to be convicts' muscles. The only economically valuable commodity of the area was the Huon Pine, a tree which because of its unique oil content resists rotting and is therefore highly valued as a ship-building material. In the years of its existence, Sarah Island became one of, if not the, major ship-building centres of Australia and even the whole of the southern hemisphere, producing some 112 ships in eleven years.

The Huon Pines were cut by the convicts and floated down the Gordon River into Macquarie Harbour and rowed over to Sarah Island where they were cut into planks (Hepper and Hepper, 1984). The sawpit was the most feared location on the island. While activity at the saw-pits simply consisted of continuous physical labour, for the 'top dog' who was sawing down through the tree, circumstances were merely bad. For the 'underdog' who was down in the bottom part of the saw-pit, conditions were horrendous. Permanently dangerous due to the potential fall of logs into a hot and confined space, the greatest discomfort was in the continuous shower of sawdust cascading down upon the unhappy prisoner. Many individuals went blind in the depths of the sawpit. In this 'place without hope', certain convicts chose to take their own lives rather than sustain what they obviously perceived of as unsupportable existence. I bring this example up not to horrify but as the most startling example I can find of life specifically designed to remove the comforts of powered machinery when it was available. Purposefully designed to be harsh in the extreme, life on Sarah Island can represent for us the shadow of a potential existence without the support of the machines we have created. One day as an underdog in the sawpits of Sarah Island would suffice to convince the most committed Arcadian that a return to life without machines would not be the 'milk and honey' adventure portrayed in some of our more florid environmental literature. With respect to machines, we have built them, we rely on them, and it is the case that we would not be who we are without them.

One of the more interesting aspects of the evolution of Sarah Island as a penal colony was the gradual change in focus from punishment to economic exploitation of the Macquarie Harbour area. It is difficult to establish whether this was ever a purposive policy. However, Sarah Island was never completely self-supporting and in 1833 it was closed because of the financial and logistical burden of supplying such a remote location. In particular, the entrance to Macquarie Harbour, known as Hell's Gates (Laney, 1989), is so narrow that it prevents the entry of any large sailing ships except in relatively rather rare, clement conditions. Given the general nature of an expansionist policy in the whole of the Australian continent at that time, it is not surprising that monetary concerns eventually overtook the concern for punishment and reform. In essence, finance and the associated greed will always supersede morality, at least for most of the human race. What is clear is that the early years of Sarah Island were an illustration of men (and some women) without machines and it is critical to recognize that this was viewed as extreme punishment, even in the early part of the nineteenth century.

❖ ❖ ❖

Port Arthur, Tasman's Peninsula, Van Diemen's Land

When the economic feasibility of supplying Sarah Island was found to be too arduous, the then colonial administration identified alternate sites for a resident penal colony (Lennox, 1996; McCulloch and Simmons, 1993). The choice fell on a harbour area on Tasman's peninsula which was named Port Arthur after the then governor. This settlement was much closer to the capital, Hobart Town, but was still easy to guard since a number of very thin isthmi, composed of a series of connecting beaches, linked the necklace of the peninsula. In particular Eaglehawk Neck, only some 200 yards across, was kept permanently guarded with a line of dogs to deter any unauthorized individual trying to cross in either direction. The location was permanently manned and was in direct contact with Port Arthur.

Port Arthur itself was a different proposition from Sarah Island. Despite a continued emphasis on hard physical labour, there was much more of what we would recognize today as a modern prison (Brand, 1975; Lennox, 1994). In particular, the nature of punishment for recalcitrant individuals had changed dramatically. Rather than prolonged physical activity in a dangerous and uncomfortable environment like the saw-pits of Sarah Island, repeat offenders were now isolated in the separate or 'model' prison (Brand, 1979). This system was itself built to emulate the Pentonville experiment in England where prisoners were kept in complete silence and complete isolation. Punishment cells in this penal system consisted of complete black out, and the now clichéd 'bread-and-water' diet. There is evidence that the prison was not just stressful for the prisoners but was almost as intolerable for the warders as well. Warders had to walk on rush matting and communicate only with hand signals. Inspection of the prisoner population was to occur once every fifteen minutes and the warder had to place a wooden peg in a specific hole in the prison clock to indicate inspection had been accomplished. Pegs could not be placed either before or after the specific inspection time, hence, the supervisor had a direct record if the warder missed his appointed round. A most cruel vigilance task indeed, the punishment for warders missing their assigned times was also rather unpleasant.

If life without machines is arduous, life without stimulation is virtually no life at all. The length of sentence to the model prison had a maximum limit but this was often violated for disfavoured offenders. It is not surprising that some convicts went insane under such a regimen (McCulloch and Simmons, 1992). Even with the magic of film and the representation given in *Papillon* we can have no real empathic understanding of what such a living death is like. Consequently, while life without machines seriously changes the nature of what humans are able to achieve, life without stimulation makes us less than human. In summary, as technology evolves it is only in very rare and exceptional cases that a society having once developed any technology then voluntarily chooses not to use it for whatever reason. In fact we see this omission as deprivation and punishment.

Men cannot survive without tools; men can survive without machines, but such an existence is little more than an extension of the observation that life is 'nasty, brutish, and short'.

❖ ❖ ❖

Directing Technology

The choice then is not machines versus no machines, or in more general terms, technology versus no technology. We can no more retreat from technology than we can relive our own existence. Rather, the choice is what technology and in what direction that technology progresses. In advocating 'human-centred' approaches to this evolution, those in the human-machine sciences have a small voice to proclaim an important message on behalf of those individuals who are expected to operate with flawless efficiency in systems currently replete with opportunities for disaster. In supporting the human operator, we must also embrace a wider responsibility in seeking to contribute our conceptions of what technology should be developed, not merely commenting upon how and why existing creations are deficient. If we can be involved in this level of meta-design, we can have a full voice in directing technology, if we can express both an intention for and a morality of technology, which is the most powerful force in our lives today, we will have a vital influence on who future human beings are and will be. I explore this moral and intentional dimension in the chapter which follows.

Chapter 8

Life, Liberty, and the Design of Happiness

Preamble

When the framers of the Constitution of the United States of America set out to codify their ideals for a free and democratic society, they did not start from square one. In fact several of these individuals, most notably Thomas Jefferson, were already well read in the classical Greek literature as to what composes the 'good' life for both the individual and the collective society. It was from those classical sources and the necessary constraints of those days that the phrase 'life, liberty, and the pursuit of happiness' was distilled. Here, I use a slightly amended version of this phraseology to trace some historical antecedents to our collective goals for human-machine systems science as a way to envisage our future. But first, I want to begin with a story. It is a story of Norfolk, Virginia.

As I turned off of Interstate 264 onto Waterside Drive, I had a distinct feeling, as Yogi Berra would have it, of '*déjà vu* all over again'. This feeling grew ever stronger as I turned into the driveway of the harbour-front, Omni Hotel in Norfolk, Virginia. As I stepped through its doors, the experience was complete – I knew I had been here before. On approaching the desk it came to me. Fifteen years before, the Omni Hotel in Norfolk had been the site of the 1983 Annual Meeting of the Human Factors Society. Norfolk is now, as it was then, a wonderful location for any scientific meeting. In 1983, I had been a first-year assistant professor with less than three months' employment under my belt at the University of Southern California (USC). In wondering what that individual would have made of his future self and, in turn, wondering what I now would have made of the fresh-faced younger version of myself, I recalled an experience at the 1983 meeting that has been a constant lesson since. I use it here as an introduction to the present chapter.

❖ ❖ ❖

Two Norfolk Stories

A First Norfolk Story

At every conference, someone has to be the last presenter and, in 1983, my turn had come. In a rather refined twist of cruelty, my session finished at 12:30 while the rest of the meeting had terminated by 12:00 noon. The town not then being a major airline hub, it was understandable that flights from Norfolk, especially to the West Coast of the US, were rather limited and in an especially piquant twist of cruelty, it was suggested to me by a fellow attendee that the 'last plane for civilization was leaving at high noon'. I do apologize to the residents of this area if they should take offence here since Norfolk is a place that I personally like very much and indeed have fond memories of. However, if you have ever been around at the end of a major conference when all the evidence disappears almost instantly you can, I think, empathize with this sentiment.

It was clear that the presenters in my particular session were painfully aware of this constraint also as they each in sequence gave their talks, made their profuse but understandable apologies and headed for the exit and their respective journeys home. Soon after 11:00, the audience was dwindling precipitately and it did not need any significant mathematical expertise to work out that the only people who were left in the room were the presenters and session chairman. As each individual presented their work and then subsequently excused themselves, the room grew a little more silent and as my turn approached I realized that this would not be a talk to a substantial proportion of the academy. The chairperson, whom I am pleased to number among my friends, got up to introduce me and then with more than some embarrassment was forced to excuse himself also since he too had a flight deadline which could not wait (although he may have a different version, please ask him, you can look him up). As I stood to announce my stunning scientific findings to the world, I was left with one audient. However, true to my self, I resolved to give full measure and for the next twenty minutes, with unstinting effort, I endeavoured to lay before my solitary listener the nuances of 'space-time and motion study' (Newell and Hancock, 1983). It is, I must add, one of the few conference proceedings papers for which I have ever had a reprint request. At the end of the twenty minutes when I had finished my talk, the lady (for it was she who was the audience) walked up to me and said in clear and ringing tones – 'Well, young man, I've only had the chance to hear one or two talks at this conference but yours was clearly the best.' My dragging spirits were raised just a little as I inquired from which institution of higher learning she came. Her reply echoes in my mind even today:

> Oh! I'm not from any university, I'm here to clean the room. Can you leave now please?

There are many lessons which I have drawn from this experience but the one that has stayed most closely with me through the years is the necessity in science for humility and humour. It does not take a philologist to recognize their common linguistic root. We are each of us much more important to ourselves than our merits support. A little deflation does no metaphorical balloon any great harm! Norfolk however, had not done with me and had more in store to offer me by way of instruction. Thus, there is a second Norfolk story.

A Second Norfolk Story

This equally instructive incident took place in the lobby of that self-same Omni Hotel just prior to commencement of the 1998 Conference which had triggered my episode of *déjà vu*. Immediately prior to this latter meeting, which was the third in the Humans and Automation series, I had been at the Human Interaction with Complex Systems symposium in Dayton, Ohio. Due to an administrative problem I was forced to switch to a very early 4:00 a.m. flight leaving from Dayton to Washington, DC, whence I proceeded to Norfolk in a rental car. I arrived around midday and had been comforting my fatigued self with the thought of a nap on a soft bed only to be told that the presence of the McDonald's All-American high-school basketball game meant that there was no room at the inn; at least no room that would be available before mid-afternoon at the very earliest. Not normally the most equitable of individuals, I found myself on the verge of significant verbal mayhem and turned from the obsequious but intransigent desk clerk, determined to do damage to the first living organism I encountered. Fortunately, the last remnants of English reserve meant that I was still partly civil as I sat next to an older gentleman in a track suit. He and I began to talk and I knew, as the course of our conversation progressed, that I was chatting with John Wooden, the legendary coach of the many UCLA Bruin Championship winning basketball teams. He turned out to be a quietly spoken and engaging individual who was kind enough to sign a treasured autograph and to converse with a strange Englishman on the problems of building teams to function in high-stress conditions. When the mass of mass media arrived wanting immediate quotes from and interviews with Wooden, he quietly pointed out that we were speaking and CNN and ESPN had to wait fifteen minutes while we talked more of cohesion and leadership. It was a conversation I treasure and an act of courtesy that I very much appreciated. Had I been able to check in as I wanted, it would have been an experience missed. I think the lesson of this second Norfolk story is that even when we do not immediately get exactly what we want it may not necessarily be all that bad and may actually lead to unexpected benefit. If you are with me to this point, you will realize that I am telling stories and I want to pursue the theme of storytelling since my presentation at the conference was itself a story, along which the pearls of fact are threaded along the strings of conjecture. In its way, the story below is only an extension of the two which precede it.

❖ ❖ ❖

Figures in the Timescape

At the beginning of my conference presentation day, I asked the rhetorical question whether an individual could kill themselves by holding their breath. In reality it would be exceptional if they could, but the question served to stimulate an audience into considering the human cardio-respiratory system and the way it automatically serves to protect us, even from ourselves. It turns out that one might be able to pass out from breath-holding, but having done so respiration most often resumes and consciousness is slowly returned to the abuser. Since there are always potential complications, I hasten to add that I would not advocate trying this, or indeed putting the challenge before a class of motivated US Marines as I once did to my subsequent chagrin. The point here being that in the actions of such physiological systems we already have very successful forms of resident automation. Thus automation is not merely an invention of the engineering realm, but is already existent in nature and has functioned for many millennia and even for millions of years in order to support the evolution of life. Human beings should be, and presumably are, very glad that they don't have to engage in volitional control of the many automated physiological life-support systems. Indeed, life as we know it would not be possible without such unconscious accomplishment of respiration, heart function and the like. Thus the first point to be made is that automation, in its different forms, has been around and working for a long time. Consequently, automation should not be seen as something new or daunting just because it is expressed now in advanced technologies.

However, even if we consider automation to be largely a technological innovation, its antecedents go back many centuries and even millennia. In respect of clockwork automata in the sixteenth century, they were largely considered to be diversions or toys as opposed to serious machines, but there are some such creations which also come from much earlier antiquity. There are many candidates that could be identified as the direct historical progeny of such clockwork mechanisms. Pre-eminent among them would probably have to be the Antijkythera Mechanism, at least in historical precedence (Freeth et al., 2006). Not far after in precedence must be the 'Wheeling Beetle' of John Dee. However, the example that I have chosen to discuss was that of the 'Golem of Prague'. The Golem is a well-known story to those of the Jewish faith (Wiesel, 1983). In legend, the Golem was an entity created by the Rabbi Loew of Prague to protect his flock from persecution, which was prevalent then as it seems to be in more modern times. Transposed from the folk stories and expressed in more modern language a list of the Golem's characteristics are noted in Table 8.1.

To put these abilities in context, the Golem was reportedly raised from clay and thus created by Rabbi Yehuda Loew, the Maharal of Prague, to help defeat the machinations of those determined to see the demise of the Jewish community there. Joseph Golem, sometimes referred to as 'Yosell the Mute', could only act in pursuit of these concerns of the community and he makes laughable errors whenever he is sent on purely secular errands. For example, the wife of the Maharal sends Joseph to obtain fish for her family. He comes back with several tons of fish which then cause a stinking mess in the home. Joseph is thus endowed with limited knowledge and essentially no self-intention and when the Maharal on Friday forgets to tell Joseph to guard the community during the Sabbath, Joseph runs amok. This uncontrolled action is eventually one element in his final 'decommissioning'. Joseph is mute and exhibits no emotion since it is said that

Table 8.1   Characteristics of a flexible function automated system: descriptive and non-exhaustive listing

Full natural language (speaker independent) interface
Full surrogate biological motion (with supra-human strength)
With correct programming – zero failure rate
Domain knowledge – extensive
Out-of-domain knowledge – highly limited
Self-intention – minimal
Out-of-domain operations – guaranteed failure
Absence of expected command – unexpected failure
Affective abilities – zero
Voice output abilities – zero

such emotion would cause him and the community significant problems. Today, we would cast such emotions in the realm of machine intentionality.

Whether the Golem was an actual creation or perhaps just a poor orphan adopted by the Maharal is a matter for historical speculation. The Golem's capabilities, when expressed in more modern terms, indicate similarities to the science-fiction robots of the 1950s and indeed also some commonalties with the character of Mr Data on the television series *Star Trek: The Next Generation* (see Scerbo, 1996). The difference being that the Golem was recorded as being created in the 1580s, four centuries before the idea for Mr Data was conceived. This story allows us to see that the conceptions of automation, even down to surrogate human beings, are not new. Indeed, many ancient cultures have employed automation-based devices. So, for example, Egyptian priest cults used heat- and steam-powered acts of object levitation in their Temples in order to impress the populous with their magic and thus control the common people.

As interesting as the Golem story is, in and of itself, it has a number of even more intriguing threads. For example, many of the scientists directly involved in the development of the modern-day computational science and machine cybernetics such as Von Neumann were from the Jewish culture and grew up on Golem stories as folk tales. Indeed, the father of cybernetics himself, Norbert Weiner, explicitly compared himself to the Golem in some of his writings. On can argue that the Golem legend was a central motif of his life (Weiner, 1954, 1964). It is therefore reasonable to suppose that the development of some forms of modern computational abilities grow from perhaps an innate desire to replicate some of the Golem's fantastic attributes as we each carry the stories of childhood with us into adulthood.

But one connection is certainly not all there is because another thread relates to the English necromancer and proto-scientist Dr. John Dee. In 1588, the fateful year of the 'Spanish Armada', Dee visited Prague. From our historical understanding it is also the case that the Maharal was in residence in Prague at that time as well. Remember, this is the John Dee of the 'Wheeling Beetle' fame. This latter entity was created by Dee during his time as a student in Cambridge and presented at a student stage production. Such was the astonishment of all at the capacities of this automated simulacrum that Dee gained the reputation as a magician and later a necromancer. As has been noted on multiple occasions, and most probably should be originally attributed to Arthur C. Clarke, any technology which is sufficiently advanced will appear to the naïve individual as magic (see Hancock and Hancock, 2008). It may therefore be possible that the creator of the 'Wheeling Beetle' and the creator of the Golem met each other. Indeed, it would seem likely that they would do so as they had another connection beyond their creative capacities.

This connection relates to the reason that Dee and his scryer Edward Kelly were in Prague in the first place. Both Dee and the Maharal were looking to the sponsorship and protection of the Emperor Rudolph II. The emperor himself was intrigued by automata and similar creations and encouraged science and technological growth within his realm. It was because of the tolerance that often accompanies science, that the Maharal had some degree of confidence in the emperor's protection. In matter of fact, Rudolph's attitude encouraged a number of influential, free-thinking individuals to visit, including Giordano Bruno and Michael Mayer (MacDonald, 2002). Most probably these and others visited Hradčany Castle in which the collection of automata was itself a wonder. Of course, the key individual here is John Dee for it is in his 'Mathematical Preface' that we find reference to the lowest form of magic which is the manipulation of the environment, essentially the first formalized foundations of human engineering. This form of action he called *thaumiturgike*. In his lifetime Dee was accused of many forms of heresy but one that is most pertinent is the accusation that he claimed human beings could be above angels. This position being attained by the three levels of magic, of which action derived by technology (of which his own exposition in the 'Wheeling Beetle' was an outstanding example) represents the lowest form. Further, Dee emphasized the crucial link between understanding and number, and it can be little wonder that this conception had an enormous effect on the young Kepler, even if we cannot show that the two actually met in Prague where they were both resident in the later 1500s.

Dee's insightful exposition in his '*Mathematical Preface*,' independent of its connections with Hermeticist philosophy, influenced Francis Bacon's *Novum Organum*, which in turn was part of a greater but unfinished work, the *Great Instauration*. Bacon, in part following Dee, advocated for the systematic empirical exploration of the world. In part reaction to the authoritarian nature of Scholasticism, Bacon advocated for the primacy of observation over authority. It was Bacon who articulated the great clearing of the detritus of accepted authority rather than experimentation and thus pre-empts Descartes in his role of Doubter General. Bacon's precepts are echoed in the foundation of the Royal Society, the first recognized scientific society, whose motto *Nulla in Verba* can be roughly translated as 'Take No One's Word For It'. What does not pass empirical muster is to be doubted. Therefore, in a chronological sense, the requirements and necessities for the creation of working automata were instrumental in the foundations of what we now recognize as the scientific method, although the influences and connections of historical figures on their academic progeny go deeper than this one effect. The confluence of each of these historical themes reaches its fruition in the fundamental question of purpose.

❖ ❖ ❖

The Purposes of Life

I like to believe that had Bacon been spared an untimely demise, he would have attempted to weld the foundations of empirical science with purpose in the unpublished portion of the *Great Instauration*, although this is something we will never know. However, the central question of purpose remains. Is life merely a neverending sequence of parturition, preservation, procreation, and putrefaction? In asserting that there can be more than this, my first claim is that there is a linkage between the design of automation and the levels of processing in the human brain and the products that those collective brains have produced. These self-similarities are thus also expressed at the level of technology, the level of human morality, and finally at the level of human society. These links are outlined in skeletal form in Table 8.2.

Table 8.2   Nested self-similarities in the substructure of the purposes of life

Brain	Technology	Philosophy	Society
Brainstem	Safety	Hobbes	Life
Paleocortex	Automation	Rousseau	Liberty
Neocortex	SIMS*	Augustine	Happiness

* Self-Intentioned Machine Systems

As with all forms of nested self-similarity, one can start in any column and transition to each of the others as desired. In the present case, let us start at the societal level since it will be that which is perhaps most familiar. This three-part distinction, and indeed essentially, the title of this present chapter, comes from the US Constitution. The fundamental right to protecting one's own life derives largely from the writings of Thomas Hobbes (1651) in *Leviathan*. Hobbes, an underrated and original intellect, asked critical questions about the basis of morality well before Descartes asked crucial questions on the origins of knowledge. Hobbes opined that the basis of moral structure was an individual's own right to their existence. Thus, one's fundamental right, even to the extent of taking the life of another, was in the defence of the self. To a large extent, we still adhere to such a precept today. In many countries the notion of self-defence is well developed and accepted as law. In some areas it is elevated beyond this idea of a last measure, especially in some of the southern United States where this self-defence principle is reified above its use in complete extremis.

In technical systems, the equivalent of self-preservation is safety. One of the first things we demand of our creations is that they not destroy either themselves or us. The epithet *primum non nocere* ('first do no harm') can be applied to the design and fabrication of most manufactured goods including, as Asimov indicated, that of robots and their actions. Indeed, the whole process of certification lies at the heart of this very issue. Bringing us back to the first point made in this chapter on automated physiological forms of defence, the human brainstem is site of many of these processes that sustain life. So, the defeat of the intention to die by holding one's breath is resident in the brainstem, which with associated brain structures, is also the centre for affect. It is from these basic needs and necessities that motivation for action often derives. In France, for example, if one commits murder under the driving force of the limbic system, there is a possibility of claiming acquittal under the terms of a 'crime of passion'. Under such circumstances, one might even be pronounced innocent because of the formal recognition of emotion as the overriding cause. However, if the murder is planned by the frontal cortex 'in cold blood' and one is found guilty, one is doomed to punishment – even in France! This is one of the very many examples in which we treat the origin of intention differently, according to our knowledge of differential brain structures and functions. The insanity defence, of course, being another example.

The next stage in each sequence is, I think, the most pertinent to the issues discussed in the present chapter. Liberty is, of course, the watchword of American society, but like so much of Jefferson there is some Montesquieu involved and I personally see Rousseau as the most influential philosopher of freedom. His stunning phrase that 'man was born free, and he is everywhere in chains' still resonates today (Rousseau, 1972; first published in 1762). At a fundamental level, automation is about freedom. In particular, it is about doing away with the drudgery of repetition and the soul-grinding boredom of invariant action simply to achieve a living wage. As always, the spectres of unemployment and its related cousin de-skilling hover ominously in the background of any such considerations.

However, within a short time, we will hopefully look back on repetitive physical and even repetitive cognitive work as such a repugnant anachronism that it will be conceived then as we now conceive of slavery. Indeed, repetition is a form of technological slavery to insensate machines and it is not a reasonable human state, as the movie *Metropolis* shows. At the level of brain function, many such processes are concerned with support of abilities such as locomotion, which like other over-learned or 'automated' (see Schneider and Shiffrin, 1977) motor abilities, allow us to accomplish a number of higher-level goals while still interacting with the predictable elements of the world. Thus, most of us are able to walk and chew gum at the same time. Consequently, although we can perform rote motions relatively independent of cognitive involvement, the question is: should we? I am suggesting here that one component of true freedom is the freedom to live life unconstrained by such a necessity, unless that is what you actively desire to do. Given that machines facilitate the efficiency of repetitive action (as noted even in the Fitts List that we have discussed previously), then the natural evolution of human-machine symbiosis is toward the machine accomplishments of such necessities.

❖ ❖ ❖

The Design of Happiness

It is the final component which needs much more detailed elaboration. Indeed, it is the goal of happiness toward which much of my contemporary thought is directed. Happiness and its near relation contentment are not solely properties of the neocortex. Indeed, all the vertical relations I have shown in Table 8.2 are better seen as nestings, in which achievement at higher levels are predicated upon fulfilment of lower levels – as is implicit in Maslow's conception. One cannot have liberty without life and similarly one cannot achieve true happiness without liberty. In respect to brain structure, the three levels are actually physically erected on top of each other and, like the societal level, are interdependent in order to function fully and effectively.

Until time flows backwards, the cleric Augustine cannot depend upon the philosopher Rousseau. However, I like to think in terms of the respective problems themselves that they are not contingent on the historical order of appearance of these respective individuals. In this sense that the mind itself can be atemporal and one of its greatest advantages is its ability to sweep across vast tracts of time, unfettered by the necessity to consider all things in a linear, chronological order. Indeed, it may be this ability to plan and 'see' ahead which is a key differentiate of humans themselves as a species (Hancock et al., 2005). In technology, our vertical integration is less clear. Indeed, it is this very question that those most interested in human-automation interaction have been struggling with. At the highest level, I have put SIMS, or self-intentioned machine systems. However, whether the full emancipation of machines, if indeed this is possible, is equated with human happiness is at present, a doubtful proposition – although it is one now often explored in many contemporary science-fiction films.

John Stuart Mill is reported to have said: '*Ask yourself if you are happy and immediately you cease to be so.*' Rousseau described the happiest time of his life as a brief sojourn on an island in which the cares of existence could be forgotten, his epitome of *dolce far niente*. Clearly, happiness is best viewed as a process rather than a goal or thing in and of itself. A crucial element of the process of happiness is the momentary or prolonged dissociation from want. Most unfortunately in our times, want has been rigidly related to materialistic mastery. In our society, we have confused the negative with the positive. That is, we have confused the absence of material needs with the presence of material desires. This confusion has been aided and abetted and perhaps even fostered by material capitalism. We are bombarded into a state of uncertainty by which we confuse that which we need (for example, air, water, food, shelter, and the like), with what we desire (for example, a new appliance, or the latest sparkling bauble to be touted as that which we cannot live without). These desires have to be constantly renewed by vendors. Each generation has their Radio Flyer, their Teddy Ruxpin, Beany Baby, or iPod. And to each generation the fads of its predecessor sequentially appear to be outdated, quaint, or just plain weird. Certainly the members of one generation have their own specific examples of where a desire was transformed to a need (just must have). But most interestingly, the examples from the previous generation of this self-same delusion are considered in the same light as their own fixation. This demonstrates the transience of this form of persuasion and thus its vacuity.

In the midst of this gross human mis-service in translating simple momentary desires to apparent absolute needs, the science of psychology in general, and one eminent psychologist in particular, stands manifestly condemned. The tenets of paired-associate learning and early behaviourist theory were promoted by John B. Watson in his second career in advertising. Rarely can so much damage have been done to a society so surreptitiously. Today, we are regaled in our communication media with omnipresent reminders that we can only experience the wonders of existence through material gain. A recent advert for a well-known product implies that one can only feel the emotion of true love by buying the latest model automobile! It is an obscene perversion of human potential to tie our future hopes to material gain. Indeed, we know that such gain does not bring happiness but the lotteries of our country continue to pour millions into the governmental coffers.

If happiness is truly pluralistic, then specification of happiness will be an arduous endeavour indeed (Hoffman and Hayes, 2004). However, if we are able to specify happiness as a process and what represents greater or lesser degrees of that process, and we can show how technology can support us in achieving those degrees, then hope does exist. For example, virtual world experiences need not necessarily affect any other individual and can provide opportunities for 'convivial' interaction (see Illich, 1973). Thus the gaming industry might well serve very useful purposes, despite the numerous detractors who decry such pastimes. As we each take small steps along the path of life, we each need to stand up and designate our own purpose. It is insufficient, now, for any human being to pass this one essential expression of self off on any other living being past, present or even future. We have no requirement to be eternally correct and, although it is tempting, we should not specify such purposes by absence alone, such as the absence of oppression. Rather, we need to articulate individual, collective, societal and indeed global goals if the future is not to be the haphazard quilt of happenstance that marks our essential past. Those who mediate between humans and technology represent a crucial bridge across these various levels of expression. For the way in which these differing aspirations can be integrated will be by technology. Only through the human-centred advances of technology will they be integrated and resolved.

Chapter 9
Mind, Machine and Morality

Introduction

Since its earliest days as a formalized pursuit there has been a continuing contention over the degree to which science should interact with purpose. As a structured method for exploring and understanding the universe about us, science has been the most useful known strategy in revealing what 'is' and, on the basis of these revelations predicting what 'will be' in the future. When confined to this role, science neither makes nor purports to make any authoritative pronouncements about what 'should be'. Science provides no value judgements or moral declarations about the course of affairs. It simply generates a progressively more precise physical specification of future conditions, given the improved understanding of the current conditions and the processes though which the future evolves.

Thus, for example, physics can tell with reasonable accuracy what will happen when sufficient amounts of uranium are crammed together into a small enough space, but as to the purposive 'fall out' of such a compaction, science itself has remained largely mute. Of course, this is not to say that particular scientists themselves do not render comments and opinions upon such activity, as individuals it is assuredly the case that some do. Rather, it is science itself which is held to be 'neutral' in respect of the issues of purpose and meaning. This propositional separation of 'what will be' from 'what should be' remains a widely perpetuated but eventually fatal fallacy (cf., Carter, 2005; Gould, 1999). For, as much as purpose predicates process, process promotes purpose. Purpose and process are thus inextricably linked together in a locked circularity. Like perception and action, their independent existence is virtually without meaning. How these respective parts of the life experience first came to be divorced is a matter of historical postulation. How they are to be reassembled and cogently integrated is the greatest human challenge of the twenty-first century (Fraser, 2007).

There are those who can afford the luxury of only studying the world as it was. Historians, paleo-anthropologists, geologists and others of similar interest seek to discover what was and try to establish some degree of truth about what actually occurred in the past. This is not to say such individuals are not interested in the present or the indeed the future; they may well be. However, their focus is on events that have already occurred. In terms of the Minkowski space-time diagram (see Chapter 1) their focus of attention is in the absolute past.

As there are those whose primary concern lies in the past, so there are many scientists who deal almost exclusively with the penumbra around the present – the 'now'. They are concerned with why things are as they are at this present moment in time. While they also may well have a pertinent interest in antecedent events and likewise in the future outfall of their discoveries their focus is the here and now. However, even when we acknowledge the respective foci of such individuals, I believe that the majority of scientists look primarily to the future. Indeed, the very act of writing itself can be characterized as a belief in the viability of the future. The models, predictions, and concerns of these latter scientists involve what will come about, either in the near term or on a longer time-scale. Further, a meaningfully large percentage of these scientists (if not all of them at least in some fashion) act as agents of change. In seeking to change the world, such individuals (and I include myself amongst them) cannot logically avoid the moral dimension of the actions which they take. In this final chapter, I want to present my perspective on this crucial issue of the expression of purpose by using an especially pointed exemplar to trigger both a visceral and a cerebral response.

❖ ❖ ❖

Design and Morality

Not many years ago we, in the United States, were on the verge of a war in the Persian Gulf. Many of the devices, the advances, methods, and technical developments made by our scientific community were about to be employed to facilitate the defeat of the enemy. In general, the better the human-machine synergy of these devices, the more the purpose-directed destruction they delivered (see also Hancock, Hendrick et al., 2006; Yuan and Kuo, 2006). How does our scientific community view this outflow of these respective efforts? How are such actions to be reconciled with our avowed purpose in Human Factors and ergonomics for example, to improve the 'quality' of human life?

When we move from a global to a more local scale of discourse, and given what we understand about the modern terrorist threat, would we publish journal papers which demonstrated techniques to avoid weapons detection in airport carry-on luggage? I suspect not. However, most of us in the behavioural science community possess just such information in one form or another expressed as antitheses to our efforts to improve detection. Is our academic freedom compromised by such restraints? More pointedly, would we accept scientific contributions to our conferences and journals concerning the ergonomics of crematoria to facilitate 'processing' time?

These questions rightly stir strong emotive responses, most especially in uncertain times like the present. Such provocative and ambiguous questions produce no easy answers. However, it is precisely because they are not easy that we need to consider the role of science in addressing them. Now as I write, the large-scale conflict is already over and the problems of winning the peace are now very much to the fore. In modern times, with the global presence of only a single military superpower, the defeat of massed armed forces in the war itself is the 'easy' part: it is the peace which is hard. Now Iraq, as a country with millennia of history behind it and a culture radically different from that of the occidental world, is undergoing major social and political reform. What role if any, should scientists undertake to contribute to the facilitation of this enforced process of political and social change?

In the past, the formal science of Human Factors and Ergonomics (HF/E), in common with many if not most other companion sciences, has been careful to avoid specific pronouncements, especially from its professional society, on issues that are so obviously 'political' in nature. Perhaps, as individuals we might believe that these are not 'appropriate' concerns upon which our scientific and professional societies should pronounce but should rather be dealt with in the larger political realm. However, in contrast to such an opinion, I believe such topics are of direct scientific concern. Thus here, I want to examine the morality of scientific advances as related to human-machine systems and especially such developments in relation to purposeful design. I do not wish to engage in any polemic based upon contemporary political alignments. This approach would almost inevitably lead to partisan disputes that are inextricably intertwined with historical as well as contemporary disagreements between entrenched constituencies. In contrast, what I do want to achieve here is the beginning of a collective discussion that brings to the fore the *moral* aspect of the discipline and profession of HF/E. This exhortation further explains why, as the bridge between science and intention expressed in the interaction of humans and technology, it is *our* branch of the scientific enterprise which *must* discuss and reconcile these extraordinarily difficult facets of human existence (see Pirsig, 1974).

I do this because I believe that the following premises to be valid ones:

1. HF/E does not seek only to understand the world as it is but aspires to shape the world as it can be. Thus those in the merging science of human-machine systems have an equal investment in what we can become as we do in what we now are.
2. HF/E affects the future either directly through its own activities, or indirectly through its relationship with designers, engineers and others who also look to create the future.
3. Technology is the most powerful contemporary, intentional force which acts to shape our world and create change in it.
4. The fundamental purpose of technology is to serve people.
5. The branch of science that currently and most evidently seeks to mediate between humans and technology is HF/E.
6. All acts of creation posses a moral dimension.

❖❖❖

The Traditional Stance

For many writers, scientists, and thinkers such as Stephen Jay Gould (1999), science and morality, or more directly, natural and moral philosophy, occupy different realms of discourse or *magesteria*. Such magesteria are purported to focus upon different orders of phenomena. Science is expectedly directed to the 'what' and the 'how' of the world and largely appeals to empirical evidence to resolve between competing possibilities posed as hypotheses about the future physical state of affairs. Morality, most frequently expressed in history as 'religion,' broadly defined, addresses the 'why' of the world. It is concerned with issues such as 'ultimate purpose' and 'first cause' (see also Chapter 2). These issues lie mostly beyond the strict empirical domain but are the subject of legitimate human discourse through purported advances and developments such as revelation and 'divine' scripture (see Carter, 2005). Using this criterion of separability, Gould can assert tacitly that the creator of a technology has no more moral right or obligation as to the eventual effect of that technology than any other individual in society. One of our HF/E luminaries, Neville Moray (1993, 1995) has also advocated the conception that science is a 'neutral' activity as have other scientists including for example the Nobel prize-winner, Steven Weinberg.

In this sense the implementation of science in society is fundamentally independent of its genesis in the process by which discoveries are made. This division between the moral dimension of creation and the moral dimension of utilization lies at the very heart of my present discourse. The traditional stance conveniently leaves the scientist with unstained hands, especially in morally ambiguous circumstances, since any subsequent 'implementation' of the scientific principles derived is a 'social' not a personal choice. This unfortunate fiction can apparently be sustained (although not on occasion without withering personal cost as was evident in the case of J. Robert Oppenheimer) by most individuals when the work is at the cutting edge and evidently remote from immediate implementation. This is especially so if the science is considered 'pure' and without evident and immediate influence (cf., e = mc^2).

In these pristine and disparate 'worlds' of science and morality, science acts rather like some dispassionate and grandiose librarian, constantly seeking to understand and catalogue the world and the universe around us and reporting and recording these conclusions in some growing fund of accumulating knowledge. In contrast morality, most often expressed collectively as religion and evermore frequently in contemporary society as secular authority, is then free to browse this library for convenient knowledge to affect the world in whatever fashion is chosen or is foisted upon the greater mass of humanity. Equally, such authorities appear free to ignore such knowledge when it appears pragmatically useful to adopt a selective form of blindness. For Gould and many others, as long as the magesteria of religion does not pronounce upon the 'facts' of science, or indeed if the tenets of science do not infringe upon the dogma of religion, all is harmony and light. This division, while practically appealing, is dangerously misguided and represents an evident form of wishful thinking. It is the prescription for the demise of our species. First, let us examine how this situation came to be, for technology and intention have not always been so divorced. Indeed, in many human cultures there has never been any such fundamental division.

Science itself is not a neutral act. No discovery ever made is a sterile event. Indeed, as Francis Bacon in his fundamental formulations observed, the very essence of science is for *the uses of life*. In accord with this view Marx indicated that the purpose of philosophy itself is not to understand the world but to change it. The simple fact is that technology, which is the active, extensive face of science, represents the primary force that shapes the world around us and has done so now for some centuries. Similarly, moral philosophy, intention, purpose, or whatever you will, finds its primary expression through these technical extensions to human capacities. Indeed, the very word 'tele-evangelist' could be regarded as the leitmotif of this latter form of marriage.

In the conception of those such as Gould, the process of science is almost a passive study of the past (and as a paleo-biologist it is little wonder that Gould himself could advocate for such separation). In the world of human-machine systems however, we are at the very confluence of science and intention. In these terms, it is *our purpose* to create the future. Thus, although in our Western past magesteria may have been seen as separable and clastic, in respect of the future they must be seen as inevitably and inextricably intertwined. The division between science and religion is commonly attributed to the times of the Renaissance and the various landmark historic cases of those times. This is a convenient historic fiction to maintain, since it provides the modern world with early scientific 'heroes' such as Gallileo. However, the distinction itself precedes even these early years of the formalization of science as a collective activity. It harks back to the division for example of the lords spiritual and the lords temporal, and emerges most clearly in the late fifteenth and early sixteenth centuries. These times saw the confluence of dissatisfaction with Scholastic authority and the nascent growth of empirical science, expressed in pursuits such as alchemy and astronomy and the crucial invention of the printing press.

❖ ❖ ❖

Separating Morality and Religion

Many readers, especially those steeped in the US Constitution, will adhere to or at least be generally supportive of a separation between church and state. In general, and despite what I have written here so far, I am also a supporter of such a separation, at least to the degree that it is procedurally possible. But this is not because I am transgressing my effort to seek a unifying principle. Rather, it is because church and state are themselves entrenched Institutions while moral and natural philosophy are fundamental attributes of each and every human individual. The central problem here is that 'religion' has traditionally been considered the arbiter of morality for so long that a putative unification of morality and science looks dangerously equivalent to the dissolution of the separation between church and state.

I would argue however that in a pluralistic society, morality cannot be the hegemony of any one single religion however powerful that single religion is. By extension, I do not believe morality has to be founded in religion at all. I would support this assertion by arguing that even those of an agnostic or even atheistic persuasion do not act without purpose or indeed on most occasions without moral rectitude and responsibility. The challenge for the unification of the type I have proposed is the distillation of a collective morality, independent of any particular religious dogma. In this quest HF/E should also have its appropriate voice. Thus, the present effort is not an attack on expressions of formalized religions. Rather, it is a search for philosophical unity.

The foregoing observations provide much to digest, especially for any practitioner who happens to be looking in this book for immediate practical help on a pressing design project. So let me illustrate my argument with an historical exposition that brings to the forefront one specific, pointed example. The example that I have chosen to use is 'the ergonomics of torture'. Again, I am seeking here to be purposely provocative. My examples of torture and its relationship to ergonomics are derived primarily from observations on fifteenth- and sixteenth-century 'technologies' in which the 'art' of torture itself was first formalized (if that is the appropriate phrase). However, the example remains unfortunately pertinent to present day issues of torture that still bedevils us, especially in the current political circumstances (Amnesty International, 2005).

❖ ❖ ❖

Torture and the Foreshadowing of Ergonomics

Perhaps the most tragic thing about torture is that I don't first have to explain what I mean by the term. The concept is so ubiquitous but so uniquely human, that I can merely mention it and there is an immediate understanding. Indeed, this observation alone perhaps means that one common moral aspiration for us collectively as a species should be to frame a world where we would eventually have to explain to our children what torture was in the same way we now have to explain to them what an eight-track tape-player was! We know that torture has been used throughout recorded history and very earliest stone-carved cartouches we possess show captured combatants undergoing a series of tortures, as opposed to simple execution. Our collective knowledge of torture and its processes increased greatly with the advent of the printing press and contemporary with its growth, the growth of systematic torture in relation to religious orthodoxy. Perhaps the most famous institutionalized form of torture was evident in the 'Spanish Inquisition'. In a seeming paradox, it is here that we can also begin to encounter the real origins of a formal science of ergonomics.

The first step in what might be termed the formal process of torture emphasizes the psychological dimension of threat. Like the anticipation of pleasure, the anticipation of pain can do much to the mind that even reality cannot match. Here, torturers use this anticipation of harm as leverage well in advance of any recourse to physical action. In the Inquisition itself, this psychological step was composed of showing the prisoner the instruments of torture (Ryley, 2003; Sabatini, 2003). This self-same sequence of first showing the instruments was adopted by many subsequent agencies who have since also sought to persuade by torture. In this, the Inquisition was a good teacher. In the vast majority of cases, this psychological threat was sufficient to cause the prisoner to acquiesce and to capitulate to whatever the torturer demanded. Indeed, in some ways the better the imagination of the victim, the better that this strategy works. One fundamental problem with this acquiescence is that it is usually total and often uninformative in the manner that the torturer desires. It is one of the crucial flaws of torture as a process of information extraction – the threatened individual will often agree to anything that is requested no matter how outlandish. But we should also remember that torture was not always for the purpose of persuasion alone but often was solely for the purpose of punishment. Thus, traditionally in the realm of formal torture, psychological threat commonly preceded any direct physical abuse.

The process of bodily torture then certainly requires the skills of the psychologist but it also necessitates the insights of the physical ergonomist. These latter skills include a thorough knowledge of anatomy and physiology as well as a detailed understanding of biomechanics. Further, the creation of torture instruments also necessitated designs of some mechanical genius on behalf of the craftsman in order to develop the antithetical 'human-centred' technologies involved (Hancock, 2003). Torture, having a variety of different goals, similarly possesses a range of different instrumental forms to achieve those goals. Such technologies, designed for the intentional *purveyance of pain*, had to be constructed most carefully and with considerable insight into the psychology of terror, the genesis of pain and the limitations of human physiological tolerance. Indeed, any failure to provide effective torture could well rebound upon the manufacturer him- or herself and a shoddy workman could readily find himself on the wrong end of this particular designer-user relationship. Thus, understanding the generation and perpetuation of pain was vital to the successful torturer of the fifteenth and sixteenth century, as indeed it unfortunately remains today.

Although the skills and knowledge required by the torturer certainly overlap to a startling extent that of the contemporary ergonomist, the essential difference lies, of course, in the purpose of the activity. It is the intention of the designer and the practitioner and therefore the morality of the participants involved which makes the difference. However, as we shall see, these divisions are neither so clear nor so pristine as we might at first hope and imagine. For we can consider many situations in which the technologies used in historical torture and the technologies of modern-day health promotion are exactly the same. Perhaps two brief examples will suffice here to illustrate this fact.

Consider for example the rack, or, more colloquially, the 'Duke of Exeter's Daughter' as it is referred to in the Tower of London. It is one of the most feared of all instruments of torture and remains today a very effective, bloodless way of administering great pain. How could such any such instrument be put to a morally positive and laudable purpose? But of course it is! There is no fundamental difference between the rack and the contemporary medical device we refer to as a 'traction bed'. Individuals unlucky enough to require a traction bed are usually in considerable pain already. The purpose of the instrument – to stretch the body – is exactly the same, and again pain can well result from the process. Thus the difference does not lie fundamentally in either the form or the function of the instrument itself. The traction bed makes a very effective rack, as was shown to us in the James Bond movie *Thunderball*. The sole difference lies in the intention of both the patient (victim) and the physician (torturer). In this respect it is manifestly the moral intention of both the administrator as well, paradoxically, as the intention of the victim themselves that creates the nature of the intercourse. The latter expression lies in whether they voluntarily submit themselves to this action or not. In the medical case, of course, we would expect to administer some form of painkiller in order that the procedure be as painless as is feasible. This duality of pain and healing is evident in the film scene between Dustin Hoffman and Laurence Olivier in the movie *Marathon Man*. Here the dualistic role of healer and torturer was played expertly by Olivier in the guise of the sadistic dentist, one minute causing agony the next administering succour. There is much more to be explored concerning this relationship between pain and healing but it is an issue that is presently beyond the direct purpose of this book.

If the rack is one example of this dualism, then a more modern illustration is the treadmill. In times past, the treadmill was a fearsome punishment for convicts at 'hard labour'. One individual to suffer under such a punishment was Oscar Wilde during his sojourn in Reading Gaol. Such was the arduous nature of the treadmill, on which individuals sometimes spent hours a day, that it was considered unlikely that a 'gentleman' such as Wilde would be able to survive the ordeal. Of course, treadmills were not originally designed for this purpose. Indeed, they were used for a variety of tasks including the raising of materials to great heights as evidence by the presence of such an instrument on the roof of Beauvais Cathedral in France. In contrast to their uses for hard physical labour, today we place these self-same instruments in local gymnasia and call them 'cardio-workout' machines. Rows of individuals can be seen daily subjecting themselves to exactly the same treatment, often at rates that would have been considered unacceptable in even the most punishing Victorian prison or Gothic cathedral! Not content with these classic treadmills, we now subject ourselves to 'elliptical gliders' and the like. Again, the parallel should be evident. It is thus the nature of the authority which imposes the action on another and the consequent inability of the individual to exercise control over their participation that provides the difference. It is not the physical form or the biomechanical function of the instrument per se but rather the context of its use, the moral compunction involved. I should note however, that this division works for only some instruments of torture. It must be absolutely acknowledged that there are certain individual instruments of torture which appear to have no redeeming social or functional possibilities whatsoever. Of these we shall pass over quickly and with as much silence as Wittgenstein can raise.

❖ ❖ ❖

For the Purposes of Life

When Francis Bacon first proposed his exploratory methods of science at around the turn of the seventeenth century he was working within living memory of the Inquisition and the English heresy trials of 'Bloody' Queen Mary (see Ridley, 2001) and indeed the punishment of Jesuits by her half-sister Queen Elizabeth I. A component of all these proceedings was the state's need for methods of physical and theological 'persuasion'. For Mary, there was as well a degree of revenge for the comparable persecution under Mary's half-brother and predecessor, Edward VI, and so for Elizabeth also after her half-sister's death. Many designers provided the ingenious instruments of torture that the then authorities required in order to achieve said purposes. Torture is the antithesis of physiological and psychological comfort and hence there is a common base of understanding between the two. In torture, one must ensure that the poor victim cannot habituate to the stimulus, since the cessation of sensory activation means the cessation of pain. Similarly, the shock of torture must fall short of instant unconsciousness, since the latter state also obviates the purposes involved. The stricture against spilling blood also generated any number of constraints on European torturers, although no such limitation was evident in other areas of the world, at that time or now in the present. One particularly trenchant example for those involved in the study of physical and cognitive ergonomics can be had by comparing the illustrations in Figure 9.1, concerning chairs.

The chair to the far right is a contemporary office chair and is designed to provide maximal seated comfort. The very self-same understanding involved in the development and construction of this chair is also intrinsic to the chair at the far left. It uses the same knowledge of pressure points, surfaces of support, and other allied anthropometric and physiological factors. But this time the purpose is to generate maximal discomfort. The two functions are again of course, the antithesis of each other. One evident difference, however, is that the latter chair was made in the very early fifteenth century while the former is a twenty-first-century creation. Of course normal chairs were made for comfort of sitting even in these earlier times and therefore the principle holds since the base knowledge remains the same.

The chair in the middle has a very different function. It is not for torture but then again neither is it for comfort. Rather, its purpose is execution. It is actually an electric chair called '*Old Sparky*' that was used by the state of New Jersey throughout most of the twentieth century. I have actually sat in this chair (although not for its prime functional purpose I am happy to report) and I can attest that in a strange way, it is actually a very comfortable chair indeed. At least that is until the switch is thrown. Even though there is much contention over this form of execution representing 'cruel and unusual punishment', there was never any intent for this type of chair to be used for the purpose of torture. In fact, during its development it was expressly designed to provide as humane a form of execution as possible.

Indeed, many forms of correction that we now consider quite egregious cases of torture were actually created as expressions primarily of public disapprobation. At the time of their genesis, there were few, if any formal prisons of the sort we know today, in which to keep those who offended against the larger social community. Thus, punishment tended to be more immediate and much more public in nature. For example, the spiked barrel shown in Figure 9.2 was used as punishment for repeated drunkenness. The other picture shown in the figure illustrates the punishment meted out to a 'nagging' woman, an instrument known as the 'branks'. Parenthetically, it is important to remember that something like 75–80 per cent of all torture was perpetrated by men against women and therefore such actions most probably involved a strong sexual element. The opportunity for sadism was also a powerful form of stimulation for torture, a facet also explored in part in Hugo's *Hunchback of Notre Dame*. Beyond these base and immoral motivations, the process of torture for nominally utilitarian purposes (for example, information extraction) can also induce significant and indeed permanent degree of psychological damage to the torturer as well as the tortured. Thus, it is a universally destructive human activity. This undermines any argument of those who would advocate for the use of torture or even extenuating interrogations to protect society in its contemporary 'war on terror'.

Figure 9.1   Three chairs, three very different purposes. The chair on the left is purposely designed primarily for discomfort and the generation of pain, the chair on the right is its material antithesis, being designed primarily for comfort. The chair in the center is for temporary occupation only

Figure 9.2   **The barrel and the 'branks' The former shown on the right side was a typical punishment for repeated public drunkenness. The heavy barrel was itself a burden but refinements such as internal spikes could very much add to the pain experienced. The 'branks', shown on the left side of the illustration, was for the 'correction' of a nagging wife**

As we have already encountered, one of the most feared forms of torture was the rack. As with some other instruments like the 'Scavenger's Daughter' (Bennett, 2007), the rack was an answer as to how to induce pain without the threat of immediate unconsciousness or death. Further, it did not spill blood which, as we have seen, was of a concern not merely to the Inquisition but for many torturers who, strangely, saw the spilling of blood as abhorrent. One fundamental problem with early rack designs was the question of tension. If one wished to inflict continuous pain on the victim, one had to be actively pulling on the handle at all times and this could be wearing on the poor torturer! Imagine the problem of carpal-torturer's syndrome! However, the ingenious incorporation of ratchet mechanisms subsequently allowed individuals to be racked in a permanent state of anguish while the torturer now no longer had to exert a constant tension, and being English could presumably go off to have afternoon tea. This also solved the problem of repeating torture which was expressly forbidden in the Inquisition rules. The relaxation of the tension on the rack provided a nice moral problem as to whether subsequent tension constituted multiple episodes of torture.

Truly the rack is an example of the very epitome of the worst form of human-centred design. Our own personal and visceral reaction to this latter observation is truly interesting, especially if one identifies with ergonomics in any professional fashion. But the development and use of such a ratchet mechanism was not confined to the realm of torture alone! Indeed, clocks would not have developed as they have without this self-same technological innovation (Greenlaw, 1999). Thus the issue of multifunctionality of discovery and innovation lies at the crux of the technology and morality issue. For, after all, as Emilio Largo, the villain in *Thunderball*, shows, everyday items can be used very effectively as instruments of torture. How then are we to judge and evaluate the morality of discovery?

❖ ❖ ❖

The Ambiguity and Emotion of Torture

There are two further aspects of torture that I want to comment on here. The first involves some facets of the curious ambiguity of the situation. In some arcane and strange way where torture is used for persuasion, it can be the case that the torturer and victim must each 'agree' to partake. By this I do not mean that the victim voluntarily walks into the torture chamber (although there are many instance especially of religious saints who seem to positively embrace the coming horror). Rather, both torturer and victim must each desperately 'believe' in some cause or issue (be it political, personal, or theological) for institutionalized torture to proceed. It is often the case that, having divulged the relevant information or reneged on some religious position, the goal of torture is achieved and is then the torture stops (McIwain, 1998). This does not preclude an individual's subsequent execution, as in cases of treason to the state. However, torture is predominantly a means to an end, and that end being achieved results in the cessation of torment. In this respect, torture bears a strange resemblance to other human conflict situations (such as baseball batters vs. baseball pitchers, or drivers involved in multi-vehicle collisions, etc.), the torturer and victim are part of a dyad of unwanted participation (sometimes by both parties). This strange and often ambiguous situation involves the interaction of 'reluctant partners' (Hancock and de Ridder, 2003).

The second curious observation concerning torture is how the emotions which are stirred can be quickly changed from revulsion to comedy. For example, in respect of the earlier discussion on chairs, who can forget the immortal *Monty Python* sketch where 'no one expects the Spanish Inquisition' and Cardinal Fang is instructed to 'get the comfy chair'. We may indeed threaten with torture but it is almost the epitome of comedy to threaten with comfort! As we look deeper into human society, we can see many occasions in which quite dreadful methods of torture can actually be converted into episodes of high comedy. We need only recall Henry Winkler as Chuck Lumley, tied to a mortuary bed in *Night Shift*, as the quintessential comedic rendering of 'water-boarding' (see Figure 9.3), or Gene Wilder as Skip Donahue relishing the torments of the prison personnel in *Stir Crazy*. This interrelationship between torture and comedy (the emotions of fear and laughter) is a very intriguing indeed as the recent James Bond movie *Casino Royale* also illustrates. It would be very elevating to say that instruments of torture do not exist in our world today but unfortunately, as we know, this is not

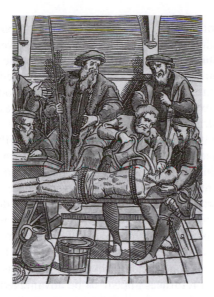

Figure 9.3   **One of the supposedly more 'benign' forms of torture in which the victim experiences the sensation of drowning. This process can be repeated at will and the largely reflex response is elicited. The word benign is carefully chosen here since such specific forms of torture can be transmuted into comedy. (For an example of transmutation of this form see the movie '*Night Shift*') Other forms of torture cannot be so transformed and their illustration remains offensive in almost any context**

so and even more sophisticated methods and technologies have been developed for the various purposes of torture still being practised (see Amnesty International, 2003). Fortunately, however, we at least appear to have progressed a little from the superstition-ridden years of the sixteenth century and can point, even in the midst of the unbridled capitalism of the nineteenth century, to some brighter facets of the human enterprise (Sagan, 1996).

Amidst our revulsion (and perhaps a degree of fascination) for the issue of torture there remains a critical awareness that the antithesis can prove any point as effectively as its positive peer. With this in mind, I'd like to now present my general consideration of morality and technology.

❖ ❖ ❖

From the Purveyance of Pain to the Pursuit of Pleasure

History is always non-linear and it is a mistake to see it as a simple chronological progression. However, we may here be justified in seeing some degree of evolution from torture to ergonomics as stops along an unlikely continuum which is illustrated in Figure 9.4. I should repeat that I do not wish to imply that this illustration shows a simple progress from savagery to morality since such an interpretation would radically distort the truth. Although these various states coexist, I think that for those in human-machine systems, writ large, it is important to consider this range of human activities.

At first, as I have been at pains to show, individuals who were involved in the design of instruments of torture might well be considered the forerunners of what is now seen as formal science of ergonomics. These human-centred designers had as much to do with torture as any other collective activity in the emerging society of the early Renaissance. The more modern incarnation of ergonomics as a branch of science would abjure this ancestry. Indeed, I think most if not all ergonomists would reject the torturer as their forebear and much rather identify pioneers such as Jastrzebowski and subsequently Murrell as the founders of the field. But as with the ascendancy of greed over other human motivations (as we have seen with the case of Sarah Island in Chapter 7), the growth of concern for worker safety and health may have been derived from legitimate caring of certain individuals, but the power of the movement was fuelled by the hope and expectation that such improvements would actually improve productivity and thus profit – 'good ergonomics' being equated with 'good economics'.

PAIN	
Purvey	Prevent
Torture	Ergonomics

PLEASURE	
Permit	Promote
Usability	Hedonomics

Figure 9.4   A continuum of affective experience from pleasure to pain and the associated areas of scientific enquiry, technology and design

Note: At left are the aspects of pain consisting of technology to purvey pain expressed as different forms of torture. Technologies and designs to moderate and prevent pain are the very foundation of ergonomics. At right of the diagram are the present developments in usability that allow the user to explore pleasurable interaction, while 'hedonomics' is that aspect of science which explicitly seeks to promote pleasurable human-technology interaction through design, and by implication to reduce its unpleasant aspects.

Early concern for the worker was thus generated by ambivalent motivations for both healthy but primarily productive individuals and several of our current efforts are still directed to convincing various strata of management that these goals are not necessarily in conflict (Hendrick, 1996). Therefore, the growth of pain prevention, laudable as this was, was not for charitable, empathic, or moral purposes alone but rather it was equally to maintain productivity by ensuring workers were the most individually efficient and productive unit that they could be. When we, in ergonomics, employ aphorisms such as 'good ergonomics is good economics', it must inevitably imply the consequent query as to who specifically this is 'good' for. Although the general wealth is thereby improved, it is an unfortunate situation at the current time that such profit that is harvested is highly mal-distributed. While good ergonomics might well result in better productivity and fewer health-related absences, the rewards go to the few and the maintained health of the individual worker is largely aimed at extracting greater effort in the future, not at the intrinsic improvement of that individual's existence. Ergonomics, as it acts to prevent harm and damage (that is, acute and chronic forms of pain and injury) is indeed good. But the 'good' thereby derived is largely not a general social good, but sub-serves the personal gain of the powerful few. In this manner, Ergonomics transgresses its aim at improving the 'quality of human life' unless that life is the pampered existence of a monetaried oligarchy. If HF/E is to succeed in its greater aim, it must also be involved not just in generating health and wealth but in addressing the ways in which that collective good is distributed. The ergonomics of politics and the politics of ergonomics are thus critical issues for the future of our science (Hancock, 2000b).

But, as we have seen in an earlier chapter, the nature of the electronic and digital revolution has changed the very nature of work itself. The physical toil of yesteryear has, in the West, been replaced largely by mental effort. The pains which are attendant to repeated heavy muscular activities have been, to a large degree, replaced by the equally aversive effects of prolonged, enforced mental concentration. However, the medium of modern work, the computer system, is much more amenable to what Ivan Illich termed 'conviviality'. From the mere prevention of pain, ergonomics has moved on to begin to explore the possibilities and potentialities involved in more flexible work organization. Most recently, we have seen this expressed as a focus on issues of 'usability'. Still couched in the capitalist, economic terms of productivity and efficiency, there has been evidence of a new dawn in which enjoyment, pleasure, and even prolonged happiness are beginning to enter into the workplace (Hoffman and Hayes, 2004). At first this happened as an informal by-product of the opportunities that computer systems present but now we are even seeing the foundation of a new face of ergonomics and perhaps a new branch of science termed 'hedonomics' which represents the formal study of pleasurable human-machine interaction (Hancock et al., 2005).

❖ ❖ ❖

The Morality of Design, the Morality of Use

No act of design is without its moral dimension. But crucially, no act of use is without its moral dimension also. The great issue that the prior, pointed examples raise is the centrality of intention. The intention of the designer may be benevolent while the intention of the (ab)user may be malevolent, or vice versa. Most often, the physical artefacts themselves that represent the technology to hand are, in human terms, morally neutral. Neutral that is until an action is undertaken with them. Some forms of technology such as weapons represent the physical instantiation of doubtful morality. However, even these items can be employed for laudable aims, as has been epitomized in the more recent Hollywood movies about destruction-threatening asteroids. In a similar manner, surgical instruments are created with the fundamental intention of healing, although this function is easily perverted by the abuser.

Thus, what we see is that the morality of technology is an emergent dimension which derives from a confluence of both the intention and action of the community of designers and the intention and action of the community of users. As an emergent property, it is hard to index and quantify on a ratio scale and because of the purported neutrality of the large majority of created designs. It should be evident now that the purported neutrality actually derives from the under-specification of what the design can do, rather than the expressed intention of what it should do. The empirical question becomes how far can designers create their technology such that it cannot do anything it is not 'supposed' to do? For example, could 'shoot by wire' firearms be designed so as not to discharge toward any human target? Although all military weapons would seem necessarily to be designed to transgress this feature! Can we design functional affordances of objects such that their abuse is so egregiously difficult that even the most malevolent of user will abandon their amoral efforts in frustration. Presumably, this aspiration would also be consistent with designing systems for the collective good, for example, low-flush toilets.

To the present, design has been judged largely on the basis of functionality and to a degree the aesthetics of the object or technology under examination. This latter expression is part of a growing concern with the more subjective and hedonistic aspects of human response to our technical creations. In respect of this, we have to broaden the concerns of the emerging human-machine sciences to understand these pervasive but often subtle influences on our collective moral behaviour. The issue of morality is deserving of much wider debate in our professional scientific societies and indeed beyond, to include the collective aspirations of all of our species (see Wilkin, 2009). It may well be the case that a satisfactory strategy for future progress mandates a much closer and intimate linkage between all of the sciences and all of the humanities (see Pirsig, 1974) who will, by necessity, have to begin to talk each other's language in a much more fluent manner (see Fraser, 2007). I sense that there is a very limited time window in which to engage this dialogue.

❖ ❖ ❖

Summary and Conclusion

While commenting on the parallel growth of ergonomics and torture, I have tried to illustrate how the processes of torture require very sophisticated ergonomics which is indeed the ultimate in a human-centred approach to technology. Indeed, the first step of almost any torturer is the practice of cognitive ergonomics in which the torturer uses anticipation and psychological menace as a preliminary to any physical action. The actual actions of physical torture then require all the skills of the ergonomist, a thorough knowledge of anatomy and physiology, biomechanics, and the ability to develop 'human-centred' technologies. Adherence to formal processes of torture and the understanding of pain and injury were vital to the successful torturer. Indeed, it is arguable that the systematic application of torture represented the first formal basis of ergonomics well before the formal definition of the name in Jastrezbowski's thesis or Murrell's more modern-day nomenclature in naming the founding scientific society and its associated publications.

I am hopeful that this expressly pointed example will serve to stimulate the discussion of purpose and the degree to which process is always contingent upon purpose, however poorly that may be expressed. On a more theoretical note, I observe that the division between natural and moral philosophy, largely formalized by the later British empiricists, derives from the assumption that perception and action can themselves be 'divorced'. In a typically pithy American expression, the savant Benjamin Franklin quoted the following concerning this issue: 'A man of words and not of deeds is like a garden full of seeds. A man of deeds and not of words is like a garden full of ... .' He was of course polite enough to omit the rhyme but the intent is clear (Japiske, 2003). It is this evident underlying divorce of perception and action to which Franklin rightly objects. Fairly obviously, the basic fracture comes from the unwarranted belief that one can view the world as a disconnected observer, independent of one's role as an actor. Indeed, the stereotype of the white-coated scientist derives from this very fallacy. While remnants of this notion of detached and dispassionate perusal persist today, such a fallacy is rapidly dissolving. In advocating for the Gibsonian emphasis on interaction, I have endeavoured to develop the argument that a philosophy of perception-action is the natural successor to the philosophical failures associated with the reification of language in the last century. A renewed philosophy of perception-action can find its prime expression in the emerging human-machine sciences, even though an explicit exposition remains underdeveloped at this time.

I know that there will be many who will, not unnaturally, be uncomfortable with the specific subject matter of torture (as indeed, I am myself uncomfortable with this subject matter). However, as Watson (1913) rightly noted, one cannot induce change without some degree of evident polarization. I am also sure that others will consider that certain of the present notions trespass over into the realms of politics and religion – both areas one is advised to avoid if one wishes to retain friends. And this is true; what I have raised here very much impinges upon these areas of the human enterprise; but then, for good or bad, so does technology. If we are not concerned with these more important interfaces of where individuals and groups meet with technology at the most important parts of their lives then what is the HF/E branch of science to represent? I, for one, refuse to see those involved in the science of human-machine systems simply as handmaids to technical systems or as a group of professionals who provide 'device advice' for an 'appliance science'.

At the start of the twentieth century, philosophy moved from its contemplation of history, memory, and logic toward the world of language. It became embroiled in a morass of relativity from which even now, it has largely failed to emerge. In our current academic institutions, philosophy has fallen from a place of honour to a minor and diminishing twilight existence. Treated as an arcane and 'unnecessary' subject in an ever-more pragmatic world, philosophy as an independent subject persistently hangs on while formal departments grow weaker or are actually abandoned. This is a tragic error, for this is to confuse the current state of the art with the value of the enterprise. At heart, we are all philosophers. Whether we are explicitly aware of it or not, we all hold philosophical positions in respect of the world around us. That the current academic philosophical perspective has apparently stagnated is a tragedy, but not an unrecoverable one. In formal terms, the fascination of philosophy with language was a turning away from its centuries old progression as the meta-study of cognition. From the empiricist focus on sensation and perception, through the Hegelian emphasis on memory to the Frege and Russell focus on logic and thus decision-making, philosophy was progressing along a line that any cognitive scientist would immediately recognize as a map of the stages of information-processing. The detour into language was one which was unfortunate but one we can now amend by beginning to base progress on the response facets of behaviour. In terms of action systems and motor control, the great insight was that of Gibson of the interlocking and inseparable dependence of perception and action. It is why we can now develop a philosophy of perception-action relations.

However, this is not enough. Our current world is one of ever more pragmatic action, driven by technological innovation. Since much of technology is only direct extensions of this perception-action linkage, the hope exists that such a philosophical renaissance based upon this latter pragmatism is now possible. But what I have indicated here is that such a step is necessary but not sufficient. It is not enough to possess the effective powers of gods if we do not have the moral capacities to temper them. In seeking a beginning to morality by design, we must acknowledge the pervasive, but as I have indicated, subtle influences of morality on technology. That is, on mind and machine. This book provides no easy, facile solutions. I suggest no easy answer will ever be forthcoming (Pirsig, 1991). But if we in HF/E are to be anything more than technological dilettantes, and if we collectively as a species intentionally seek to survive, it is an effort we must embrace – and quickly.

Permissions

Permission to reproduce the following material is gratefully appreciated. For 'Convergent Technological Evolution', The Future of Function Allocation', and 'The Future of Work', each of which originally appeared in *Ergonomics in Design*, the Human Factors and Ergonomics Society. For 'The Sheepdog and the Japanese Garden', Springer-Verlag. For 'Teleology for Technology', 'On Human Factors', and 'Men Without Machines', Lawrence Erlbaum. I am grateful for each of the publishers' agreement to reproduce these works. Although each of the chapters is based upon one or more previous works, many have had added amendments including in some cases, considerable change.

Chapter 1, 'The Science of Human Factors', is based on an earlier work entitled 'On Human Factors' which appeared in J. Flach, P.A. Hancock, J.K. Caird and K. Vincente, (eds) (1995) *Global Perspectives of the Ecology of Human-Machine Systems* (Hillsdale, NJ: Lawrence Erlbaum).

Chapter 2, 'Teleology for Technology', is based on an earlier chapter of the same title which appeared as Hancock, P.A. (1996) 'Teleology for Technology', in: R. Parasuraman and M. Mouloua (eds) *Automation and Human Performance: Theory and Applications* (Hillsdale, NJ: Lawrence Erlbaum).

Chapter 3, 'On Convergent Technological Evolution', is based on an earlier work which appeared in 1996 in *Ergonomics in Design* 4:1, 22–9.

Chapter 4 is derived from the paper 'The Future of Function Allocation', which appeared in *Ergonomics in Design* as Hancock, P.A. and Scallen, S.F. (1996) 'The Future of Function Allocation', *Ergonomics in Design* 4:4, 24–9.

Chapter 5 is derived from 'The Future of Hybrid Human-Machine Systems', which appeared in J.D. Wise, V.D. Hopkin and P. Stager (eds) (1993) *Verification and Validation of Complex Systems: Human Factors Issues* (Berlin: Springer-Verlag).

Chapter 6 is derived from the paper 'On the Future of Work', which appeared in 1997 in *Ergonomics in Design* 5:4, 25–9.

Chapter 7 is derived from 'Men Without Machines' which appeared in M. Mouloua and J. Koonce (eds) *Human-Automation Interaction: Research and Practice* (Mahwah, NJ: Lawrence Erlbaum).

Chapter 8, 'Life, Liberty and the Design of Happiness', began life as Hancock, P.A. (1999) 'Life, Liberty and the Design of Happiness' in M. Scerbo and M. Mouloua (eds) *Automation, Technology, and Human Performance: Current Research and Trends* (pp. 42–7) (Mahwah, NJ: Lawrence Erlbaum). The chapter has changed considerably from that earlier version.

Chapter 9, 'Mind, Machine and Morality', began life as Hancock, P.A. (2003) 'The ergonomics of torture: The moral dimension of evolving human-machine technology', *Proceedings of the Human Factors and Ergonomics Society* 47, 1009–11. As can be seen, the chapter has evolved from that early beginning.

References

Amnesty International (2005). <http://web.amnesty.org>.

Anderson, A.R. (ed.) (1964). *Minds and Machines*. Upper Saddle River, NJ: Prentice-Hall.

Akins, K. (1993). What is it like to be boring and myopic? In: B. Dahlbom (eds) *Dennett and his Critics*. Oxford: Blackwell.

Ashby, E. (1958). *Technology and the Academics: An Essay on Universities and the Scientific Revolution*. London: Macmillan.

Asimov, I. (1950). *I, Robot*. New York: Doubleday.

Aurelius, M. (1964). *To Himself: Meditations* (trans. M. Staniforth). London: Penguin. (Written in 120.)

Bainbridge, L. (1983). Ironies of automation. *Automatica*, 19, 775–9.

Bedini, S.A. (1964). The role of automata in the history of technology. *Technology and Culture*, 5 (1), 24–42.

Bekey, G.A. (1970). The human operator in control systems. In: K.B. DeGreene (ed.) *Systems Psychology*. New York: McGraw-Hill.

Bennett, C.H. and Landauer, R. (1985). The fundamental physical limits of computation. *Scientific American*, 253, 48–56.

Bennett, K.B. and Flach, J.M. (1992). Graphical displays: Implications for divided attention, focused attention and problem solving. *Human Factors,* 34, 513–33.

Bennett, V. (2007). *Portrait of an Unknown Woman*. New York: HarperCollins.

Beringer, D.B. and Hancock, P.A. (1989). Exploring situational awareness: A review of the effects of stress on rectilinear normalization. *Proceedings of the International Symposium on Aviation Psychology*, 5, 646–51.

Billings, C.E. (1989). Toward a human-centered aircraft automation philosophy. In: R.S. Jensen (ed.) *Proceedings of the Fifth International Symposium on Aviation Psychology*. Columbus, OH: Ohio State University Department of Aviation.

Billings, C.E. and Woods, D.D. (1994). Concerns about adaptive automation in aviation systems. In: M. Mouloua and R. Parasuraman (eds) *Human Performance in Automated Systems: Current Research and Trends*. Hillsdale, NJ: Erlbaum.

Birmingham, H.P. and Taylor, F.V. (1954). A design philosophy for man-machine control systems. *Proceedings of the IRE,* 42, 1748–58.

Booch, G. (1991). *Object Oriented Design with Applications*. Redwood City, CA: Benjamin Cummings.

Brand, I. (1975). *Port Arthur 1830–1877*. Launceston, Tasmania: Regal Publications.

Brand, I. (1978). *Escape from Port Arthur*. Launceston, Tasmania: Regal Publications.

Brand, I. (1979). *The 'Seperate' or 'Model' Prison, Port Arthur*. Launceston, Tasmania: Regal Publications.

Brand, I. (1990). *Sarah Island*. Launceston, Tasmania: Regal Publications.

Broadbent, D. (1993). (ed.) *The Simulation of Human Intelligence*. Oxford: Blackwell.

Bronowski, J. (1958). *William Blake*. London: Cox and Wyman Ltd.

Bronowski, J. (1973). *The Ascent of Man*. Little, Brown and Company: Boston.

Bronowski, J. (1978a). *The Common Sense of Science*. Cambridge, MA: Harvard University Press.

Bronowski, J. (1978b). *Magic, Science, and Civilization*. New York: Columbia University Press.

Budiansky, S. (2000). *The Truth about Dogs*. New York: Penguin.

Butler, R. (1975). *The Men that God Forgot*. London: Hutchinson.

Butler, S. (1872). *Erewhon or Over the Range*. London: Trubner.

Caird, J.K. and Hancock, P.A. (2002). Contributing factors to left turn and gap acceptance crashes. In: R.E. Dewar and P. Olson (eds) *Human Factors in Traffic Safety*. Tucson, AZ: Lawyers & Judges Publishing.

Calasso, R. (1994). *The Marriage of Cadmus and Harmony*. New York: Vintage Books.

Capek, K. (1923). *RUR (Rossums Universal Robots)*. Oxford: Oxford University Press.

Card, S.K. (1989). Human factors and artificial intelligence. In: P.A. Hancock and M.H. Chignell (eds) *Intelligent Interfaces: Theory, Research, and Design*. Amsterdam: North-Holland.

Carmody, J., Harder, K. and Hancock, P.A. (2000). Designing safer transportation environments. Paper presented at the 31st Annual meeting of the Environmental Design Research Association. San Francisco, CA, May.

Carter, J. (2005). *Our Endangered Values: America's moral crisis*. New York: Simon & Schuster.

Chapanis, A. (1965). On the allocation of functions between men and machines. *Occupational Psychology*, 39, 1–11.

Chapanis, A. (1970). Human factors in systems engineering. In: K.B. DeGreene (ed.) *Systems Psychology*. New York: McGraw Hill.

Chignell, M.H. and Hancock, P.A. (1989). Intelligent interfaces. In: M. Helander (ed.) *Handbook of Human-computer Interaction*. Amsterdam: North-Holland.

Chignell, M.H., Loewenthal, A. and Hancock, P.A. (1985). Intelligent interface design. *Proceedings of the IEEE International Conference on Systems, Man and Cybernetics*. Piscataway, NJ: IEEE.

Corkindale, K.G. (1971). Man-machine allocation in military systems. In: W. Singleton, R.S. Easterby, and D.C. Whitfield (eds) *The Human Operator in Complex Systems*. London: Taylor & Francis.

Craik, K.J.W. (1947a). Theory of the human operator in control systems. I: The operator as an engineering system. *British Journal of Psychology*, 38, 56–61.

Craik, K.J.W. (1947b). Theory of the human operator in control systems. II: Man as an element in a control system. *British Journal of Psychology*, 38, 142–8.

Csikszentmihalyi, M. (1990). *Flow: The psychology of optimal experience*. New York: Harper.

De Cortis, F. (1988). Dimension temporelle de l'activité cognitive lors des démarrages de systèmes complexes. *Le Travail Human*, 51, 1215–38.

Defanti, T., Sandin, D. and Cruz-Neira, C. (1993). A 'Room' with a 'View'. *IEEE Spectrum*, October, 30–3.

Dekker, S.W.A. (2003). Illusions of explanation: A critical essay on error classification. *International Journal of Aviation Psychology*, 13 (2), 95–106.

Dekker, S.W.A. and Woods, D.D. (2002). MABA-MABA or abracadabra? Progress on human automation coordination. *Cognition, Technology and Work*, 4, 240–4.

Dennett, D.C. (1991). *Consciousness Explained*. Boston: Little, Brown and Co.

Dirkin, G.R. and Hancock, P.A. (1984). Attentional narrowing to the visual periphery under temporal and acoustic stress. *Aviation, Space and Environmental Medicine*, 55, 457.

Easterbrook, J.A. (1959). The effect of emotion on cue utilization and the organization of behavior. *Psychological Review*, 56, 183–201.

Eiseley, L. (1960). *The Firmament of Time*. New York: MacMillan.

Eiseley, L. (1973). *The Man Who Saw Through Time*. New York: Scribner.

Fischer, C.S. (1994). *America Calling: A Social History of the Telephone to 1940*. Berkeley: University of California Press.

Fitts, P.M. (ed.) (1951) *Human Engineering for an Effective Air Navigation and Traffic Control system*. Washington, DC: National Research Council.

Fitts, P.M. (1954). The information capacity of the human motor system in controlling the amplitude of movement. *Journal of Experimental Psychology*, 47, 381–91.

Fjermedal, G. (1986). *The Tommorrow Makers*. Washington, DC: Tempus.

Flach, J. (1994). *Going with the Flow*. Personal communication.

Flach, J.M. (1989). The ecology of human-machine systems. Technical Report, Engineering Psychology Research Report, EPRL-89-12. Urbana, IL: University of Illinois.

Flach, J.M. and Bennett, K.B. (1992). Graphical interfaces to complex systems: Separating the wheat from the chaff. *Proceedings of the Human Factors Society*, 36, 470–4.

Flach, J.M. and Dominguez, C.O. (1995). Use-centered design: Integrating the user, instrument, and goal. *Ergonomics in Design*, July, 19–24.

Flach, J.M., Hancock, P.A., Caird, J.K. and Vicente, K. (1995). (eds) *Global Approaches to the Ecology of Human-machine Systems*. Hillsdale, NJ: Erlbaum.

Flach, J.M. and Hoffman, R.R. (2003). The limitations of limitations. *IEEE Intelligent Systems* (January/February), 94–7.

Flach, J.M. and Vicente, K.J. (1989). *Complexity, Difficulty, Direct Manipulation and Direct Perception*. Engineering Psychology Research Laboratory Report 89-03. Urbana, IL: University of Illinois.

Flink, J.J. (1975). *The Car Culture*. Cambridge, MA: MIT Press..

Ford, H. and Crowther, S. (1922). *My Life and Work*. Garden City, NJ: Doubleday.

Fraser, J.T. (ed.) (1966). *The Voices of Time*. New York: Braziller.

Fraser, J.T. (2007). The integrated study of time: A call for reciprocal literacy. *Time's News*, 38 (February), pp. 1, 14–15.

Freeth, T., et al. (2006). Decoding the ancient Greek astronomical calculator known as the Antikythera Mechanism. *Nature*, 444 (30 November), 587–91.

Fuld, R.B. (1993). The fiction of function allocation. *Ergonomics in Design* (January), 20–24.

Garrett, G. (1925). *Ouroborous or the Mechanical Extension of Mankind*. New York: E.P. Dutton.

Gibson, J.J. (1966). *The Senses Considered as Perceptual Systems*. Boston: Houghton Mifflin.

Gibson, J.J. (1975). Events are perceivable but time is not. In: J.T. Fraser and N. Lawrence (eds) *The Study of Time II*. Berlin: Springer-Verlag.

Gibson, J.J. (1979). *The Ecological Approach to Vision Perception*. Hillsdale, NJ: Lawrence Erlbaum.

Gibson, J.J. and Crooks, L.E. (1938). A theoretical field analysis of automobile driving. *American Journal of Psychology*, 51, 453–71.

Gladwell, M. (2008). *Outliers*. New York: Little, Brown and Co.

Gleick, J. (1988). *Chaos*. London: Heinemann.

Goldberg, M.H. (1984). *The Blunder Book*. New York: William Morrow.

Goldiez, B., Ahmad, A.M. and Hancock, P.A. (2007). Effects of augmented reality display settings on human way-finding performance. *IEEE Transactions on Systems, Man, and Cybernetics, Part C: Applications and Reviews*, 37 (5), 839–45.

Gooddy, W. (1988). *Time and the Nervous System*. New York: Praeger.

Gould, S.J. (1980). *The Panda's Thumb: More Reflections in Natural History*. New York: W.W. Norton.

Gould, S.J. (1999). *Rocks of Ages: Science and Religion in the Fullness of Life*. New York: Ballantine.

Greenlaw, J. (1999). *Longcase Clocks*. Princes Risborough, England: Shire Publications.

Gregory, R. L (1981). *Mind in Science*. London: Penguin.

Haddon, W. (1970). On the escape of tigers: An ecologic note. *Technology Review*, 72, 44–7.

Hamilton, J.E. and Hancock, P.A. (1986). Robotics safety: Exclusion guarding for industrial operations. *Journal of Occupational Accidents*, 8, 69–78.

Han, S.H. and Hong, S.W. (2003). A systematic approach for coupling user satisfaction with product design. *Ergonomics*, 46 (13/14), 1441–61.

Hancock, P.A. (1991). On operator strategic behavior. *Proceedings of the International Symposium on Aviation Psychology*, 6, 999–1007.

Hancock, P.A. (1993). Body temperature influences on duration estimation. *Journal of General Psychology*, 120, 197–216.

Hancock, P.A. (1999). On Monday, I am an Optimist. *Human Factors and Ergonomics Society Bulletin*, 42 (11), 1–2.

Hancock, P.A. (2000a). Can technology cure stupidity. *Human Factors and Ergonomics Society Bulletin*, 43 (1), 1–4.

Hancock, P.A. (2000b). Is truth soluble in politics. *Human Factors and Ergonomics Society Bulletin*, 43 (4), 1–4.

Hancock, P.A. (2002). The time of your life. *Kronoscope*, 2 (2), 135–65.

Hancock, P.A. (2003). Individuation: Not merely human-centered but person-specific design. Paper presented at the Panel on Considering the Importance of Individual Differences in Human Factors Research: No Longer Simply Confounding Noise at the 47th Annual Meeting of the Human Factors and Ergonomics Society, Denver, October.

Hancock, P.A. (2005). Time and the privileged observer. *Kronoscope*, 5 (2), 177–91.

Hancock, P.A. (2007). On time and the origin of the theory of evolution. *Kronoscope*, 6 (2), 192–203.

Hancock, P.A. (2009). The future of simulation. In: D. Vincenzi, J. Wise, M. Mouloua, and P.A. Hancock (eds) *Human Factors in Simulation and Training*. Boca Raton, FL: CRC Press, Taylor & Francis.

Hancock, P.A. and Chignell, M.H. (1987). Adaptive control in human-machine systems. In: P.A. Hancock (ed.) *Human Factors Psychology*. Amsterdam: North-Holland.

Hancock, P.A. and Chignell, M.H. (1988). Mental workload dynamics in adaptive interface design. *IEEE Transactions on Systems, Man, and Cybernetics*, 18, 647–58.

Hancock, P.A. and Chignell, M.H. (eds) (1989). *Intelligent Interfaces: Theory, research, and design*. Amsterdam: North-Holland.

Hancock, P.A., Chignell, M.H. and Loewenthal, A. (1985). An adaptive human-machine system. *Proceedings of the IEEE International Conference on Systems, Man and Cybernetics*, 627–30.

Hancock, P.A. and de Ridder, S. (2003). Behavioral response in accident-likely situations. *Ergonomics*, 46 (12), 1111–35.

Hancock, P.A., Dewing, W.L. and Parasuraman, R. (1993). A driver-centered system architecture for intelligent-vehicle highway systems. *Ergonomics in Design*, 2, 12–15, 35–9.

Hancock, P.A. and Diaz, D. (2001). Ergonomics as a foundation for a science of purpose. *Theoretical Issues in Ergonomic Science*, 3 (2), 115–23.

Hancock, P.A., Flach, J., Caird, J. and Vicente, K. (eds) (1995) *Local Applications of the Ecology of Human-machine Systems*. New Jersey: Lawrence Erlbaum.

Hancock, P.A. and Hancock, G.M. (2008). Is there a super-hero in all of us? In: R.S. Rosenberg and J. Canzoneri (eds) *The Psychology of Super-heroes*. Dallas, TX: Benbella Books.

Hancock, P.A., Hendrick, H.W., Hornick, R. and Paradis, P. (2006). Human factors issues in the design and operation of firearms. *Ergonomics in Design*, 14 (1), 5–11.

Hancock, P.A., Hurt, H.H., Jr., Ouellet, J.V. and Thom, D.R. (1986). Failures of driver sustained attention in the etiology of motorcycle-automobile collision. *Proceedings of the Annual Meeting of the Human Factors Association of Canada*. Vancouver, Canada.

Hancock, P.A. and Meshkati, N. (eds) (1988). *Human Mental Workload*. Amsterdam: North-Holland.

Hancock, P.A., Mouloua, M. and Senders, J.W. (2008). On the philosophical foundations of driving distraction and the distracted driver. In: M.A. Regan, J.D. Lee and K.L. Young (eds) *Driver Distraction: Theory, Effects and Mitigation*. Boca Raton, FL: CRC Press.

Hancock, P.A. and Newell, K.M. (1985). The movement speed-accuracy relationship in space-time. In: H. Heuer, U. Kleinbeck and K.H. Schmidt (eds) *Motor Behavior: Programming, Control and Acquisition*. Berlin: Springer.

Hancock, P.A., Pepe, A. and Murphy, L.L. (2005). Hedonomics: The power of positive and pleasurable ergonomics. *Ergonomics in Design*, 13 (1), 8–14.

Hancock, P.A. and Scallen, S.F. (1996). The future of function allocation. *Ergonomics in Design*, 4, 24–9.

Hancock, P.A. and Sheridan T.B. (2008). The future of driving simulation. In: Fisher, D., Lee, J., Caird, J., and Rizzo, M. (eds) *Handbook of Driving Simulation for Engineering, Medicine and Psychology*. Boca Raton, FL: CRC Press.

Hancock, P.A., Simmons, L., Hashemi, L., Howarth, H. and Ranney, T. (1999). The effects of in-vehicle distraction upon driver response during a crucial driving maneuver. *Transportation Human Factors*, 1, 295–309.

Hancock, P.A., Szalma, J.L. and Oron-Gilad, T. (2005). Time, emotion, and the limits to human information processing. In: D. McBride and D. Schmorrow (eds) *Quantifying Human Information Processing*. Boulder, CO: Lexington Books.

Hancock, P.A. and Warm, J.S. (1989). A dynamic model of stress and sustained attention. *Human Factors*, 31, 519–37.

Hansen, J.P. (1995). Representation of system invariants by optical invariants in configural displays for process control. In: P.A. Hancock, J. Flach, J. Caird and K. Vicente (eds) *Local Applications of the Ecology of Human-machine Systems*. Hillsdale, NJ: Lawrence Erlbaum.

Hardy, R. (1990). *Callback*. Washington, DC: Smithsonian Institution Press.

Harper's Weekly (1899). The status of the horse at the end of the century. *Harper's Weekly*, 43, 1172.

Harris, W.C., Hancock, P.A., Arthur E. and Caird, J.K. (1991). Automation influences and performance, workload, and fatigue. *Human Factors Research*

Laboratory, Technical Report, 91-N01. Minneapolis, MN: University of Minnesota.

Hekkert, P., Snelder, D. and van Wieringer, P. (2003). 'Most advanced, yet acceptable': Typicality and novelty as joint predictors of aesthetic preference in industrial design. *British Journal of Psychology*, 94, 111–24.

Helander, M.G. (2002). Hedonomics: Affective human factors design. *Proceedings of the Human Factors and Ergonomics Society*, 46, 978–82.

Helander, M.G., Khalid, M. and Tham, M.P. (eds) (2001). *Affective Human Factors Design*. London: Asean Academic Press.

Helander, M.G. and Tham, M.P. (2003) Hedonomics: Affective human factors design. *Ergonomics*, 46 (13/14), 1269–72.

Hendrick, H. (1987). Macroergonomics. In: P.A. Hancock (ed.) *Human Factors Psychology*. Amsterdam: North-Holland.

Hepper, J. and Hepper, K. (1984). *The Gordon River Book*. Hobart: Mercury Walch.

Herzberg, F. (1966). *Work and the Nature of Man*. Cleveland, OH: World Publishing Company.

Hoc, J-M. (1995). Planning in diagnosing a slow process. *Zeitschrift für Psychologie*, 203, 111–15.

Hoffman, R.R. (1990). Remote perceiving: A step toward a unified science of remote sensing. *Geocarto International*, 2, 3–13.

Hoffman, R.R., Bradshaw, J.M., Hayes, P.J. and Ford, K.M. (2003). The Borg hypothesis. *IEEE Intelligent Systems*, September/October, 73–5.

Hoffman, R.R. and Deffenbacher, K.A. (1993). An ecological analysis of the relations of basic and applied science. *Ecological Psychology*, 5, 315–52.

Hoffman, R., Hancock, P.A., Ford, K. and Hayes, P. (2002) The triples rule. *IEEE Intelligent Systems*, 17 (3), 62–5.

Hoffman, R.R. and Hayes. P.J. (2004). The pleasure principle. *IEEE Intelligent Systems*, 19 (1), 86–8.

Hoffman, R.R. and Yates, J.F. (2005). Decision (?) making (?). *IEEE Intelligent Systems*, July/August, 76–83.

Holland, J.F., Leary, J.J. and Sweeley, C.C. (1986). Advanced instrumentation and strategies for metabolic profiling. *Journal of Chromatography*, 379, 3–26

Holland, J.H. (1992). *Adaptation in Natural and Artificial Systems*. Cambridge: MIT Press (first published by the University of Michigan, 1975).

Hollnagel, E. (1993). The art of efficient man-machine interaction: Improving the coupling between man and machine. In: J-M. Hoc., P.C. Cacciabue and E. Hollnagel (eds) *Expertise and Technology*. Mahwah, NJ: Lawrence Erlbaum.

Hopkin, V.D. (1988). Air traffic control. In: E.L. Wiener and D.C. Nagel (eds) *Human Factors in Aviation*. San Diego, CA: Academic Press Inc.

Hughes, R. (1987). *The Fatal Shore*. London: Random House.

Hume, D. (1739). *An Enquiry concerning Human Understanding: A critical Edition*. John Noon, at the White Hart, near Mercer's Chapel in Cheapside, London.

Hurt, H.H.Jr., Ouellet, J.V. and Thom, D.R. (1981). *Final Report: Motorcycle Accident Cause Factors and Identification of Countermeasures*. DOT HS-805 862, DOT-NHTSA. Washington, DC: National Highway Traffic Safety Administration.

Hutchins, E. (1994). *Representation*. Paper presented at the Department of Psychology, University of Minnesota, Minneapolis, MN.

Iberall, A.S. (1992). Does intention have a characteristic fast time scale? *Ecological Psychology*, 4, 39–61.

Illich, I. (1973). *Tools for Conviviality*. New York: Harper and Row.

Jacob, R.J.K. (1989). Direct manipulation in the intelligent interface. In: P.A. Hancock and M.H. Chignell (eds) *Intelligent Interfaces: Theory, Research and Design*. Amsterdam: North-Holland.

Jacob, R.J.K., Egeth, H.E. and Bevon, W. (1976). The face as a data display. *Human Factors*, 18, 189–200.

James, W. (1890). *Principles of Psychology*. New York: Holt.

Japikse, C. (2003). *Fart Proudly: Writings of Benjamin Franklin You Never Read in School*. Berkeley, CA: Frog Limited: Berkeley.

Jastrzebowski, W.B. (2000). *An Outline of Ergonomics, or the Science of Work*. Warsaw: Central Institute for Labour Protection. (First published in 1857.)

Jenkins, J.J. (1978). Four points to remember: A tetrahedral model of memory experiments. In: L. Cermak and F. Craik (eds) *Levels of Processing and Human Memory*. Hillsdale, NJ: Erlbaum.

Jordan, N. (1963). Allocation of functions between man and machines in automated systems. *Journal of Applied Psychology*, 47, 161–5.

Jordan, P.W. (2000). The four pleasures: A framework for pleasure in design. In: P.W. Jordan (ed.) *Proceedings of the Conference on Pleasure Based Human Factors Design*. Groningen, The Netherlands: Phillips Design.

Julen, H. (1976). *The Penal Settlement of Macquarie Harbor*. Launceston, Tasmania: Regal Publications.

Kant, I. (1787). *The Critique of Pure Reason*. Riga: Hartnocht.

Kantowitz, B.H. (1989). Interfacing human and machine intelligence. In: P.A. Hancock and M.H. Chignell (eds) *Intelligent Interfaces: Theory, Research, and Design*. Amsterdam: North Holland.

Kantowitz, B.H. and Sorkin, R.D. (1987). Allocation of functions. In: G. Salvendy (ed.) *Handbook of Human Factors*. New York: Wiley.

Karasek, R.A. (1979). Job demands, job decision latitude and mental strain: Implications for job redesign. *Administrative Science Quarterly*, 24, 285–308.

Kauffman, S.A. (1993). *The Origins of Order: Self-organization and Selection in Evolution*. Oxford: Oxford University Press.

Karwowski, W. (2000). Symvatology: The science of an artifact-human compatibility. *Theoretical Issues in Ergonomic Science*, 1, 76–91.

Khalid, H.M. (2004). Conceptualizing affective human factors design. *Theoretical Issues in Ergonomic Science,* 5 (1), 1–3.

Kirlik, A. (1995). Requirements for psychological models to support design: Towards ecological task analysis. In: J.M. Flach, P.A. Hancock, J.K. Caird, and K.J. Vicente (eds) *Global Perspectives on the Ecology of Human Machine Systems*. Hillsdale, NJ: Erlbaum.

Klein, G. (2007). Flexecution as a paradigm for replanning. *IEEE Intelligent Systems*, September/October, 79–83.

Klein, G.A., Orasanu, J., Calderwood, R. and Zsambok, C.E. (1993). *Decision Making in Action: Models and Methods*. Norwood, NJ: Ablex Publishing Co.

Koestler, A. (1964). *The Act of Creation*. New York: Hutchinson.

Koestler, A. (1972). *The Roots of Coincidence*. New York: Vintage Books.

Koestler, A. (1973). *The Sleepwalkers: A History of Man's Changing Vision of the Universe*. New York: Hutchinson.

Koestler, A. (1978). *Janus: A Summing Up*. New York: Vintage Books.

Kozak, J.J., Hancock, P.A., Chrysler, S. and Arthur, E. (1993). Transfer of training from virtual reality. *Ergonomics*, 36, 777–84.

Krippendorff, K. (2004). Intrinsic motivation and human-centered design. *Theoretical Issues in Ergonomic Science,* 5 (1), 43–71. Kugler, P.N. and Turvey, M.T. (1987). *Information, Natural Law, and the Self-assembly of Rhythmic Movement*. Hillsdale, NJ: Lawrence Erlbaum.

Kurtz, P. (1992). *The New Skepticism: Inquiry and Reliable Knowledge*. Buffalo: NY: Prometheus Books.

Kurtz, P. (1994). The new skepticism. *Skeptical Inquirer*, 18, 134–41.

Kurzweil, R. (2005). *The Singularity is Near*. New York: Penguin.

Laney, J. (1989). *Wreck's at Hell's Gates*. Portarlington, Australia: Marine History Publications.

Lashley, K.S. (1951). On the problem of serial order in behavior. In: L.A. Jeffress (ed.) *Cerebral Mechanisms of Behavior*. New York: Wiley.

Lee, J. and Moray, N. (1992). Trust, control strategies and allocation of function in human-machine systems. *Ergonomics*, 35, 1243–70.

Lennox, G. (1996). *A Visitor's Guide to Port Arthur and the Convict Systems*. Tasmania: Rossetta.

Lewin, R. (1992). *Complexity: Life at the Edge of Chaos*. New York: Macmillan.

Licklider, J.C.R. (1960). Man-computer symbiosis. *IRE Transactions on Human Factors in Electronics*, HFE-1, 4–11.

Liu, Y. (2003) The aesthetic and the ethic dimensions of human factors and design. *Ergonomics,* 46 (13/14), 1293–305.

Locke, J. (1959). *An Essay concerning Human Understanding*. New York: Dover. (First published in 1690.)

Loomis, J.M. (1992). Distal attribution and presence. *Presence*, 1, 113–19.

MacDonald, A.S. (2003). Affective technology and affective human factors design in an era of rapid technological change. Proceedings of the XVth Triennial Congress of the International Ergonomics Association and the 7th Joint Conference of Ergonomics Society of Korea/Japan Ergonomics Society. Seoul, Korea, 24–29 August.

MacDonald, P.S. (2002). Descartes: The lost episodes. *Journal of the History of Philosophy*, 40 (4), 437–60.

Mackworth, N.H. (1961). Researches on the measurement of human performance. In: H.W. Sinaiko (ed.) *Selected Papers on Human Factors in the Design and Use of Control Systems*. New York: Dover. (Reprinted from: Medical Research Council Special Report Series No. 268. London: HM Stationery Office, 1950.)

Malthus, T.R. (1798). *An Essay on the Principle of Population, as it Affects the Future Improvement of Society with Remarks on the Speculations of Mr. Godwin, M. Condorcet, and other Writers*. London: J. Johnson.

Maslow, A.H. (1954). *Motivation and Personality*. New York: Harper and Row (revised edition published by R. Frager in 1987).

Maslow, A.H. (1964). *Religions, Values, and Peak Experiences*. New York: Penguin.

McConica, J. (1991). *Erasmus*. Oxford: Oxford University Press.

McCorduck, P. (1979). *Machines who Think*. New York: Freeman.

McCormick, E.J. and Sanders, M.S. (1982). *Human Factors in Engineering and Design*. New York: McGraw-Hill.

McCulloch, J. and Simmons, A. (1992). *Ghosts of Port Arthur*. Port Arthur, Tasmania: A.D. Simmons.

McCulloch, J. and Simmons, A. (1993). *A Guide to Port Arthur*. Port Arthur, Tasmania: A.D. Simmons.

McIlwain, J. (1998). *Dungeons and Torture*. Norwich, England: Jarrold.

McKibben, W. (1989). *The End of Nature*. New York: Random House.

McPhee, J. (1989). *The Control of Nature*. New York: Farrar Straus Giroux.

Meister, D. (1985). *Behavioral Analysis and Measurement Methods*. New York: Wiley.

Minkowski, H. (1923). Space and time. In: H.A. Lorentz, A. Einstein, H. Minkowski. and H. Weyl (eds) *The Principles of Relativity*. London: Dover. (Originally delivered as an address at the 80th Assembly of German Natural Scientists and Physicians. Cologne, Germany, 21 September 1908.)

Minsky, M. (1985). *The Society of Mind*. New York: Simon and Schuster.

Moore, G.E. (1965). Cramming more components onto integrated circuits. *Electronics*, 38 (8), April, 19.

Moore, M. (2001). *Stupid White Men*. New York: Regan Books.

Moravec, H. (1988). *Mind Children: The Future of Robot and Human Intelligence*. Cambridge, MA: Harvard University Press.

Moray, N. (1986). Monitoring behavior and supervisory control. In: K.R. Boff, L. Kaufman and J.P. Thomas (eds) *Handbook of Perception and Human Performance*, Vol. II. New York: Wiley.

Moray, N. (1990). Application of human factors to identified world problems. Plenary Address to the Fifth Mid-Central Ergonomics/Human-Factors Conference. Dayton, OH, May.

Moray, N. (1993). Technosophy and humane factors. *Ergonomics in Design,* 1, 33–7, 39.

Moray, N. (1994). Ergonomics and the global problems of the 21st century. Keynote address given at the 12th Triennial Congress of the International Ergonomics Association, Toronto, August.

Moray, N.P. and Hancock, P.A. (2009). Minkowski spaces as models of human-machine communication. *Theoretical Issues in Ergonomic Science,* in press.

Moray, N., Lee, J., Vicente, K.J., Jones, B.G. and Rasmussen, J. (1994). A direct perception interface for nuclear power plants. *Proceedings of the Human Factors and Ergonomics Society,* 38, 481–5.

Moray, N. (1995). Ergonomics and the global problems of the twenty-first century. *Ergonomics,* 38 (8), 1691–707.

More, T. (1965). *Utopia.* New York: Washington Square Press. (First published in 1516.)

Morrison, P., Morrison, P., Eames, C. and Eames, R. (1982). *Powers of Ten: About the Relative Size of Things in the Universe.* New York: Scientific American Library.

Murphy, L.L., Stanney K. and Hancock, P.A. (2003). The effect of affect: The hedonomic evaluation of human-computer interaction. *Proceedings of the Human Factors and Ergonomics Society,* 47, 764–7.

Mutter, S. (1993). *Surrational Images.* Corte Madera, CA: Portal Publications.

Nagel, T. (1974). What is it like to be a bat? *The Philosophical Review,* 83 (4), 435–50.

Nagge, J.W. (1932). Regarding the law of parsimony. *Journal of Genetic Psychology,* 41, 492–4.

Naimark, M. (1990). Realness and interactivity. In: B. Laurel (eds) *The Art of Human-computer Interface Design.* Reading, MA: Addison Wesley.

National Research Council (1997). *Tactical Displays for Soldiers.* Washington, DC: National Academy Press.

National Safety Council (1999). *Injury Facts.* Chicago, IL: National Safety Council.

Neisser, U. (1976). *Cognition and Reality.* San Francisco: Freeman

Newell, A. (1990). *Unified Theories of Cognition.* Cambridge, MA: Harvard University Press.

Newell, K.M. (1986). Constraints on the development of coordination. In: M.G. Wade and H.T.A Whiting (eds) *Motor Development in Children: Aspects of Coordination and Control.* Dordrecht: Martinus Nijhoff.

Newell, K.M. and Hancock, P.A. (1983). Space-time and motion study. *Proceedings of the Human Factors Society,* 27, 1044–8.

Nickerson, R.S. (1992). *Looking Ahead: Human Factors Challenges in a Changing World.* Hillsdale, NJ: Lawrence Erlbaum.

Norman, D.A. (1988). *The Psychology of Everyday Things.* New York: Basic Books.

Norman, D.A. (1991). Cognitive artifacts. In: J.M. Carroll (ed.) *Designing Interaction: Psychology at the Human-computer Interface*. Cambridge: Cambridge University Press.

Norman, D.A. (2004). *Emotional Design: Why Do We Love (or Hate) Everyday Things*. New York: Basic Books.

Oakley, K.P. (1949). *Man the Tool Maker*. London: British Museum.

Parasuraman, R. (1986). Vigilance, monitoring, and search. In: K.R. Boff., L. Kaufman. and J.P. Thomas (ed.) *Handbook of Perception and Human Performance*. New York: Wiley.

Parasuraman, R. (2003). Neuroergonomics: Research and practice. *Theoretical Issues in Ergonomics Science*, 4 (1–2), 5–20.

Parasuraman, R. and Davies, D.R. (1976). Decision theory analysis of response latencies in vigilance. *Journal of Experimental Psychology*, 2, 578–90.

Parasuraman, R., Molloy, R. and Singh, I. (1993). Performance consequences of automation-induced complacency. *International Journal of Aviation Psychology*, 3, 1–23.

Parasuraman, R. and Mouloua, M. (1995) (eds) *Automation and Human Performance*: *Theory and applications*. Hillsdale, NJ: Lawrence Erlbaum.

Parasuraman, R., Sheridan, T.B. and Wickens, C.D. (2008). Situation awareness, mental workload, and trust in automation: Viable, empirically supported cognitive engineering constructs. *Journal of Cognitive Engineering and Decision Making*, 2 (2), 140–60.

Pepperberg, I.M. (1999). *The Alex Studies: Cognitive and Communicative Abilities of Grey Parrots*. Cambridge, MA: Harvard University Press.

Perrow, C. (1984). *Normal Accidents: Living with High-risk Technologies*. New York: Basic Books.

Petroski, H. (1992). *The Evolution of Useful Things*. New York: Vintage.

Pirsig, R.M. (1974). *Zen and the Art of Motorcycle Maintenance: An Inquiry into Values*. London: Bodley Head.

Pirsig, R.M. (1991). *Lila: An Inquiry into Morals*. New York: Bantam.

Poppel, E. (1988). *Mindworks: Time and Conscious Experience*. Boston: Harcourt, Brace, and Jovanovich.

Porter, R. (ed.) (1988). *Man Masters Nature: Twenty-five Centuries of Science*. New York: Braziller.

Powers, W.T. (1974). *Behavior: The Control of Perception*. London: Wildwood House.

Powers, W. T. (1978). Quantitative analysis of purposive systems: Some spadework at the foundations of scientific psychology. *Psychological Review*, 85, 417–35.

Rahimi, M. and Hancock, P.A. (1986). Optimization of hybrid production systems: The interaction of robots into human-occupied work environments. In: O. Brown, Jr. and H. Hendrick (eds) *Human Factors in Organizational Design and Management II*. Amsterdam: North-Holland

Rasmussen, J. (1986). *Information Processing and Human-Machine Interaction: An Approach to Cognitive Engineering*. Amsterdam: North-Holland.

Raup, D.M. (1986). Biological extinction in earth history. *Science*, 231, 1528.

Raup, D.M. (1991). *Extinctions: Bad Genes or Bad Luck?* W.W. Norton: New York.

Reason, J. (1990). *Human Error*. Cambridge: Cambridge University Press.

Reed, E.S. (1988). *James J. Gibson and the Psychology of Perception*. New Haven: Yale University Press.

Reed, T.J. (1984). *Faust*. Oxford: Oxford University Press.

Ridley, J. (2001) *Bloody Mary's Martyrs*. New York: Caroll & Graf.

Rifkin, J. (1988). *Time Wars*. New York: Bantam.

Riley, V. (1994). *Human Use of Automation*. Unpublished doctoral dissertation. University of Minnesota, Minneapolis, MN.

Rousseau, J.J. (1972). *The Social Contract*. London: Penguin. First published 1752.

Rothenberg, D. (1993). *Hand's End: Technology and the Limits of Nature*. Berkeley, CA: University of California Press.

Russell, B. (1915). On the experience of time. *Monist*, 25, 212–33.

Russell, B. (1952). *The Impact of Science on Society*. New York: Allen and Unwin.

Russell, P. (1992). *The White Hole in Time*. San Francisco: Harper.

Ryley, G.S. (2003). *The History of Torture Throughout the Ages*. Columbia, SC: Columbia University Press.

Sabatini, R. (2003). *Torquemada and the Spanish Inquisition: A History*. New York: Kessinger Publishing.

Sagan, C. (1996). *The Demon-haunted World: Science as a Candle in the Dark*. New York: Random House.

Sagan, C. and Druyan, A. (1992). *Shadows of Forgotten Ancestors*. New York: Balantine.

Salvendy, G. (ed.) (1987). *Handbook of Human Factors*. New York: Wiley.

Sanquist, T.F. (2008). Human factors and energy use. *Human Factors and Ergonomics Society Bulletin*, 51 (11), 1–3.

Sawin, D.A. and Scerbo, M.W. (1993). Vigilance: Where has all the workload gone? *Proceedings of the Human Factors Society*, 37 (2), 1383–7.

Scerbo, M.W. (1995). Adaptive automation. In: M. Mouloua and R. Parasuraman (eds) *Automation and Human Performance*. Mahwah, NJ: Lawrence Erlbaum Associates.

Scerbo, M (1996). Theoretical perspectives on adaptive automation. In: R. Parasuraman and M. Mouloua (eds) *Automation and Human Performance*. Mahwah, NJ: Lawrence Erlbaum.

Schneider, W. (1985). Training high performance skills: Fallacies and guidelines. *Human Factors*, 27, 285–300.

Schneider, W. and Shiffrin, R.M. (1977). Controlled and automatic human information processing I: Detection, search, and visual attention. *Psychological Review*, 84, 1–66.

Schrodinger, E. (1944). *What is Life?* Cambridge: Cambridge University Press.

Schroots, J.J.F. and Birren, J.E. (1990). Concepts of time and aging in science. In: J.E. Birren and K.W. Schaie (eds) *Handbook of the Psychology of Aging*. San Diego, CA: Academic Press.

Scriven, M. (1953). The mechanical concept of mind. *Mind*, 62 (246), 230–40.

Searle, J. (1984). *Minds, Brains, and Science*. Cambridge, MA: Harvard University Press.

Sedgwick, J. (1993). The complexity problem. *The Atlantic Monthly*, March, 96–104.

Segal, L.D. (1994). Actions speak louder than words: How pilots use nonverbal information for crew communications. *Proceedings of the Human Factors and Ergonomics Society*, 38, 21–5.

Seligman, M.E.P. and Csiksentmihalyi, M. (2000). Positive psychology: An introduction. *American Psychologist,* 55 (1), 5–14.

Servan-Schreiber, J.L. (1988). *The Art of Time*. New York: Addison-Wesley.

Shakespeare, W. (1977). *Complete Works of William Shakespeare*. Secaucus, NJ: Historic Reprints, Inc. Book Sales: Secaucus, N.J. (As You Like It, Act II, scene, vii).

Sharit, J. (1988). Issues in modeling supervisory control in flexible manufacturing systems. In: W. Karwowski, H.R. Parsaei, and M.R. Wilhelm (eds) *Ergonomics of Hybrid Automated Systems*. Amsterdam: Elsevier.

Shaw, G.B. (1929). *Back to Methuselah: A metabiological pentateuch*. New York: Bretano's.

Shaw, R. and Kinsella-Shaw, J. (1988). Ecological mechanics: A physical geometry for intentional constraints. *Human Movement Science*, 7, 155–200.

Shelley, P.B. (1818). Ozymandias. *The Examiner*, 11 January.

Sheridan, T.B. (1990). Telerobotics. *Automatica*, 25, 487–507.

Sheridan, T.B. (2002). *Humans and Automation: Systems design and research issues*. Santa Monica, CA: Human Factors and Ergonomics Society.

Shneiderman, B. (1983). Direct manipulation: A step beyond programming. *IEEE Computer*, 16, 57–69.

Sidney, P. (1593). *The Countess of Pembroke's Arcadia*. London: Ponfonbie.

Simon, H.A. (1981). *The Science of the Artificial*, 2nd ed. Cambridge, MA: MIT Press.

Simon, C.W. (1987). Will egg-sucking ever become a science? *Human Factors Society Bulletin,* 30 (6), 1–4.

Smith, K.U. (1987). Origins of human factors science. *Human Factors Society Bulletin*, 30 (4), 1–3.

Smith, K. and Hancock, P.A. (1995). Situation awareness is adaptive, externally-directed consciousness. *Human Factors*, 37 (1), 137–48.

Snow, C.P. (1964). *The Two Cultures and a Second Look*. Cambridge: Cambridge University Press.

Sparrow, W.A. (1985). The efficiency of skilled performance. *Journal of Motor Behavior*, 15 (3), 237–61.

Steinbeck, J. (1952). *East of Eden*. New York: Viking Press.

Stevens, S.S. (1975). *Psychophysics: Introduction to its Perceptual, Neural, and Social Prospects*. New York: Wiley.

Stevenson, R.L. (1946). *Treasure Island*. London: Puffin. First published 1883.

Stoffregen, T.A. (2000). Affordances and events. *Ecological Psychology*, 12 (1), 1–28.

Stroud, J.M. (1955). The fine structure of psychological time. In: H. Quastler (ed.) *Information Theory in Psychology*. Glencoe, IL: Illinois Free Press.

Suedfeld, P. (2001). Applying positive psychology in the study of extreme environments. *Human Performance in Extreme Environments*, 6 (1), 21–5.

Swain, A.D. and Wohl, J.G. (1961). *Factors affecting Degree of Automation in Test and Checkout Equipment*. Stanford, CN: Dunlap & Associates.

Sweeley, C.C., Holland, J.F., Towson, D.S. and Chamberlin, B.A. (1987). Interactive and multi-sensory analysis of complex mixtures by an automated gas chromatography system. *Journal of Chromatography*, 399, 173–81.

Swenson, R. and Turvey, M.T. (1991). Thermodynamic reasons for perception-action cycles. *Ecological Psychology*, 3, 317–48.

Tattersall, A.J., (1990). Effects of system induced stress on total system performance. In: *Automation and Systems Issues in Air Traffic Control: Draft Papers*. Dayton, FL: NATO, Embry-Riddle Aeronautical University Printing Department.

Taylor, F.V. and Garvey, W.D. (1958). The limitations of a Procrustean approach to the optimization of man-machine systems. *Ergonomics*, 2, 187–94.

Teague, R.C. and Whitney, H.X. (2002). What's love got to do with it: Why emotions and aspirations matter in person-centered design. *User Experience*, 1 (3), 6–13.

Thomas, B. and McClelland, I. (1994). The development of a touch screen based communications terminal. *Proceedings of the Human Factors and Ergonomics Society*, 38, 175–9.

Thompson, J.M. and Stewart, H.B. (1986). *Nonlinear Dynamics and Chaos*. New York: Wiley.

Teilhard de Chardin, P. (1959). *The Phenomenon of Man*. New York: Harper and Row.

Tolkkinen, K. (1994) Machines are making us soft. *Minnesota Daily*, Thursday, 27 January.

Torczyner, H. (1979). *Magritte: the True Art of Painting*. Paris: Draeger.

Toulmin, S. and Goodfield, J. (1965). *The Discovery of Time*. New York: Harper and Row.

Turing, A.M. (1950). Computing machinery and intelligence. *Mind*, 59, 433–60.

Turvey, M.T. (1992). Affordances and prospective control: An outline of the ontology. *Ecological Psychology*, 4, 173–87.

Tzu, S. (1983). *The Art of War*. New York: Dell. (Originally published c.500 BC.)

Vallee, J. (1982). *The Network Revolution*. Berkeley, CA: And/Or Press.

Vicente, K.J. (1995). A few implications of an ecological approach to human factors. In: J.M. Flach, P.A. Hancock, J.K. Caird and K.J. Vicente (eds) *Global*

Perspectives on the Ecology of Human-Machine Systems. Hillsdale, NJ: Erlbaum: Hillsdale.

Vicente, K.J. (2004). *The Human Factor*. New York: Routledge.

Vicente, K.J. and Rasmussen, J. (1990). Ecology of human-machine systems II: Mediating 'direct perception' in complex work domains. *Ecological Psychology*, 2, 207–49.

Vicente, K.J. and Rasmussen, J. (1992). Ecological interface design: Theoretical foundations. *IEEE Transactions on Systems, Man, and Cybernetics*, 22, 589–606.

Vroon, P.A. (1974). Is there a quantum in duration experience. *American Journal of Psychology*, 87, 237–45.

Waddington, C.H. (1957). *The Strategy of the Gene*. London: Allen & Unwin.

Waldrop, M. (1992). *Complexity*. New York: Simon and Schuster.

Walker, N., Fisk, A.D., Phipps, D. and Kirlik, A. (1994). Training perceptual-rule based skills. *Proceedings of the Human Factors and Ergonomics Society*, 38, 1178–82.

Watson, B. (1993). For a while, the Luddites had a smashing success. *Smithsonian*, April, 140.

Watson, J.B. (1913). Psychology as the behaviorist views it. *Psychological Review*, 20, 158–77.

Warm, J.S. (ed.) (1984). *Sustained Attention in Human Performance*. New York: Wiley and Sons.

Warm, J.S., Dember, W.N., Gluckman, J.P. and Hancock, P.A. (1991). Vigilance and workload. *Proceedings of the Human Factors Society*, 35, 980–1.

Weiser, M. (1991). The computer of the 21st century. *Scientific American*, 265, September, (3), 94–100.

Westrum, R. (1991). *Technologies and Society: The Shaping of People and Things*. Belmont, CA: Wadsworth.

Whitfield, D. (1971). Human skill as a determinate of allocation of function. In: W. Singleton, R.S. Easterby., and D.C. Whitfield (eds) *The Human Operator in Complex Systems*. London: Taylor and Francis.

Wickens, C.D. (1984). *Engineering Psychology and Human Performance*. Columbus, OH: Merrill.

Wiener, E.L. (1985). Beyond the sterile cockpit. *Human Factors*, 27, 75–90.

Wiener, N. (1954). *The Human Use of Human Beings*. Boston: Da Capo Press.

Wiener, N. (1964). *God and Golem Inc*. Cambridge, MA: MIT Press.

Wiesel, E. (1983). *The Golem*. New York: Simon & Schuster.

Wilce, H. (2006). Young minds in hi-tech turmoil. *Independent*, 6 December, <http://education.independent.co.uk/schools/article2024769.ece>.

Wilkin, P. (2009). The ideology of ergonomics. *Theoretical Issues in Ergonomic Science* (in press).

Winsch, B.J., Atwood, N.K. and Quinkert, K.A. (1994). Using a distributed interactive simulation environment to investigate machine interface and training requirements. *Proceedings of the Human Factors and Ergonomics Society*, 38, 1033–7.

Wise, J.A. and Fey, D. (1981). Principles of centaurian design. *Proceedings of the Human Factors Society*, 25, 245–53.

Wolfe, T. (1979). *The Right Stuff*. New York: Farrar, Straus, Giroux.

Wolozin, B. (2007). The art of persuasion in politics (and science). *Skeptical Inquirer*, 31 (1), 15–17.

Woods, D.D. and Hancock, P.A. (2000). Dumb voters or bad design at the root of the ballot confusion? Available at: <http://www.decadeofbehavior.org/policyseminars/er_voters-or-design.pdf>.

Wulf, G., Hancock, P.A. and Rahimi, M. (1989). Some causes of automobile-motorcycle collisions. *Proceedings of the Human Factors Society*, 33, 910–14.

Yates, F.E. (1988). The dynamics of aging and time: How physical action implies social action. In: J.E. Birren and V.L. Bengston (eds) *Emergent Theories of Aging*. New York: Springer.

Yuan, C.K. and Kuo, C.K. (2006). Influence of hand grenade weight, shape and diameter on performance and subjective handling properties in relation to ergonomic design consideration. *Applied Ergonomics*, 37, 113–18.

Index

Figures are indicated by **bold** page numbers, tables by *italic* numbers.